SOME BEGINNINGS
The Cape Times
(1876–1910)

SOME BEGINNINGS

The Cape Times

(1876–1910)

GERALD SHAW

Oxford University Press

LONDON   CAPE TOWN   NEW YORK

1975

Oxford University Press

OXFORD LONDON GLASGOW NEW YORK
TORONTO MELBOURNE WELLINGTON CAPE TOWN
DELHI BOMBAY CALCUTTA MADRAS KARACHI LAHORE DACCA
KUALA LUMPUR SINGAPORE JAKARTA HONG KONG TOKYO
NAIROBI DAR ES SALAAM LUSAKA ADDIS ABABA
IBADAN ZARIA ACCRA BEIRUT

ISBN 0 19 570071 6

Copyright © Gerald Shaw 1975

⚆ SET, PRINTED AND BOUND IN THE REPUBLIC OF SOUTH AFRICA BY THE RUSTICA PRESS
(PTY.) LTD., WYNBERG, CAPE
PUBLISHED BY THE OXFORD UNIVERSITY PRESS, OXFORD HOUSE, BUITENCINGLE STREET,
CAPE TOWN

FOREWORD

By the Editor of the *Cape Times*

FREDERICK YORK ST LEGER established the *Cape Times* in March 1876, some 50 years after the battle for the freedom of the Press had been won in South Africa.

Fairbairn's *South African Commercial Advertiser*, which was never a daily newspaper, had died five years earlier. Saul Solomon's *Cape Argus* was already in the field, appearing three times a week. But no one had yet succeeded in establishing a daily newspaper on a sound and permanent footing. And the *Cape Times* remains the oldest daily newspaper in South Africa which has a record of publication as a daily since its inception.

St Leger was the founder of a South African tradition of vigorous, independent daily journalism. This book is a memoir of the first Editor of the *Cape Times* and of two successors, Edmund Garrett and Maitland Park, against the background of South African history in the tumultuous era from 1876 to 1910. It is a retrospective glance at the birth and growth of a tradition.

Newspapers are human institutions, with human failings, and the *Cape Times* has endured its vicissitudes, periods when the ideals of its founder were in eclipse and the newspaper's fortunes at a low ebb. But the tradition survived.

This volume, which covers the years of crisis before Union, is going to press as Southern Africa enters another difficult period potentially as grave as any in its history. South African newspapers, in seeking to uphold a public responsibility, are being severely tested. And it is my hope that this book, which tells of human frailty as well as significant achievement, will promote public understanding of the value of a free Press, independent of official or other extraneous control.

This is not a work of propaganda, nor a 'house' publication. It has been thoroughly researched and written in the limited time that the author, himself a *Cape Times* journalist, could spare from the treadmill of daily newspaper production. The

author has had access to the records of the *Cape Times* and has
been given complete co-operation by the board of the company
including a generous grant of sabbatical leave in which to complete the work. But the responsibility for the text, an unindulgent
memoir of our founding fathers, is his.

A. H. HEARD

Cape Town, September 1975

CONTENTS

		page
Foreword		v
Introduction		xi
1	FREDERICK YORK ST LEGER	1
2	COUNTING PENNIES	9
3	MORAL POLTROONS	14
4	CONFLICTS OF INTEREST	19
5	ENGLISHING THE TRANSVAAL	28
6	AN ANCIENT AND FISH-LIKE SMELL	35
7	VALEDICTORY	43
8	EDMUND GARRETT	61
9	THE JAMESON RAID	74
10	RECESSIONAL	96
11	THE SOUTH AFRICAN WAR	107
12	OATMEAL AND COMMONSENSE	125
13	UNION OF SOUTH AFRICA	146
	Postscript	160
	Appendix 1 (Directors of Cape Times & S.A.A.N., 1975)	167
	Appendix 2 (A Plain Talk with Oom Paul)	168
	Appendix 3 (Cecil Rhodes—An Interview)	179
	Acknowledgements	185
	Sources	187
	Index	191

ILLUSTRATIONS

Plate		facing page
1	Frederick York St Leger	2
2	The *Cape Times* office, *circa* 1880	3
3	The young Canon St Leger	18
4	Three generations of St Legers	19
5	Cecil John Rhodes	34
6	Sir James Rose Innes	34
7	John X. Merriman	34
8	J. W. Sauer	34
9	Sir James Sivewright	35
10	Cartoon from *Cape Punch*	50
11	Frederick Luke St Leger	51
12	Robert Arthur St Leger	51
13	J. D. Logan	51
14	F. Rutherfoord Harris	51
15	Edmund Garrett	66
16	Memorial to Edmund Garrett	67
17	Letter from Rhodes to Garrett	82
18	Agnes Garrett	83
19	Olive Schreiner	83
20	Cartoon from the *Cape Times*	98
21	Crowds outside the *Cape Times* building	99
22	Meeting in Greenmarket Square	99
23	Arrival of Lord Kitchener at Cape Town docks	114
24	Group of Boer troops	114
25	Sketch of Kruger consultation	115
26	Cartoons of Maitland Park	146
27	Caricature of Maitland Park	147
28	Rudyard Kipling	162
29	Maitland Park	162
30	Letter from Rudyard Kipling to Maitland Park	162
31	Frederick York St Leger	163
32	Edmund Garrett	163
33	Sir Maitland Park	163
34	B. K. Long	163
35	G. H. Wilson	163
36	Victor Norton	163
37	A. H. Heard	163
38	E. R. Syfret	163
39	Gerald Orpen	163
40	Sir Alfred Hennessy	163
41	Clive Corder	163

INTRODUCTION

CAPE TOWN in the 1870s did not commend itself to visitors from the old world. Anthony Trollope, a celebrated tourist in 1877, pronounced it a ragged place. A contemporary guide-book compiled by John Noble describes a prospect of flat-roofed dwellings with a few church towers and scattered villas, gardens and vineyards on the outskirts, adjoining the silver tree and pine plantations at the base of Table Mountain. Adderley Street, a wide and dusty thoroughfare, led to the Government Gardens, with its oak-shaded avenue and Government House, the official residence of Her Majesty Queen Victoria's representative in the Cape Colony.

The population of Cape Town and suburbs at this time was estimated at 50 000—'both white and coloured races, with all their varieties of nationality, and gradations of blood, from fairest Saxon to darkest Ethiopian', as Noble expressed it.

There was little industry. But Cape Town was beginning to share in the economic growth and prosperity which the discovery of diamonds brought to the Colony. The Cape's exports at this time were mainly wool and some wine, with diamonds becoming increasingly important. The great age of railway expansion was beginning, triggered by the discovery of diamonds. First Kimberley was to be the magnet which drew the railways as, a decade later, the discovery of gold on the Rand would attract competing lines from the coast. Economic forces were being unleashed which would strengthen the movement towards South African unification.

There were also new political forces stirring. Britain, the major world power, was feeling the stress of competition from the Continent. The Empire acquired in a 'fit of absence of mind' was imposing new and onerous burdens and responsibilities. A new, fervent doctrine of Imperialism was beginning to take hold of the popular imagination, influencing the decisions of policy-makers. But expansionism still alternated with fits of economy and the old philanthropic and humanitarian tradition remained vigorous.

In 1874, Lord Carnarvon had become Colonial Secretary. The fidgety and anxious Carnarvon, 'Twitters' to his colleagues, had set his heart on achieving a confederation of South Africa and was preparing to send his emissary, James Anthony Froude, historian and apostle of Imperial unity, to prepare the way. But Carnarvon's inept diplomacy, following the annexation of the diamond fields and Basutoland and culminating in the annexation of the Transvaal, quickly soured the atmosphere. In reaction, sharp resentment and an awakening sense of Afrikaner national consciousness grew in the Republics and in the Cape Colony.

For the next two decades, South African politics were dominated by three remarkable men: Cecil Rhodes, with his dream of spreading British law and justice across the face of the earth; Paul Kruger and his vision of a free and independent South African Republic; and J. H. 'Onze Jan' Hofmeyr, whose moderate middle course would recede in the aftermath of the Jameson Raid and the tragedy of the South African War—before reasserting itself in the South African Party at the time of Union

At this time Cecil Rhodes, not yet a member of the Cape Parliament, was completing his education at Oriel College Oxford, while buying up claims at the diamond fields and profitably working an ice-machine for the comfort of the diggers. In Pretoria, Paul Kruger was preparing for the next presidential election. In Cape Town, J. H. Hofmeyr was editing the *Zuid Afrikaan*, pressing the claims of the Dutch language and drawing attention to inequalities in the political and educational system. He had yet to establish the Boeren Beschermings Vereeniging, his movement of farmers' associations, which in time he was to merge with the strongly republican Afrikaner Bond, transforming the Bond in the process and moulding the most powerful political force in the Cape Parliament.

Hofmeyr's Afrikaner Bond, on a course of moderate South Africanism, was to become the maker and unmaker of ministries in the Cape, backing Cecil John Rhodes in a remarkable exercise in English–Dutch co-operation. The Rhodes–Hofmeyr alliance was to be blown apart by the Jameson Raid with Rhodes betraying the confidence of Hofmeyr and leaving an enduring legacy of mistrust.

But in the 1870s, there were still no clearly defined political parties in the Cape Parliament. Responsible government had been granted in 1872 and the first Prime Minister, J. C. Molteno, was still in office. Saul Solomon, in spite of his diminutive size and physical handicap, was at the height of his powers and was probably the outstanding figure in the House, noted for his outspoken liberalism and his concern for the interests of Africans.

In this setting, Frederick York St Leger established the *Cape Times*, producing the first issue on 27 March 1876. It was an unpretentious beginning—a four-page sheet, of small format, printed by a commercial printer until the new press and steam-engine to run it arrived from England. With St Leger at the start was R. W. Murray, Junior, son of one of the founders of the *Cape Argus*. The initial capital of a few hundred pounds was provided by a solicitor, Mr Halford Brown, who shared St Leger's belief that the time was right for the establishment of a new morning newspaper, to be published daily and to be entirely independent in policy. The values and standards of the new paper were to be St Leger's own.

CHAPTER 1

FREDERICK YORK ST LEGER

Liberty in deed is so far a law of nature to us, individually and
nationally, that, once the stage of dependence is passed, there
can be no moral or political health without it.

The *Cape Times*, 1 July 1882

FREDERICK YORK ST LEGER was born in Limerick, Ireland,
on 20 March 1833, the third surviving son of Robert St Leger of
Glenview, Co. Limerick, whose family traced its descent to
Robert St Leger, who came out of Normandy with William the
Conqueror.

At the age of ten, he went to live with his uncle, William
Nassau St Leger, Rector of St Mary le Tower, Ipswich. After
attending St Paul's School, London, he won a scholarship to
Corpus Christi College, Cambridge, was a gold medallist in the
Classical Tripos and became classics master at Oundle School.
In March 1856, at St Mathias, Stoke Newington, he married
Christian Emma, eldest daughter of John Muddelle of Shirley,
Hants., a purser in the East India Company who had often called
at Cape Town on voyages to the Far East.

In the early 1850s Robert Gray, Bishop of Cape Town, had
visited Britain to arrange for the division of his vast diocese and
the creation of new Sees of Grahamstown and Natal. Bishop
Gray was also successful in stirring up interest in the work of the
missions, raising funds and recruiting for the mission field.
Among those who responded was St Leger, who sailed for the
Cape soon after his marriage, taking up an appointment as
second master at the new St Andrew's College, Grahamstown,
then a frontier town with memories of bloody warfare.

In the Bishopscourt archives there is a letter to St Leger from
Bishop Gray, dated 14 November 1856, inviting St Leger to
Cape Town to be ordained as deacon. As the See of Grahams-
town was vacant, Bishop Gray said he felt bound by his promise

1

to receive St Leger as a candidate for Holy Orders. But he pointed out that a new Bishop of Grahamstown was about to be appointed: 'You may therefore judge for yourself whether it would be desirable for you to make so long a journey.'

It seems that St Leger did not make the journey, as his ordination to the priesthood in fact took place in the Grahamstown diocese.

In Grahamstown, St Leger was soon appointed headmaster of St Andrew's, succeeding the Reverend Frederick Bankes, who had retired on account of ill-health. The historian of St Andrew's, R. F. Currey, tells us that St Leger built a classroom with dormitory and kitchen and improved the school in other ways, in spite of grave financial difficulties. When he left St Andrew's in 1862, the College had been saved from extinction. In 1861 Bishop Cotterill had been able to tell the first Diocesan Synod that at St Andrew's 'boys may now receive an education such as in England can only be obtained in the best grammar schools'.

In January 1863, St Leger became second rector of St Michael's, Queenstown. The church, a small rectangular building with narrow Gothic windows and a thatched roof, had been built in 1855, two years after the foundation of Queenstown.

The diary of Canon Matthew Norton gives us a somewhat jaundiced impression of St Leger in the next few years. An entry on 12 September 1868 records: '. . . St Leger is said to be a good preacher; but I can scarcely think so from his manner of speaking and reading in the Synod. He is a clever man, I believe probably one of the cleverest in the diocese. But I scarcely think he is an orator.'

30 October 1868: 'On Wednesday I received a letter from the Rev. F. Y. St Leger exceedingly kind in its tone; but whether it was because he was making requests on behalf of a friend, or because he may have learned that his hauteur towards me can do me no harm and himself no good, I cannot determine. . . . In St Leger's letter I remarked his crest was a winged animal, and the motto "Haut et Bon". . . .'

13 July 1869: 'I have been to the fourth Synod of the diocese. . . . St Leger kept his good standing though he appeared a good

I. Frederick York St Leger as Editor of the *Cape Times*.

2. The *Cape Times* office in St George's Street, *circa* 1880.

deal more uppish than ever. I heard him preach at the Cathedral, a really good sermon; full of thought expressed in terse classical English. He is certainly a leading man in the Diocese.'

In 1867, St Leger had been appointed a canon and had accompanied Bishop Cotterill as his chaplain on a voyage to England. He was presented on his departure with an address by his congregation and a purse of 150 guineas. Returning to Queenstown, St Leger brought with him a set of stained-glass windows. These are now in the apse of the new St Michael's; the central window represents the Good Shepherd, on the left is a teaching or healing scene and on the right, the Last Supper.

By 1870, the St Legers had six children: Frederick Luke, born in 1857; John (1859); Emma Jane (1863); Robert Arthur (1865); Stratford Edward (1868); and Ellen Mary (1870).

In February 1870, Canon St Leger represented the Grahamstown diocese at the first provincial synod of the Church of the Province of South Africa, the historic gathering at which the constitution of the Church of the Province was drawn up. St Leger was appointed secretary of the Synod. The minutes, which are preserved at Church House, Cape Town, are recorded for the most part in St Leger's own handwriting.

Then, in December 1871, there was a turning-point in St Leger's life; he resigned his living and set out by wagon with his wife and six children for the diamond fields. For a canon of the Anglican Church, this was an extraordinary change of course. No written records can be traced which explain his decision to abandon pastoral work; the Bishopscourt archives are silent and there is no correspondence between St Leger and the Bishop of Grahamstown in the archives of that diocese.

Anthony York St Leger, the youngest son—born at the diamond fields—said in later years that the reasons for his father's resignation were uncertain but were 'thought to be connected with the split in the Church, influenced by the difficulty of providing for a growing family on a small stipend'.

The 'split in the Church' was obviously the Colenso controversy and the maze of ecclesiastical and juridical disputes concerning the status and jurisdiction of colonial bishoprics which raged in the last century. Colenso's advanced theological views had led to a charge of heresy against him in 1863 and the controversy had repercussions in the Church for decades.

St Leger himself left no collection of personal papers. But some insight into his attitudes can be gleaned from his leading articles in the *Cape Times* in later years.

On 14 July 1880, a *Cape Times* editorial, in a style unmistakably St Leger's, expressed this view:

> It is far better and happier for the world that an unquestioning faith should prevail, provided it be such as to rightly influence thought and conduct, than that every half-taught lad should be disturbing his grandmother's soul with vauntings of trumpery doubts about Noah's ark or talking donkeys. Scepticism should be as earnest in its way as omnivorous belief. And those who have parted from the old moorings should say as little as possible about their scheme of navigation until they have found good holding-ground elsewhere.

On the jurisdictional controversy, the *Cape Times* on 1 July 1882 took the view that responsible government in the ecclesiastical economy was the necessary complement of responsible government in the political system. St Leger favoured the establishment of the Church of the Province of South Africa 'essentially one with the Church of England, deriving from it its order and mission and accepting its doctrinal standards, formalities and ritual, free to adapt itself in ministrations and discipline to the circumstances which it may from time to time experience . . . .'. Even if liberty had sometimes proved to be a dubious boon, 'who amongst us would now surrender it?' The miscalculations of the earlier days of liberty could not be turned into an argument against liberty itself—either in the body politic or in the Church.

'Liberty indeed is so far a law of nature to us, individually and nationally, that, once the stage of dependence is passed, there can be no moral or political health without it.'

St Leger's decision to resign his living might have been prompted by disenchantment with the whole climate of controversy, as it manifested itself in the Church of his time. The

Grahamstown diocese seems to have been a hotbed of feuds and wrangles.

And there might have been another factor. It is known that some time after their marriage Mrs St Leger became a convert to the Roman Catholic faith. It is possible that his wife's conversion, in the climate of the time, was felt by St Leger to be incompatible with his role as an Anglican clergyman. If there were any other factors which might explain his leaving the priesthood so abruptly, no record appears to have survived. Whatever his reasons for resigning his living, St Leger remained a committed Christian until his death and was a familiar figure for more than 20 years in the pews of St George's Cathedral, Cape Town.

The discovery of diamonds in 1869 had drawn men to the banks of the Vaal from the ends of the earth. The further discovery of the so-called dry diggings, notably De Beer's 'New Rush', now the Big Hole at Kimberley, started a stampede. St Leger resigned his living in 1871 and set out for the New Rush camp. R. A. St Leger, the third son known as Bob, later recalled that he slept under the wagon during the roadside stops at night, while mother and daughters slept in the wagon itself.

John X. Merriman, who had yet to make his name in South African politics, has left us a picture of New Rush camp in 1872 as an 'awful place. About two or three miles long. No order or anything else—a sort of canvas London; for no one seemed to know their next-door neighbours. . . . Nothing is more common than to see the canteens adorned with a row of dead-drunk corpses at 10 a.m. Policemen there are none and they (the drinkers) never appear in the streets until three parts gone, but quarrels are generally settled by a stand-up fight. . . .'

This was indeed a radical change of environment for the St Legers and their young family, a far remove from the ordered routine of a Queenstown rectory. They had one wood-and-iron room—Mrs St Leger's bedroom—and one or two tents. R. A. St Leger once recounted to his own children a memory of his seventh birthday in New Rush camp in 1872. There were no toy shops, and his birthday presents consisted of a tin soldier, a large currant bun and a shilling which Bob spent at the local 'sweetshops', the dried-fruit wagons that used to come up from the Oudtshoorn district with peaches, apricots and raisins.

St Leger worked as a diamond buyer while the two eldest boys, Fred and John, dug for diamonds without particular success.

St Leger then turned his hand to writing for newspapers and from April 1873 was Editor of the *Diamond Field*. But he resigned the following year after a dispute with the proprietors and, in 1875, took his family to Cape Town, travelling part of the way by Gibson's coach but mainly by ox-wagon to the railhead at Worcester. In Cape Town, he became Editor of the newly-established Cape Town *Daily News*, and it was soon apparent that he had found a new vocation.

But once again he resigned in a dispute with proprietors, on this occasion after refusing to write a leading article according to instructions. Now there was only one course left—to become a proprietor himself. The time had come for the foundation of the *Cape Times*.

St Leger was well equipped for the task. His experience of the Eastern Province frontier and of the diamond diggings would be invaluable in assessing the events of the 1870s and 1880s. He was now 44, his idealism and scholarship leavened by contact with all sorts and conditions of men. In politics, he described himself as a Radical although, as he wrote to his son Bob some years later, 'I don't see why Radicals should make fools of themselves'.

His contemporaries in Cape Town found the Editor-to-be aloof and reserved, with little taste for general society. But he did enjoy club life and, as a founder member of the City Club in Cape Town, helped to establish its library. He was to become a well-known figure in the city, immaculate in spats and topper and sporting a silver-headed cane.

At least one of St Leger's clerical brethren in the Grahamstown diocese had pronounced him to be 'uppish'. The pencil sketch of the young Canon St Leger (facing p. 18) certainly suggests a touch of hauteur. And he was a rather forbidding figure to those who did not know him well, with Victorian side-whiskers and military bearing. But he is remembered in the St Leger family as a devoted father and grandfather, gentle in speech and manner, with the distinctive grey-blue eyes that recur frequently among the St Legers.

St Leger had few close friends and was not a man who gave his confidence easily. The man he chose to succeed him as Editor of the *Cape Times*, Edmund Garrett, spoke of the 'singular charm, once known, of his mind, in which the sense of honour and the sense of humour were equally delicate'.

After retiring from the editorship in 1895, St Leger became active in public affairs, as a town councillor and member of Parliament. He held the rank of major in the Duke of Edinburgh's Own Volunteer Rifles.

He also became first chairman of the Cape Town Irish Association, in which he presided over a remarkable group of Cape Town Irishmen—Protestant, Catholic and Jewish—who, under his leadership, pledged themselves to avoid all religious and political disputation in their St Patrick's Night gatherings, which took place at the Mount Nelson Hotel or other hostelries. The members included the Roman Catholic coadjutor Bishop, the Rt Reverend John Rooney, and Rabbi A. P. Bender, and set a striking example in an era not always noted for social and religious tolerance.

St Leger was active on a number of other public bodies, including the boards of the Woodstock and Somerset Hospitals. While Editor of the *Cape Times*, however, he took no part in public life and adhered strictly to the practice of editorial anonymity.

James Rose Innes, who was prominent in Cape politics in the 1890s and one of the few men who did gain St Leger's confidence, said of the founder of the *Cape Times* that he was content that his 'opinions, his scholarship and his delicate fancy should impersonally permeate the paper he controlled'.

St Leger's style was ornate by contemporary standards, and reflected his own oblique and ironic personality. He had frequent recourse to Biblical and classical quotation, writing as a cultivated man for other cultivated men. As an editor for the most part he shunned close contact with the politicians of the day, but he did maintain some sort of rapport in politics with James Rose Innes, whose outlook accorded closely with his own.

John X. Merriman, who seems to have admired St Leger as much as he disliked his successor, Edmund Garrett, once dubbed St Leger 'blind old Dandolo', after Enrico Dandolo, a Doge of Venice and reputedly a man of weak sight. Merriman was noted for coining apt, semi-malicious nicknames for his political contemporaries. But St Leger was an elusive personality and Merriman's tag never stuck.

To his staff at the *Cape Times*, St Leger was the 'Old Saint', to distinguish him from his son Fred, who later joined the management of the newspaper after a wild youth at the diggings. And, as the *Cape Times* grew steadily in stature and influence to become the leading newspaper in South Africa by the early 1890s, it was as the 'Old Saint' that St Leger became known in Cape Town and beyond.

Victor Sampson, a freelance contributor to the *Cape Times* in its early days, recalled in his reminiscences that 'it was the wit and brilliant writing of St Leger that made the leaders in the paper a joy in the morning to anyone who appreciated the "Saint's" good things'.

CHAPTER 2

COUNTING PENNIES

We will do our utmost to deserve public support, following our
own independent line and only asking indulgence for such shortcomings as are inevitable, until we have fairly worked into our
groove.

The Cape Times and Daily Advertiser, 27 March 1876

IN a house in Buitengracht Street, Cape Town, on the evening
of 27 March 1876, the St Leger children sat around a table and
helped their father in 'counting the pennies', the proceeds of the
first day's sale of *The Cape Times and Daily Advertiser*, as the
newspaper was initially styled. This was to become a regular
family custom. Excitement mounted as the piles of pennies grew
larger by the day and the new paper, as a penny daily, made
steady headway against Mr Saul Solomon's threepenny, tri-
weekly *Cape Argus*, the *Cape Town Daily News*, and the other
rival newspapers.

St Leger's first office was in a small building in St George's
Street where the ABC Branch of the Standard Bank now stands.
After a few months, there was a move across the road to 56
St George's Street and, later, extensions which took the offices
right through to Burg Street.

Right from the start, the newspaper found a point of sympathetic contact with its readers. The first letter to the Editor
was from a man who signed himself 'A Londoner', writing to
complain of the lack of restaurants in Cape Town. 'Living out of
town one cannot get home for a one o'clock meal and our circumstances prohibit the luxury of one at a hotel.'

The newspaper supported the reader in an editorial but noted
that 'as public spirit is slow of motion' this correspondent and
others like him 'must munch their biscuits and sigh for the
succulent chop'.

By September 1876, the newspaper had outgrown its original

9

small format and now appeared in standard newspaper size, printed on the press which had arrived from England. The old title, *The Cape Times and Daily Advertiser*, had become simply *Cape Times* and the Royal coat of arms had been incorporated in the title, where it would remain until the advent of the Republic in 1961.

The newspaper was showing considerable enterprise in news-gathering, becoming the first paper in the country to use the telegraph as a means of getting news for publication. Until this time, only shipping movements from East London and Port Elizabeth were obtained by telegraph. The rest of the news came by the infrequent mail steamer or by post-cart from up-country contemporaries and correspondents.

By October 1876 the *Cape Times* was proudly proclaiming:

The *Cape Times* has the largest circulation of any newspaper published in Cape Town, is issued daily, and contains reports of all public events, the latest telegrams from all parts of the country, reliable commercial and shipping intelligence, whilst all political and other questions, which come under the review of public opinion, are dealt with in an impartial spirit.

Another sign of progress at this time was an advertisement calling for the services of newspaper boys and an office boy. But, for all the brave words and grandiose claims, the paper was having a hard time. St Leger's efforts to build a good news service were costing a lot of money. There were times when there was no money to pay the printing staff, some of whom, confident that St Leger would ultimately pull through, went without pay. St Leger himself, with only R. W. Murray helping him at the start, had to develop an astonishing capacity for hard work. His working routine has been described in the reminiscences of G. A. L. Green, a reporter on the *Cape Times* in the 90s who later became a distinguished Editor of the *Cape Argus*.

As Green tells it, St Leger would spend the greater part of the morning in the office, reading and writing letters and preparing manuscripts for publication. Two-thirty found him in the Press Gallery of the Cape Parliament, seated at the far end at the right of the Speaker, and there he would stay for solid hours unbroken but for a hurried cup of tea in Kamp's café nearby. While listening to the debates, at odd intervals he would scribble a few sentences with a stub of pencil—the famous 'Notes in the House', a feature carried on in later years by G. H. Wilson, Victor Norton, Angus McKenzie, Anthony Delius and, in our time, John Scott. As Green recalled of St Leger's original 'Notes in the House', few who admired their pith and irony or who laughed over the clever personal touches and allusions would have guessed that they were dashed off all ready for the printer while the debate proceeded.

On a dull afternoon in the Press Gallery, St Leger would work off reviews of books which he had read in bed before going to sleep. After an early dinner at his home in the suburbs, by eight o'clock, if there was no night sitting in the House, the Editor would be at his office ready to fill the leading columns. It may be that the finer shades of his irony sometimes escaped the general reader, but Green believed that St Leger was probably the most polished writer who had ever supplied regular copy to the Press of South Africa. Green held that the secret of St Leger's facility lay in his retentive memory. He rarely needed to hunt up references or verify quotations. Yet he seldom erred. And his regard for accuracy was almost obsessive. He was greatly perturbed if a wrong date, a name misspelt, an incorrect initial or some fatuous remark crept into the paper. 'But such was his habitual reserve that his annoyance found vent only in a brief note of reproof, spiced with faint sarcasm, addressed not to anybody in particular, but impersonally "to whom it may concern".'

Green remembered St Leger as austere in manner. He rarely spoke to any of his staff unless he was spoken to first, when he was invariably courteous. 'His attitude of aloofness was due to shyness, for he was free from intellectual arrogance and beneath the cold exterior lay a heart of gold. We, his subordinates, though at times irreverent, looked up to our chief. We knew that he was a great journalist—the greatest of his day.'

The qualities which would rapidly make St Leger's *Cape Times* the most influential newspaper in South Africa were already evident in the early days of March and April 1876. The general tenor of those calmly argued first leaders discussing the annexation of the diamond fields was that the British Government had shown neither consideration nor a sense of justice in its dealings with the Republics. But there was also an insistence in the leading columns that the British Government remained committed to its traditional policy of protecting the interests of the tribal African peoples.

On the 'native question', as the *Cape Times* then described it, the newspaper was advocating a 'true and fair course' lying 'between the extremes'. This placed the *Cape Times* to the right of Saul Solomon's philanthropic *Cape Argus*. The political duels between St Leger and Solomon and their respective newspapers in the next few years would become memorable.

There began, also, in these early months the vigorous *Cape Times* involvement in municipal affairs which continues in the present day. On 3 April 1876, the *Cape Times* chided the municipal authorities:

> By the kindness of Providence in making South-Easters the city is protected from the visitation of pestilence, which in the course of nature should follow (the Municipality's) neglect. The invincible patience of citizens still bears with their lethargic tardiness in making the streets fit for the pedestrian and in supplying houses with the means of ordinary cleanliness.

The editorial spurred the Municipality to greater efforts in nosing out dead rats and cleansing the city of their remains.

If its economic basis was still somewhat shaky, the *Cape Times* continued to put on a bold front. As another early advertisement declared:

> As an advertising medium, the *Cape Times* has not its equal. The paper is delivered in Cape Town and Green Point early each morning to subscribers. At all stations along the Wynberg line, subscribers obtain their papers after the arrival of the first train; papers are also for sale at each station.
> At all the principal stations on the Worcester line *The Times*

is sold, and it is delivered in such towns as Somerset West, Stellenbosch, the Paarl, Wellington, Worcester, Malmesbury and Simon's Town, at the same rate of subscription as in Cape Town.

R. W. Murray, who combined the duties of business manager and political correspondent in the early years, seems to have been an early advocate of vigorous promotion as a means of building circulation. By 1877, the *Cape Times* was well established.

CHAPTER 3

MORAL POLTROONS

As long as the sun shines, the Transvaal will be British territory, and the Vaal river shall flow back to its sources before the Transvaal is again independent.

Sir Garnet Wolseley on becoming High Commissioner
of the Transvaal, 1879

ON 22 January 1877, Sir Theophilus Shepstone rode into Pretoria with an escort of 25 Natal mounted police. His instructions from Lord Carnarvon at the Colonial Office required him to annex the Transvaal—with its consent, if possible.

The *Cape Times* had eyed Shepstone's mission with some misgivings, noting that there was no possible advantage to be gained if one flag was flying from Agulhas to the Zambezi, 'unless that flag be in honest truth a symbol of one broad principle of loyalty and justice'. Yet when the annexation came, the newspaper accepted it without much demur, apparently satisfied that the Transvaal, with 12s 6d in the Treasury, and ill-equipped to withstand a war with Cetewayo or Sekukuni, was well advised to accept the benefits of British protection. In time, the *Cape Times* revised this judgement. Shepstone's annexation of the Transvaal came to be seen as a monumental blunder. And the Transvaal was on the verge of war with Britain when the *Cape Times*, by now thoroughly disillusioned with the Downing Street policy-makers, spoke its mind:

> We as a community are not in a position to offer counsel just now to the Imperial government, nor is the government in a frame of mind to profit by our admonitions, however timely or wise. Let them settle with the Transvaal as best they may the account they have industriously swelled. . . . At the time of the annexation we were told that they [the Boers] had become a nuisance and a source of danger; that they were irritating the native tribes to a war which could involve

14

Her Majesty's subjects and that the general peace of South Africa required the extinction of the Republic. But afterwards we learned how utterly false and absurd these representations were; and we witnessed the painful spectacle of British protection entailing more serious and more disastrous native disturbances than had been experienced aforetime . . . (15 December 1880).

There had been the ill-starred Zulu War, provoked by Sir Bartle Frere, the High Commissioner, who was intent on removing what he conceived to be obstacles to confederation. The *Cape Times*, from the start a supporter of confederation, and firmly committed to the extension of British influence and civilization in South Africa, was usually inclined to give Sir Bartle the benefit of the doubt, defending him against the 'canting negrophilism' of Saul Solomon's *Cape Argus*. The *Cape Argus's* treatment of the disaster of Isandhlwana, when it came out in mourning in black borders, evoked St Leger's scorn. Attacking what it saw as a change of front by the *Argus*, a *Cape Times* leader concluded: 'No wonder the worthy creature turns black like a chameleon on an Ethiopian's head' (27 January 1879).

But the vagaries of Imperial policy brought disillusionment. When the Gladstone ministry decided to end the Transvaal War and restore the Republic's independence, the *Cape Times* declared:

The rivers have not flown towards their sources, nor has the sun ceased to warm the earth, and yet despite the hyperbole of an eminent soldier and the more prosaic asseverations of statesmen, the British flag has been virtually struck in the Transvaal. . . . The sense of humiliation to which these terms of peace have exposed men who cherish national sentiment is not associated with the least feeling of bitterness towards the insurgents. Believing that they were fighting for their liberty, they fought bravely and with determination. They have gained their end; it would be a superhuman exercise of virtue if they were to exhibit no pride in their success . . . There is nothing in this unhappy story, now we trust closed, to hinder us from working together for the welfare of our adopted land, or from building up in concert a community which will one day hope to have traditions of its own worthy of a place in history (29 March 1881).

But the story was by no means closed. The Transvaal's victory at Majuba, which the *Cape Times* had seen as a salutary lesson in political wisdom for the Gladstone ministry—'instilled into them by the sharp-shooting of a few rock-protected marksmen'—was to fire the imagination of Afrikaner South Africa. In the Cape, the Afrikaner Bond was given the impetus that would soon make it the dominant power in Colonial politics. The *Cape Times* had regarded the stirrings of nationalism at the Cape—S. J. du Toit's *Afrikaanse Patriot* and Hofmeyr's farmers' movement—with uneasy suspicion. It saw the latter as 'a new sort of Fenians' who proposed to extend the ramifications of their conspiracy to every part of the Colony (14 August 1878).

Hofmeyr's aim was to achieve the full political recognition of Afrikaners yet, at the same time, it was to be his role to modify republican tendencies in the new nationalist movement. By 1882, as Hofmeyr was emerging to gain control of a flourishing Afrikaner Bond, the *Cape Times* would view with equanimity, if not much enthusiasm, the recognition of Dutch as a language for use in Parliament, while noting that English was not accorded similar privileges in the Orange Free State.

In 1884, Hofmeyr, now with a strong following in the Cape Parliament, was asked by the Governor, Sir Hercules Robinson, to form an administration. But Hofmeyr, believing that his presence at the head of a ministry would 'raise the racial issue', stood back for Sir Thomas Upington, and threw the weight of his supporters behind the Upington ministry. The *Cape Times* welcomed the arrangement and said the time was opportune for a rest from strife:

> The present is emphatically a time for building up our own colonial interests and developing whatever we may possess in the way of factors of prosperity. To this end we have the best of all aids, as perfect a system of constitutional liberty as any nation or community in the world.

Cecil Rhodes was now also establishing himself in Cape politics, having floated the De Beers Mining Company at Kimberley and entered the House in 1881, at the age of 28, as member for Barkly East. Rhodes had also bought an interest in the *Cape Argus* when Saul Solomon relinquished control in 1881, putting up the money for Francis Dormer to buy the paper. One of Rhodes's biographers, Basil Williams, says that he bought a share in the *Argus* to make certain of a paper that would always print his speeches and any information he might give it, '. . . at the same time assuring the Editor he would never attempt to interfere with the opinions expressed in its columns'.

As Saul Solomon withdrew, the *Cape Times* took up the cause of the Zulu monarch Cetewayo, who was now in detention in Cape Town, having been stripped of his kingdom after the Zulu War. Solomon had been Cetewayo's champion in all his misfortunes. But now it was the *Cape Times* that was calling for Cetewayo's release from detention and his restoration in Zulu-land. Cetewayo had appealed to the Colonial Secretary, Lord Kimberley, but without success.

There was a *Cape Times* editorial:

> Some may be right in asserting that Cetewayo would never have injured an English colony, just as they might have taken an optimistic view of Cetewayo and avowed that he was not such a bloodthirsty monster as represented. . . . Others, again, might have seen in the Zulu power the darkest phases of barbarity, a standing menace to Natal, and a stumbling-block in the way of civilization. Whatever, however, our previous views with regard to the Zulu kingdom and its rulers may have been, we have had for the last year or so a practical insight into the character of the despot himself, and it cannot be denied that he has carried himself with a certain air of nobility. . . . It is with amusement, not unmixed with pity, that we hear of the terrible despot subjecting himself to the intricate hardships of an English primer, learning the language of his captors in a strange land, growing fond and affectionate towards his guardians, and maintaining throughout a kingly demeanour in what he calls his grave. . . . His appeal to Lord Kimberley

was perfectly reasonable. . . . We might wish to have been spared the spectacle of a fettered King appealing to the magnanimity of a clique of moral poltroons who grovel before the strong to the lowest depth of apologetic disgrace but only dare to be resolute and firm when they strike down the hopes of a captive which they have previously done everything to raise (25 July 1881).

Lord Kimberley's decision would be bitter news for Cetewayo, the *Cape Times* said. Cetewayo 'may have gathered hope from the general tenor of radical retrocession that an *amende honorable* for previous injustices might be made to himself as well as to the Boer Republic'.

Cetewayo's cause was also supported by Bishop Colenso of Natal, and eventually he went to England to put his case, causing quite a stir. In formal dress, Cetewayo called on Queen Victoria and Lord Kimberley and, eventually, the British Government decided to restore the Zulu king—but in only part of his former kingdom. Cetewayo accepted this arrangement under protest and returned to Zululand in January 1883. He died a year later.

Rev. Frederick York. St. Leger. B.A.
Rector 1863 — 1871.
Canon of Grahamstown.

3. The young Canon St Leger. A pencil sketch by an unknown artist.

St Michael's Church, Queenstown

4. Three generations of St Legers—Frederick York St Leger with his son Bob and his grandson Bi
A photograph taken in Purley, Surrey, where Bob was practising medicine.

CHAPTER 4

CONFLICTS OF INTEREST

It seems to us that while it is commendable to encourage youthful talent and honourable ambition, it is at the same time advisable to mark with disapproval the introduction of political principles which Machiavelli would have envied.

The *Cape Times*, 11 August 1881

ON 19 April 1881, 'Notes in the House' recorded the first speech in the Cape Parliament by Cecil John Rhodes. As a parliamentary debut, the speech—on the Basuto troubles of the early 80s—was not a conspicuous success. The new member for Barkly East addressed fellow members by name, in defiance of parliamentary custom. As spokesman for the diamond lobby in the House, Rhodes had an interest in Basutoland, as the territory was a major source of labour for the fields. But he was also concerned to speed up the progress of the railway line to Kimberley. The Basuto War, provoked by attempts of the Cape Government to enforce a disarmament law, was draining funds which Rhodes now felt would be better expended on railway construction. A speech by Rhodes on the Basutoland troubles, delivered at a rowdy banquet in Kimberley later in the year, was received with wild enthusiasm. It was not so received in a *Cape Times* leader:

It is a matter of no great moment that Mr Rhodes should have considered it necessary to have recourse to sophistry in vindicating his conduct on the occasion of his startling political conversion; but it is a matter of the gravest consequence that such sophistry should come into common use in political discussion and that it should meet with the success that followed it at the Kimberley banquet. We do not blame Mr Rhodes, who in political warfare is at liberty to practise any of the ordinary artifices of debate, but we should be sorry to think that any of our legislators have acted, or may hereafter act,

19

upon the doctrine enunciated by him as the ground of his justification . . . (11 August 1881).

Meanwhile, Rhodes would be devoting his extraordinary energies to keeping open his route to the North, amalgamating the Kimberley diamond mines and forming the British South Africa Company. He was also cultivating the friendship and goodwill of J. H. Hofmeyr, in the knowledge that the latter's support was essential if his schemes were to be backed in the Cape Parliament. Rhodes was to take up the confederation plan where the Imperial factor had left off, working towards a southern African confederation of states, and employing rather more finesse than the statesmen of Downing Street. His plan called for the isolation of Paul Kruger's Transvaal, denying the South African Republic an outlet to the sea and, in time, bringing the Transvaal into a united South Africa.

As Kruger became increasingly wary of Hofmeyr, the understanding between Hofmeyr and Rhodes grew into a working alliance. Hofmeyr gained much from the alliance, although Rhodes was to remark cynically after the Jameson Raid: 'He thought I was serving his object; he finds he was serving mine.' The alliance was founded on a basis of close personal friendship and a common belief in the goal of a united South Africa. It led to Rhodes's championing the interests of Cape farmers, who were the bulk of the support of Hofmeyr's Afrikaner Bond, and taking a conservative line on racial policies. It meant support for tariff policies which favoured agricultural rather than urban interests.

In return, Rhodes gained Hofmeyr's support in his plans to develop Rhodesia with a Royal Charter granted to the British South Africa Company. As Hofmeyr's biographer notes, if Hofmeyr and his followers in the Cape Parliament had opposed the Chartered Company, Rhodes's schemes could have been checked. If Paul Kruger had adopted a less suspicious attitude to Hofmeyr and the economic aspirations of the Cape Colony, it is possible that the Rhodes–Hofmeyr alliance would never have developed. But when Rhodes became Prime Minister of the Cape in July 1890, on the fall of the Sprigg Cabinet, he was able to form a government with the support of the Afrikaner Bond.

Now, at 38, Cecil John Rhodes wielded immense power as Prime Minister of the Cape Colony, Chairman of De Beers and of Consolidated Goldfields and of the British South Africa Company. His Kimberley consolidation was paying huge dividends. His Goldfields Company was prospering. His Chartered Company had occupied Mashonaland.

St Leger at first questioned the wisdom of such a man becoming Prime Minister. What troubled the *Cape Times* was the conflict of interests that could arise between Rhodes, Prime Minister of the Cape Colony; Rhodes, Chairman of the Chartered Company; and Rhodes, Chairman of De Beers. The newspaper argued that it would be unfair to Rhodes to put him in a position in which—however patriotic his intentions—a suspicion might attach to him of sacrificing the one interest to the other. Initially, the *Cape Times* was disposed to think that he would not in fact take office, except, perhaps, as a temporary expedient.

It was not that St Leger minimized Rhodes's remarkable achievements. As the *Cape Times* said on 18 July 1890, whatever success Rhodes had attained was due in the first place to honourable and courageous enterprise. 'He meditates great projects and exercises a noble ambition in carrying them out. This bent of mind differs by the whole semi-circle from the mean passion for gain which stimulates the activities of the share market. . . . To speak of Mr Rhodes as a speculator is to betray an almost ridiculous ignorance of his influence upon South African industry and upon South African history. . . .'

St Leger was of the view that Hofmeyr, as leader of the Afrikaner Bond, should have been called upon to form a government. He now distrusted Hofmeyr's preference for working behind the scenes and believed that the Bond should accept the responsibility of office. But Hofmeyr's aversion to taking office was well established and so the *Cape Times* favoured J. W. Sauer as Prime Minister. The newspaper argued that Rhodes could be as effective out of office, if not more so, in advancing the objects of a united South Africa. But when this view did not prevail and

Rhodes did accept office, the *Cape Times* expressed the hope that he might receive the fair consideration he sought at the hands of Parliament:

> We have already stated our reasons for preferring that Mr Sauer should have formed a Cabinet; and that reason does not yield to the might of the British South Africa Company. None can desire more earnestly than we do the success of the Company or the co-operation of the Cape Colony in its magnificent designs. Nevertheless, contingencies may arise in which the Colony and the Company are at issue in matters of detail; and in that event Mr Rhodes would be in a false position as managing director of each party to the dispute . . . (18 July 1890).

St Leger disliked an arrangement in which a strong bloc of members—the Afrikaner Bond—could dictate policy while not accepting formal constitutional responsibility. The day before, the *Cape Times* had noted:

> Under such conditions the most honest politician in the world is tempted to palter with his honesty, to assume some principle which fits him ill or to dissemble his strong conviction. The honest plan is to reject the system altogether. But this is a counsel of perfection; and we must only hope that by impulses of honesty here and there, now and again, the system may be jerked into a fair track; for otherwise it will drag our political constitution to ruin (17 July 1890).

The Rhodes Cabinet was a remarkably able if rather ill-assorted team. There was John X. Merriman with his intellectual brilliance and outspoken courage; there was Sauer, superb parliamentarian; and there was James Rose Innes, of whom a *Cape Times* leader noted: 'An honest lawyer and conscientious to a fault . . . cured of the extreme negrophilism which would have unfitted him for responsible office.' Of the Bondsmen, there were P. H. Faure and J. Sivewright, Rhodes's man-of-all-work, who would be knighted for his achievements as a railway negotiator with the Transvaal and, as Sir James Sivewright, would follow questionable standards in the award of railway contracts, wrecking the first Rhodes Cabinet.

The *Cape Times* gave the new Cabinet its broad support; but it was often at odds with Rhodes in his domestic policies.

On 31 July 1890, the *Cape Times* commended the majority of members in the House who had spoken and voted against the 'brutal and retrogressive' Strop Bill, which had been rejected at its second-reading stage in the Cape Parliament on the previous day. The measure would have made whipping mandatory in cases where fines could not be paid by offenders against the Masters and Servants Act.

If a servant or farm labourer had been found guilty of impertinence towards his master, or some small infraction of duty or error of judgement 'interpreted by some cross-grained master or mistress into a deliberate offence', and if the employee was not able at that moment to pay the fine imposed, magistrates would be obliged to inflict what the *Cape Times* regarded as 'degrading corporal punishment'.

The *Cape Times* was not surprised that James Sivewright 'should have taken his place with the slave-driving section'. But the Premier himself, Cecil Rhodes, had also voted for the Bill. As the *Cape Times* said, Rhodes had missed an opportunity of 'proving himself superior to the influences which drag men down in our parliamentary life. It was a melancholy conclusion to a debate which will do more harm to the country in the opinion of those whose approval is best worth having than anything within recent Colonial experience.'

Rhodes's Cabinet was divided when the vote was taken. Rhodes, Faure and Sivewright voted in favour. Merriman, Rose Innes and Sauer voted against, even though the mandatory provision was made permissive by the Bill's sponsors in a bid to gain majority support. The Strop Bill had been introduced during the term of office of the previous Ministry. Rhodes's support of the measure was dictated by the need to cement his alliance with the Afrikaner Bond.

The *Cape Times* was also unenthusiastic about another important Rhodes measure—the Franchise and Ballot Bill of 1892—which raised the qualifications for the franchise in the Cape although it maintained its traditional non-racial character.

The measure was introduced by Rhodes under pressure from the Bond, on whom he continued to rely for his parliamentary majority. The liberal wing of the Rhodes Cabinet, and notably James Rose Innes, had accepted the measure as a compromise. Rose Innes believed that opposition to the compromise measure would have meant a Cabinet split, with the moderates having to withdraw and the way being opened for more drastically retrogressive franchise legislation.

On the day the Bill was to be introduced by Rhodes, the *Cape Times* said it saw no pressing need for tampering with the constitution. If this was inevitable, however, the major priority was redistribution—the delimitation of constituencies at the time gave great weight to the country vote—and reform of the Upper House in the Cape Parliament. The *Cape Times* was not opposed to franchise qualifications as such—the introduction of a simple educational test, in fact, had been its own proposal—but the newspaper was strongly opposed to piecemeal constitutional changes. Accordingly the *Cape Times*, as a leader expressed it, had opposed the Bill as strenuously as the 'deadness of popular feeling' in the matter would permit.

In the Cape Assembly, Rhodes claimed that the Bill enjoyed general support. He cited the *Cape Times*'s advocacy of an educational test and declared 'no one could consider the *Cape Times* a warm supporter' of his government.

James Rose Innes, in later years, said that he had never regretted the compromise in the 1892 Bill, '. . . if we could abate a demand which it was impossible to resist and could prevent any real injustice by so doing, it was the part of wise statesmanship to consent'. In this, Rose Innes enjoyed the support of the *Cape Times*, which believed that the moderating presence of Innes, Merriman and Sauer in the Rhodes Cabinet was worth the price of compromise.

But before the decade was out, St Leger's initial reservations about Rhodes's accepting the premiership would be shown to be amply justified—as Rhodes compounded his conflicts of interest in the folly of the Jameson Raid.

The *Cape Times* was now at the pinnacle of success. St Leger jealously guarded its independence against all comers—including 'the might of the British South Africa Company'—and cherished its reputation for accuracy, fairness and good faith in its dealings with its readers. So much so that he had a few years earlier success-fully instituted an action for libel when his integrity as an editor had been questioned.

The case, *St Leger* v *Rowles and Co.*, was heard before the Chief Justice of the Cape, Sir J. H. (later Lord) de Villiers, KCMG, on 18 February 1888. With the Chief Justice on the Bench were Mr Justice Smith and Mr Justice Buchanan. James Rose Innes appeared for St Leger and, with him, M. W. Searle, later Sir Malcolm Searle, who was to marry St Leger's daughter, Emma Jane. The defendants, the publishers of a King William's Town newspaper, the *Kaffrarian Watchman*, were Thomas William Robertson, of the S. E. Rowles estate, and Horatio Dunsterville Blewitt, trading under the style of S. E. Rowles and Company.

The *Watchman* had said in a series of vigorous editorials that the *Cape Times* reports of Parliament were manipulated and cooked for political purposes and that these reports were then designedly used as the basis for leading articles in the *Cape Times*. Referring to the *Cape Times* as 'our bilious contemporary', the *Watchman* said the *Cape Times* had manipulated reports of parliamentary proceedings 'to suit its own disordered propensities, so much so that a simple comparison of the *Argus* reports with those of the *Cape Times* must convince any observer of the design which underlines the latter's double shuffle of *suppressio veri* and *suggestio falsi* . . .'.

Rose Innes, addressing the court, said that Mr St Leger would not accept any damages in the case. 'He simply desires to clear himself; he comes to the Court to have these charges refuted and to have it declared that there is nothing dishonest in the *Cape Times* reports or in the articles founded upon those reports', he added.

Mr Edmund Powell, Editor of the *Cape Argus*, told the court that he clearly understood the articles in the *Watchman* to refer to St Leger, who was so identified with the *Cape Times* and his style so well known that he did not think that there could be any doubt to whom the *Watchman's* articles referred.

Mr Powell said he considered the *Cape Times* reports complained of by the *Watchman* to have been quite fair reports. It would be mere chance if the *Argus* reports were fuller than the *Times* reports.

The Chief Justice: 'Did you ever find the Editor of the *Cape Times* manipulating reports?'

Mr Powell: 'Oh, no. I am working side by side with the *Cape Times* staff in the gallery and I am confident that Mr St Leger never sees the reports. Mr Aubin [a *Cape Times* reporter] has the whole thing in hand.'

St Leger's own evidence indicated that, while he exercised supervision over the staff as a whole, he never saw the parliamentary reports or interfered with them. He occupied a seat in the reporting gallery during the session. The leading articles on the parliamentary proceedings were written by him on his own knowledge, most of them in the Press Gallery itself. He was accused of having gone out of his way as editor of a newspaper to make reports published as reports—not as comments—false and misleading. 'And I say that is a most damaging charge to bring against a journalist. I do not complain of being accused of writing strongly or of forming wrong judgements, but I complain of being charged with manipulating reports. . . .'

Mr Horatio Dunsterville Blewitt, Editor of the *Watchman*, went into the witness-box to say that he no longer believed there had been a systematized perversion of the reports. He withdrew the allegations and was quite willing to accept Mr St Leger's statement.

The Chief Justice: 'Is that not enough, then, for your purposes, Mr Innes?'

Mr Innes: 'Of course, that will perfectly clear Mr St Leger. . . .'

In giving judgment in favour of St Leger and awarding nominal damages of one shilling, the Chief Justice said that, however severe Mr St Leger might be in criticizing other public men, 'we cannot let that deprive him of the right to come into this Court and claim damages for imputations of his character'.

St Leger's vindication of his good name (and that of his newspaper) was noted in a cartoon in the contemporary periodical, *Cape Punch*, showing an elegant Editor of the *Cape Times* holding at arm's length a wriggling, bat-like creature—Horatio Dunsterville Blewitt, Editor of the *Kaffrarian Watchman*.

CHAPTER 5

ENGLISHING THE TRANSVAAL

Realize that for the sort of Imperialism which means the Divine
Right of Downing Street there is indeed, in Sir Hercules
Robinson's words, no more room in South Africa.

Edmund Garrett, in the *Pall Mall Gazette*, 1890

IN December 1889, Sir Henry Loch, the new Governor of Cape
Colony and High Commissioner for South Africa, landed at
Table Bay and made solemn progress to Government House
through a Cape Town gay with bunting and triumphal arches.

In the crowd lining Adderley Street was a young English
journalist, Edmund Garrett, special correspondent of W. T.
Stead's *Pall Mall Gazette*, who had arrived a few days earlier.
Garrett's health had broken down. His doctor, in the fashion of
the time, suggested his lung trouble might benefit from a spell
in the South African air. Garrett's travel letters, published in the
Pall Mall Gazette, attracted considerable notice in England and
elsewhere. They would also catch the eye of St Leger.

On that December day, Garrett recorded the excitement of the
new Governor's arrival in the colloquial and rather breathless
prose of Stead's 'new journalism', noting the hundreds of school-
children—'bands of boys and girls of every conceivable hue;
from black to brown; from brown to yellow; from yellow to
white'—who were drawn up in the Avenue to sing the National
Anthem. At the railway station, he found a crowd taking leave
of friends with ringing English cheers:

> You might fancy yourself at Charing Cross seeing off a
> Continental Mail, only there is rather more hand-grasping and
> handkerchief-waving here. This train is packed with English-
> men—engineers, speculators, doctors, clerks, every trade and
> craft that a growing community require. A few of them are
> for Kimberley, many more are bound for the Rand. Their

goal is the Eldorado of the Transvaal and it is the Englishing of the Transvaal that they are going to help.

The 24-year-old Garrett was inclined to be enthusiastic about the Empire. And he was to become increasingly enthusiastic about South Africa as he journeyed north to Kimberley and the Rand, meeting President Reitz of the Free State, President Kruger of the Transvaal, J. H. Hofmeyr of the Afrikaner Bond— and Cecil Rhodes, buttonholing the great man in a railway carriage and holding him in conversation for hours.

Garrett spoke to Hofmeyr in the latter's study, 'hung with the portraits of the men who led at Laing's Nek and Majuba'. He found him shrewd and cautious, but kindly, and he went away with the impression that there was no longer a 'Dutch question' at the Cape. Reitz, who in later years would say that he had an almost affectionate regard for Garrett, impressed the young correspondent as a sincere advocate of closer South African union.

Garrett was captivated by Rhodes—'a bundle of inconsistencies'— and wrote the first of the adulatory but perceptive character sketches which would later be quarried by historians:

I have heard Mr Rhodes defined as a cynic whose one formula for success was 'Find the man's price'. If you read price in a large enough sense, I am not disposed to dispute that, nor to deny that even when the price is of the most sordid quality Mr Rhodes will often use the man for ends worthy of a better instrument. But if he is a cynic, he is also an enthusiast, and he presses the former's quality into the latter's service. Money, either to hoard or to hold, he does not care for. Power is his idol; creative power, efficient energy, control over men and things in the mass. In the British Empire he recognizes the most perfect and far-reaching machine for this purpose which the world has yet seen and the Empire, accordingly, is his religion. 'Sentiment', he once said to me, when I objected that some idea or other, on which he had laid stress, was 'mere sentiment', 'sentiment rules half the world'. We have seen what is the sentiment which rules Mr Rhodes. . . . For some millionaires it is enough to run a yacht. Mr Rhodes's hobby is running an Empire. He has that inclusiveness of mind, that passion for the grand scale, for generalizing and combining in the gross, which goes to make Newtons, and Napoleons, and Darwins, and Bismarcks—each in his own field of thought and action. He is always thinking of the next move but one; he is a general who carries the whole line of battle in his head.

Garrett also noted the conflicts of interest implicit in Rhodes's chairmanships of the Chartered Company and De Beers and his position as Prime Minister of the Cape. He was confident that Rhodes would resign the premiership if these conflicts became overt.

His tastes are simple to a fault. He cares not a pin what he eats or drinks, so there be enough of it, or wherewithal he shall be clothed, so there be not too much of it. The Premier's is the dowdiest hat in the House of Assembly. He lives in chambers and at the club. His unconventionality shocks the sticklers. They were opening an extension of the Cape Town suburban railway the other day—an extension at the edge of one of those tempting blue bights that fret the Cape Peninsula. Suddenly the central figure of the ceremonies was missed—and descried a short way off, stalking out of the water to rejoin his clothes. Lastly, Mr Rhodes is still an unappropriated match, and not, so friends declare, 'a marrying man'; which is a pity, for the man would be none the worse for a few more feminine traits about him. . . . One day some six years ago, Mr Rhodes, then busy with the amalgamation of the diamond mines, was looking at a map of Africa hung in the office of a Kimberley merchant. After gazing intently at it for some time, he placed his hand over a great slice of Southern and Central Africa, right across the continent; and turning to a friend at his side, 'There,' said Mr Rhodes, 'all that British! That is my dream.' 'I give you ten years', returned the friend—who told me the story himself on the very scene of the incident. More than half the allotted term has passed, and more than half of Mr Rhodes's dream is already accomplished.

Garrett's interview with Paul Kruger was conducted at

six o'clock on a sultry January morning. Mr Johann Rissik, acting Surveyor-General of the South African Republic, the man who surveyed Johannesburg, was the interpreter and the interview took place on the stoep of the President's house, with Kruger puffing away at a long pipe, a 'hale old man' who, as Garrett noted, as a youth was said to have been able to keep pace with a horse. Garrett set the scene:

Oom Paul, as his own people affectionately dub him, is a strong man and a shrewd. He has matched that strength and that shrewdness against English proconsuls and English statesmen and for a time he did not come off worst. But no man or President is strong enough to grapple Fate; and Fate just now is engaged in the experiment of planting out the Englishman, *malgré lui*, over some large regions of the world. We—the English—certainly did our best to forfeit any share in that particular tract which lies between the Vaal and the Limpopo. From the annexation of the Transvaal to its retrocession— from Shepstone with his two dozen policemen and his proclamations, to poor Colley with his mob of panic-stricken redcoats on Amajuba Hill—it all reads like one mad abdication, on the part of our statesmanship and of our arms alike, of any title to shape, create and govern. Yet five short years had scarcely passed when the whole situation changed. To burrow for a precious metal English men with English money and English enterprise swarmed into the country. . . . Meanwhile there are dangers and difficulties and delays, and the Englishing of the Transvaal is a process to which Oom Paul has still quite enough to say to make it worth John Bull's while to be closer acquainted. At the time of my talk with him, Mr Rhodes's company had but newly cut him off from the North, and the old man's eyes were turned to the one opening left him on his south-eastern marches, where the barbarous little Swazi country, already made over to White adventurers and overrun by his own Boers, interposes between him and the Indian Ocean. . . .

After some wary talk of newspapers and their influence on

political questions—Kruger conceding that a well-informed
newspaper might have great influence in England—Garrett
mentioned Majuba and the conversation took a most happy turn:

'Amajuba!' repeated the President, with warmth. 'It is all
wrong about Amajuba. I am sorry that the English people
seem to keep up such a foolish feeling about that. People say
that we think we conquered the English. I'll tell you what we
do think—and not one man, two men, but all the men in the
Republic.' The President paused a moment and blew a cloud
of smoke with great energy. He has no Dutch phlegm, by
the way, in conversation, but is forcible, voluble, prone to
gesture. 'We think that the English did not know what were
the wishes of our people when they took our country away
from us. Then we said: "We will show them that we do love
our country." We knew that England was much stronger; but
we said, "Sooner than our country be taken away from us
unjustly, we will fight until we die". Then the English people
saw that they were wrong, and so they gave us back our
country. You can tell the English people that is what we think.
It is the busybodies that write to England, and make out that
we are always boasting about Amajuba, who do the harm.
But you can go and talk to the farmers, and you will find that
what I say is the truth.'

'Down in Cape Colony,' said I, encouraged by the President's speech about the war, 'I found that the Dutch and the
English are growing more and more to be friends and to work
together for their common interests. Cannot this be so in the
Transvaal also?'

'If,' returned the President, deliberately, 'if I find the English
government willing to work with me, and help me to promote
the interests of this country, then I will do the same for
England. But if not, I must go my own way. Each hand must
wash the other, you know', he added with a characteristically
homely metaphor. . . .

Eventually, Garrett asked the President a direct question:

'If we frankly give up some day the policy of distrust and
isolation—if we recognize as nowise inimical the desire of this

Republic to touch the seaboard—if we throw absolutely open the path through Swaziland and Tongaland to the sea, and invite the Transvaal to work out its own ambition with British coast protection, how far then will you, on your part, fall in with a scheme of cordial South African co-operation?'

'Then,' exclaimed Oom Paul, with the greatest emphasis, 'if England works together with me in that way, I will do everything to work together with England and the Colonies. I will come into a Customs Union; I will give free leave for railways to be built wherever it will pay anyone to build them; I will do my best to make the South African states in one; I will do everything together with the Colonies, for I believe their interests are the same as the interests of this country. But what can I do,' he cried, catching himself up—'what can I do as long as England persists in shutting me up like this?'

He put two brawny hands together, finger tips to finger tips, in illustration. A moment later our conversation was cut short by a voice from within doors summoning the President to breakfast. But the look of the old man as he made these memorable declarations and the quaint gesture that accompanied them stuck in my mind. I noticed on the left hand that the thumb was wanting. It seems it was shattered by a gun which burst when Kruger as a lad went out hunting. It was in the early days of the *voortrekkers* (for Paul's parents were among the first in the country, whither they brought him as a boy of ten, teaching him, no doubt, some Hannibal's oath against the English, from whose rule they fled). Surgeons, therefore, there were none. Paul pulled out his pocket knife and with his right hand coolly whipped off the offending member at the joint. It was characteristic of the iron resolution of the man.

Oom Paul is a bad enemy, as we have learned to our cost. He has proved to us of late that he can also be a leal friend. Slowly but surely, I believe, my countrymen are coming to realize that his friendship is worth having.

Garrett, returning to England, was elated about his South African journey and wrote in optimistic strain about the future;

believing that the drift was in the direction of South African union:

> Realize that for that sort of Imperialism which means the Divine Right of Downing Street there is indeed, in Sir Hercules Robinson's words, no more room in South Africa. . . . Once grasp these things here in England, put in the stocks the people who talk or write about 'keeping down the Boers' or 'hemming in the Boers', as if they were rat-hunting rather than seeking to cement a political alliance; gag, in the occasional aberrations of those good men, the Aborigines Protection Society; and you will have gone a long way towards that unity through which alone South Africa can grapple with its future. Only we must not hurry.

Garrett would return to South Africa five years later and would have another interview with Paul Kruger—as Editor of the *Cape Times*.

5. Cecil John Rhodes. From a photograph in *The Story of the Cape to Cairo
Railway and River Route* 1887–1922.

6. Sir James Rose Innes

7. John X. Merriman

8. J. W. Sauer

9. Sir James Sivewright

CHAPTER 6

AN ANCIENT AND FISH-LIKE SMELL

I was astounded the other day to find it stated in the papers that
Logan had been granted the monopoly of supplying refreshments
at all stations upon the entire system for a term of years.

James Rose Innes in a letter to
Cecil John Rhodes, 8 November 1892

ON Saturday morning, 5 November 1892, a letter appeared in
the *Cape Times* which was signed 'An Astonished Colonist'. The
correspondent said that the holders of the refreshment rooms
along the line of the Cape railways from Cape Town to the
Free State had been given peremptory notice to vacate their
means of livelihood. The contract for bars and refreshment rooms
along the line were to be given to one man, a Mr Logan.

Logan, who ran the bar and refreshment room at Matjiesfontein, was undoubtedly an energetic man. A great deal of
public money had been spent on Matjiesfontein station. But
why should Mr Logan have every refreshment room under his
control? One of the holders of a refreshment room on the Cape
railways had been for more than ten years at one station and had
given every satisfaction. Now he had been given notice. It was
strange that the public should countenance a monopoly of this
sort. Who was interested in the financial success of the proprietor
of Matjiesfontein that such undoubted favouritism should be
shown to him?

Other letters to the Editor followed, with one of 8 November
asking why the government had not called for tenders for the
refreshment contract. There was a 'very ancient and fish-like
smell' connected with the business. The correspondent expressed
the hope that some independent member of the House of Assembly
would call for the relevant papers to be laid on the table. Then,
on 18 November, there appeared the first of a series of editorials
in the *Cape Times* demanding that the contract be cancelled and
that tenders be called for in the ordinary way. A 'vicious pre-

cedent' would be set up if the arrangement, as reported, went through.

The stage was set for the break-up of the first Rhodes Cabinet. Within a few months, Rhodes was to lose the services of his best colleagues—James Rose Innes, Attorney-General; J. W. Sauer, Colonial Secretary; and John X. Merriman, Treasurer. The three refused to sit any longer in the same Cabinet as Sir James Sivewright, Commissioner of Crown Lands and Public Works, who had given the refreshment contract to his friend, J. D. Logan—without calling for tenders.

Both Rhodes and Sivewright were abroad and it was not until May the following year that the crisis was resolved. Rhodes could have retained the others by dropping Sivewright. But Rhodes resigned and, to avoid taking sides with Innes, Sauer and Merriman, left all the parties to the dispute out of the new Cabinet. In so doing, Rhodes alienated Innes, Sauer and Merriman, but kept the goodwill and co-operation of Sivewright. Sivewright was indispensable in Rhodes's plans. As a prominent English-speaking member of the Afrikaner Bond, he was needed by Rhodes to ensure the Bond's continued backing for his plans of Northern expansion. And he had proved invaluable as a railway negotiator with the Transvaal. But his support could be retained only if Rhodes was prepared to break with Innes, Merriman and Sauer. For Sivewright remained unrepentant about his actions in the Logan contract and Rhodes declined to demand his resignation.

It was a fateful decision, which some have seen as the decisive turning-point in Rhodes's career, marking a moral decline and an increasing carelessness about the means used in achieving his aims. By now, it seems, Rhodes no longer had any doubts at all that the end justified the means. But it is possible that the first Rhodes ministry would have broken up anyway. Innes, particularly, as a liberal in politics, and Sauer and Merriman were never fully at ease in the Cabinet. Nevertheless, Vere Stent, special correspondent of the *Cape Times* and later Editor of the *Pretoria News*, who was an admirer of Rhodes, accounted the Logan affair as his first great mistake, allowing Innes, Sauer and Merriman to leave his Cabinet 'rather than abandon Sivewright before their charge of corruption and the sacrifice of public welfare to personal and private interests'.

When we consider the outstanding reputation of Innes, his integrity and impartiality; the brilliance of Sauer—if only in debate and upon a public platform; and the scholarly frankness of Merriman and his hatred of humbug, it is obvious that Rhodes's decision was infinitely to be regretted. High honesty and a nice sense of honour, brilliant biting wit and moral courage, erudition and fearless criticism, left Rhodes's Cabinet and the door was open for sycophancy, opportunism and time-serving.

In November 1892, however, Rhodes was abroad. James Rose Innes wrote to him in terms of great urgency, pointing out that Logan was to have a monopoly for 15 years and 'practically had the option for running the whole show for 20 years'. Innes enclosed the newspaper cuttings—'merely the first droppings of a shower'—and said he declined to share any responsibility in the matter, unless Sivewright could provide a satisfactory explanation. As he told Rhodes, 'I do not like hanky-panky'. Rhodes agreed to the cancellation of the contract, whereupon Logan successfully sued the Cape Government for non-performance, being awarded £5 000. But Sivewright, unrepentant, steadfastly refused to resign.

Meanwhile, the *Cape Times* was refraining from further comment, anxious that the crisis should be satisfactorily resolved without the Cabinet losing its liberal wing. But the *Star* and the *Argus* began taking Sivewright's part against Merriman, Innes and Sauer, and the *Argus*, on the day that the Cabinet broke up— 3 May 1893—launched a violent attack on the 'machinations' of Sivewright's colleagues, 'the three mutineers', accusing them of conspiring against him in his absence and bringing down a ministry which enjoyed the fullest public confidence. The *Argus* spoke of their conduct as motivated either by personal jealousy or disappointment or, possibly, in other cases, by a 'mistaken sense of personal and political honour'. Merriman was singled

out for particular criticism as the 'ringleader' and a man who had
already wrecked three ministries.

On the following day the *Cape Times* sprang to the defence
of the 'mutineers', declaring that their motives had been set in a
false and confusing light, 'as though the revolt had been organized
under the sting of personal jealousy . . .'.

> Never did ministers go forth, we do not hesitate to say, with
> less hope of any near—nay even of remote—advantage than
> did Messrs Merriman, Sauer and Innes when they took part
> in the Cabinet exodus of Tuesday last. They have no party
> waiting them with open arms. . . . The Ministers who threw
> up a work in which they were doing excellent service to the
> country virtually abandoned all hope—within present vision—
> of return to public employment. They are neither so opulent
> as lightly to surrender a comfortable income, nor so feather-
> headed as to court disaster upon the impulse of a capricious
> animosity. Public men who incur a sacrifice of means and
> ambition . . . in their jealousy for the honour of the State and
> its administration deserve to be better spoken of. If we were
> running perilously near the example of a neighbouring State
> in other things, we may at least claim for this Colony the unique
> dignity of such a sacrifice. And whether the Ministers have been
> guided by a right judgement or not this recognition is no more
> than their just due. . . . We claim for the Ministers who forced
> the breaking-up credit for a strong sense of public duty. The
> sacrifice that they have made is the most eloquent argument of
> an honest cause.

The Logan affair had consequences which went beyond its
intrinsic importance. Vere Stent believed that Rhodes's break
with Rose Innes, Merriman and Sauer helped to create the circumstances which made the Jameson Raid possible.

A dangerous phase in Rhodes's life began. He grew domineer-
ing, says Stent, and began to prefer as his helpers men with no
opinions of their own. He sought willing obedience, not wholesome advice. Deprived of the counsel and company of men like
James Rose Innes and Merriman and surrounded by sycophants,

Rhodes became embroiled in what Stent called the 'stupendous folly' of the Jameson Raid.

Hoping to repair the breach, Rhodes wrote to Merriman a few days after the Cabinet break-up that 'needless to say' he had no knowledge of 'certain Press articles that have come under my notice'. The reference, obviously, was to the attacks on Merriman, Innes and Sauer which had appeared in Argus newspapers. Rhodes expressed the hope to Merriman that they could continue having their accustomed morning rides. But Merriman's confidence was shaken. As he wrote to his friend Currey, he felt that Rhodes had acted a dastardly part, 'seeing a thief and consenting to him' and sacrificing three honest men.

Rhodes was now at the height of his political power, having included the then Leader of the Opposition, Sprigg, in his new Cabinet and having the support of the Bond as well. There was no means of welding together a powerful opposition party and the situation would remain confused until the polarization on English–Dutch lines that took place in the wake of the Jameson Raid.

The Cape Times was still supporting Rhodes's schemes of Northern expansion and South African confederation. Indeed, St Leger always claimed that the Northern expansion had been first broached in the columns of the Cape Times and that the newspaper was the first to give Rhodes's schemes encouragement. But the Cape Times continued to be critical of his domestic policies and on occasion found fault with his methods. Yet the paper did not turn against Rhodes after the Logan affair, arguing (3 May 1894) that the country 'at present is especially in need of a strong man at the head of affairs'. Rhodes 'owed it to the country to continue to give it the benefit of his far-seeing sagacity and of his inflexible will'.

This did not inhibit St Leger from criticizing De Beers, for instance, when he deemed it to be acting contrary to the public interest. At the same time as the Logan affair was attracting attention, the Cape Times was questioning the activities of De Beers in denuding sections of Bechuanaland of wood to provide fuel for its mining machinery at Kimberley. The newspaper argued that it should not have been difficult in a paternally-governed province to impose an effectual check on the destruction of timber. 'The effect on climate and soil of such despoliation is a thing of common knowledge; and if the annexation of British Bechuanaland to the Cape Colony is contemplated (as is said), it would be prudent on the part of the Government to make a formal representation of the damage being done to property of which we hold the reversion. . . . British Bechuanaland would not be worth taking over as a bare and barren desert.'

And on the following day, concluding another long leader on the subject, the *Cape Times* said: 'It is likely that the De Beers Company desires to cultivate the friendship of the Cape Colony; and it would be no mean evidence of that disposition if they could so far control the commercial instinct as to reduce the temptation to needy landowners in Bechuanaland to make profit at the expense of the country.'

One consequence of the Logan affair, which persisted for years, was a feud between the *Cape Times* and Sir James Sivewright —which blew up into a national controversy in March 1894.

On 6 March, the *Cape Times* published an interview with Dr Leyds, State Secretary of the Transvaal, in which Leyds denied a statement by Sivewright that President Kruger had promised him (Sivewright) that no railway would enter the Transvaal on better terms than those negotiated for the Cape by Sivewright. The *Cape Argus*, by now a daily newspaper, immediately sent a wire to Sivewright at his country seat, Lourensford, Hottentots Holland, asking for his comment. As the *Argus* noted, Sir James's reply did not err on the side of prolixity.

He wired back: 'The *Cape Times* or Dr Leyds lies, and I cannot believe it is Dr Leyds.'

St Leger's blood was up. The following day there was a leader in the *Cape Times* under a headline: 'The usual denial from Sir James Sivewright':

> The extent to which reliance may be placed on Sir James Sivewright's denials may be gathered from the following statements of fact; some few weeks ago, on the occasion when Mr Hofmeyr addressed the electors of Somerset West, Sir

James Sivewright declared that Mr Rhodes 'ordered' Messrs Innes, Merriman and Sauer to resign. This was duly reported in the next issue of this journal; in the afternoon, an inspired denial appeared in our contemporary, with the additional statement that the reporter's shorthand notes of Sir James Sivewright's speech had been consulted and no such word as 'ordered' could be found. The statement respecting the search was, of course, accepted; but as two expert shorthand writers present at the meeting in question had the word 'ordered' in their notes of Sir James's speech, our statement was repeated the following day—and there was no further denial.

At this point, Sir James addressed a letter to the Editor of the *Cape Times*, a missive of extraordinary length and prolixity, which insisted that President Kruger had given the promise in question—but had added a rider to the effect that this would only hold good as long as all remained well between the Transvaal and the Cape Colony. The *Cape Times* dismissed this as an afterthought and defended itself against Sir James's charge that it was motivated by spite.

Sir James Sivewright knows, no one better, the extent of the indulgence that has been granted to him in the past two years. Every possible opportunity has been given to him to explain his position. . . .

On 20 March, the *Cape Times*'s Pretoria correspondent reported President Kruger's comment: He could not for the world understand why such a noise was being made by his friend, Sir James, over a matter upon which he never had any doubt. What he had said at the time was: 'I do not wish to privilege any other State, or promise you anything whatsoever, for I must first see what events the future brings us.' At no time was a verbal or other promise made.

By this time, just about every newspaper in the country had taken a stand—for or against Sir James Sivewright or the *Cape Times*. The *Star* and the *Argus* backed Sir James, with the *Star* declaring that Sivewright had fully vindicated himself against the 'gross and scandalous charge of having said the thing that was not'. The *Star* conceded, however, that Sir James had not presented his case as well as a more practised controversialist might have done. The East London *Daily Dispatch* saw the *Cape Times*'s stand as 'an exercise of untimely spleen'. The *Standard and Diggers' News*, a pro-Kruger organ in Johannesburg, said it would be hard on the Transvaal if it transpired that Sir James was trying to cover the failure of his historic mission in its most important details 'at the expense of Dr Leyds and the Transvaal's reputation for truth-telling and trustiness'. Sir James had yet to demonstrate that there had been lying by Dr Leyds or by the *Cape Times*. So the *Cape Times* found itself momentarily on the side of President Kruger's Transvaal in a dispute with an influential Cape politician. St Leger was once again concerned to vindicate his newspaper's reputation for accuracy and good faith.

The 'solemn promise' controversy, as it came to be known, was not the last brush between Sir James and the *Cape Times*. In 1897, Sivewright delivered a speech at Ashton which the *Cape Times* reporter, G. H. Wilson, considered to be remarkably friendly to President Kruger in the (post-Raid) circumstances. Wilson in his reminiscences noted that he expected the speech to cause a sensation when published the next day in the *Cape Times*. He was writing it out in a railway carriage when Sir James Sivewright looked in, produced a flask of Mountain Dew whisky, and asked Wilson what he thought of the speech. Wilson said he thought it would cause considerable astonishment and he read Sivewright the passage in question. Sivewright listened gravely and then declared: 'I never said anything of the sort.' Wilson replied that this undoubtedly was what Sivewright had said: 'Oh, no,' said Sir James. 'Now please take down what I really did say', and he dictated. 'Now,' he said, 'will you kindly substitute that for your inaccurate account of my speech.' Wilson said he could not possibly do that but he undertook to send a telegram to the *Cape Times*, in addition to his report, saying that Sivewright claimed to have spoken in different terms and appending Sivewright's version—which the *Cape Times* published the next day as a footnote to Wilson's report.

CHAPTER 7

VALEDICTORY

They are not likely to abandon their republicanism; and it would be not merely a crime but a blunder to force the Imperial allegiance upon unwilling peoples.

F. Y. St Leger, 1898

ON Monday morning, 24 June 1895, readers of the *Cape Times* were startled to find that the leading article was signed by the Editor. Departing for the first and last time from his strict practice of editorial anonymity, St Leger addressed his readers personally to announce his retirement.

He had been planning withdrawal from the active editorship of the newspaper for several years. In 1890 he had travelled to England in the same ship as Edmund Garrett. The time he spent with Garrett on shipboard and later in London convinced St Leger that he was an ideal successor. A year later he asked his former partner, R. W. Murray Junior, who had moved to London, to recruit Garrett as Assistant Editor, but the latter was out of reach in Egypt. St Leger remained convinced that Garrett was his man.

Meanwhile, he had set about rebuilding the *Cape Times* office and works, and in September 1892 a new building had come into use on the St George's Street site—a three-storey edifice with Tudor gable and the Colonial coat of arms and the motto 'Spes Bona' prominent on the façade. The premises now extended right through to Burg Street. The undertaking was flourishing; *Cape Times* Daily, Weekly and Mail editions were being produced and there was also an extensive general printing business. As the newspaper had proudly announced in a supplement on 4 September 1892: 'The building will be lighted throughout by electricity, which will give the building a brilliant appearance at night. . . .'

But the *Cape Times* was under-capitalized and there was an

43

overdraft at the bank. St Leger accepted, though very reluctantly, a suggestion by his son Fred, the business manager, that Dr Rutherfoord Harris, his brother-in-law, should be allowed to put some capital into the *Cape Times*.

As far as St Leger was concerned, this was purely a financial transaction, designed to relieve him of dependence on borrowed capital. He insisted on a deed of partnership which stipulated that the newspaper's policy and its editorial control were in no way affected by the arrangement. As G. A. L. Green expressed it, St Leger, at the time of his retirement, exercised 'absolute and exclusive control of the newspaper which his transparent honesty, incessant hard work and sound judgement had made easily the greatest organ of opinion in South Africa'.

St Leger was to have cause for regretting his decision to give Harris a share in the newspaper. Harris, as the events of the next few years would demonstrate, was unscrupulous and unprincipled in politics. He had been a doctor in Kimberley and an early associate of Cecil Rhodes, and had become secretary of Rhodes's Chartered Company. As he later told the South Africa Committee, there was nobody more intimately associated with Rhodes's affairs, private, political and public, than himself. He did everything for Rhodes, said Harris.

If this was so, as Basil Williams has noted, it did not indicate much discrimination on Rhodes's part. And Harris was to become deeply embroiled in the conspiracy which preceded the Jameson Raid. His connection with the Raid, when it became known, severely embarrassed the *Cape Times* in its standing as an independent newspaper.

After the 1898 elections, Harris's role in securing Rhodes's re-election in Barkly West was the subject of a petition to the Supreme Court seeking to have the result set aside on grounds of bribery. Although the petition was unsuccessful, the Chief Justice, Lord De Villiers, described Harris's role as 'very reprehensible'. But St Leger, at this stage, was blind to Harris's shortcomings and placed great faith in his son's judgement, a faith that was not vindicated by subsequent events.

In offering Edmund Garrett the editorship, St Leger gave him a contract between himself and Harris as proprietors of the *Cape Times*, and Garrett as Editor, guaranteeing Garrett's editorial independence. The new Editor's position was strengthened by a stipulation that he could be discharged only on 12 months' notice whereas Garrett was able to resign, if he wished, at three months' notice. In St Leger's time, any question of interference by Harris or anyone else would have been unthinkable, such was St Leger's standing and prestige. But Garrett was young and relatively untried.

As St Leger withdrew from the editorial chair, it was soon plain that Harris had no intention of abiding by the spirit of the agreement. Garrett was subjected to severe pressures by Harris, who persistently tried to interfere in editorial policy to promote what he conceived to be the interests of Cecil Rhodes.

By 1898, when it was decided to transform the *Cape Times* into a company, a somewhat disillusioned St Leger took further steps to safeguard the independence of the newspaper, placing the position beyond doubt by insisting that the following agreement between himself and the Company be included in the Articles of Association:

'F. Y. St Leger shall during his lifetime have the sole control over the editorial management of the *Cape Times* newspaper, it being understood that it shall be in his power to appoint any person whom he may choose as editor or acting editor provided that the persons appointed shall be instructed and bound to conduct the paper in all respects on similar lines to which the paper has been conducted by the said F. Y. St Leger.'

In the partnership, St Leger held 56 per cent of the capital and Harris 44 per cent, and this proportion appears to have been maintained in the shareholding of the new *Cape Times* Company. After April 1898, then, Garrett was answerable in law to F. Y. St Leger and, as he put it, his own conscience. But Harris and, initially, Fred St Leger, made it necessary for Garrett to fight every inch of the way to maintain the paper's independence.

Now, in June 1895, however, St Leger was confident that the independence of the paper was secure, and he was happy to withdraw in favour of his chosen successor. As the time came for the change of editors, rumours were rife in Cape Town that, with Garrett's appointment, Cecil Rhodes had gained control of the *Cape Times*. Rhodes's substantial interest in South African newspapers was felt by his political opponents to be contrary to the public interest.

As Eric Walker has pointed out in his biography of W. P. Schreiner, Rhodes-ian interests were at this time in control of the Argus Company, which included the *Cape Argus*, the Johannesburg *Star* and 'at least one paper in every state or colony south of the Zambesi'. The suggestion that the staunchly independent *Cape Times* was coming under the same control caused a public outcry.

By this time Harris's connection with the *Cape Times* had become known and it was assumed, probably correctly, that Harris's investment in the newspaper had been made on Rhodes's behalf. It had been reported that Rhodes had tried, unsuccessfully, to get Edmund Garrett appointed as Editor of the *Cape Argus* and had then found a place for him at the *Cape Times*.

At least part of this was true. Rhodes had, in fact, suggested Garrett's name to Francis Dormer, Managing Director of the Argus Company. But Dormer was implacably opposed to the appointment. This is confirmed in an acrimonious exchange of letters between Garrett and Dormer which survives, curiously enough, in the Michell papers at the Cape Archives.

There was a violent quarrel between Rhodes and Dormer which seems to have been a factor in the latter breaking his long association with Rhodes and resigning, in February 1895, as Managing Director of the Argus Company and Editor of the *Star*. Dormer was also increasingly at odds with Rhodes about the latter's attitude to Paul Kruger's Transvaal, and the row over Garrett seems to have been the last straw. Dormer disliked Garrett and questioned his judgement, although he conceded his brilliance as a writer.

As Dormer wrote later in *Vengeance as a policy in Afrikanderland* [*sic*], Rhodes had wanted him to displace a valued colleague in favour of Garrett, whom he described as 'glib and hysterical'. But Dormer felt that 'a man with a weak chest and strong con-

victions, particularly when they did not accord with my own'
would not make a good editor of an Argus publication. So the
Argus appointment fell through.

Garrett's subsequent appointment to the *Cape Times* suited
Rhodes, of course, but there is no doubt that Garrett was St
Leger's personal choice as his successor. Now, on the eve of
Garrett's arrival at the *Cape Times*, it was being said that he was
'Rhodes's nominee' for the job, and the paper's independence
was being questioned.

This, more than anything else, probably persuaded St Leger to
depart from his invariable custom and sign his valedictory
leading article. His decision to retire had been hastened by the
threat of formidable competition from the *South African Telegraph*,
a new morning paper which was being started by the pro-Kruger
millionaire, J. B. Robinson. Robinson had earlier tried,
unsuccessfully, to buy the *Cape Times*. Now he was determined
to break it.

St Leger believed that new blood and new methods would be
needed to meet the challenge. As he said in his valedictory article,
it was all very well for the old horse to amble along at his own
pace as long as nobody else was in any particular hurry. St Leger
told of his attempts to recruit Garrett a few years earlier and his
gratification when his cabled offer to him had been accepted.

St Leger also explained the terms of the partnership arrangement, without mentioning Harris by name, and appealed 'without fear to the record of the last two years in evidence of independence and candour in dealing with public questions'.

It would argue a certain benevolence on the part of 'the
monopolist' (obviously Cecil Rhodes was indicated) 'to have
borne with my perversity for so long. But on the monopolistic
assumption, it is sad to think that my successor is even a more
perverse fellow than myself.'

Introducing Garrett to readers of the *Cape Times*, St Leger
said he was as honest, independent and fearless a craftsman as he
could have found with the aid of Diogenes's lantern itself. And
Garrett would be assured of complete independence in his
editorship of the newspaper.

It has been objected to him that he believes in Mr Rhodes; it has been said that he invented Mr Rhodes. I, too, have had the misfortune to incur rebuke because, with all my criticism of Rhodes's policy, I have still retained an affection for his personality. To turn against Mr Rhodes, to vituperate him as one who has developed monstrous qualities since the period of his domestication in the Happy Family, is the one way of salvation, according to the critics of smoking room and club. Be it so. I have known Mr Rhodes for 24 years; and I do not feel called upon to revise my estimate of his character because he had the misfortune to differ from his former colleagues about the character of one who had shared his confidence. Mr Garrett starts with a fair appreciation of those qualities in Mr Rhodes which have lifted him to distinction. I am sure that the appreciation will not hoodwink the critical eye or diminish lucidity of judgement in matters of daily discussion.

Now St Leger was withdrawing from the editorial chair. Freed from the daily—and nightly—labours of nearly 20 years as Editor, he began for the first time to take part in public affairs. He became a town councillor and in November 1895 we find him opposing the construction of the new town hall, arguing that slum clearance and housing for the poorer classes deserved priority over prestige projects, given the state of municipal finances.

The *Cape Times*, meanwhile, was keeping up its vigorous interest in municipal affairs, declaring on 25 November: 'For once the Town Council of Cape Town has shown a disposition to listen to outside critics.' The newspaper was elated at having persuaded the Mayor, Mr Atwell, to agree to the publication of a quarterly statement setting forth the financial condition of the Council. The paper also hailed the Council's acceptance of a proposal by St Leger for a slum inquiry, noting the 'terrible death rate' recorded in the report of the Medical Officer of Health. 'Mr St Leger, in making this proposal, is true to his *Cape Times* record, and the *Cape Times* can only wish him and his fellow-councillors all success in their humane labours.'

St Leger was soon also involved in politics—on the platform of James Rose Innes's South African Political Association, a body which reflected Innes's own liberal views and was fighting for the abolition of protective duties on meat, wheat and foodstuffs—duties which Rhodes's government, in deference to the Afrikaner Bond's farming constituency, steadfastly refused to abolish. The cost-of-living at the time was crippling city-dwellers and the 'cheap food' issue would be a consistent theme of politics in the next few years. The subject was dear to St Leger's heart. He had made a study of the theory and practice of taxation in all its forms and held that taxation of the necessities of life was iniquitous.

On 13 December 1895, St Leger was welcomed at a meeting of the South African Political Association by Innes, who said that their guest held an 'almost unique position' in the affections of Cape Town. St Leger told the audience that most reforms had to be first fought out on public platforms. 'No expediency, no plea of utility, could ever justify a policy, whether social or fiscal, which was essentially unjust.'

But now a political tornado was about to break. In a few weeks, the Jameson Raid would bring Rhodes down and smash the Rhodes–Hofmeyr alliance, inflaming English–Afrikaans animosity and setting the scene for the South African War. James Rose Innes and the moderates who thought like him now became increasingly ineffectual, forming an uneasy liberal wing in a Progressive Party which would soon be under the dominance of Rhodes in a new guise—this time as the leader of a largely English-speaking party, militantly ranged against an Afrikaner Bond which it accused of 'Krugerism'.

This was the atmosphere in which St Leger became increasingly active in politics, seeking election for the Upper House, the Legislative Council, sponsored by the South African Political Association. Meanwhile, however, he had developed a painful affliction of the throat. At first, the diagnosis was not alarming and, at his doctor's suggestion, he travelled to England for several months' holiday.

Garrett wrote to his cousin Agnes in London urging her to take St Leger—'poor, dear old boy'—under her wing and be kind to him. 'He is rather a sad old man. He has just resigned from his Town Council in a huff. They didn't run the election properly and let the bounders get the upper hand. . . .'

He followed this with another letter in June 1897 saying that St Leger and Rose Innes were coming over in the same ship, the *Dunvegan Castle*, and urging Agnes to have them to dinner together. 'Be nice to the old man and speak so as to make him feel that we appreciate his kindness to me and make him see that I feel I am carrying on *his* line after my own way. . . .'

When St Leger returned to Cape Town, he picked up his public activities, becoming deeply engrossed in preparations for his election campaign in the Legislative Council. He drafted an election statement which the *Diamond Fields Advertiser* hailed as a manifesto in the best sense, expressing sentiments which were 'almost an echo of those which Mr Rhodes professed in his earlier and saner days before he was led astray by the temptation to take a short cut'.

St Leger's manifesto, a characteristic document, declared in part:

> In our relations with the Republics I have always advocated the policy of doing all things that make for practical unity; and to this policy I adhere. They are not likely to abandon their republicanism; and it would be not merely a crime but a blunder to force the Imperial allegiance upon unwilling peoples. But by a patient continuance in unifying policy—as in railway matters, customs, law—an advance may be made in which we may at all events realize harmony, if it is not possible to be wholly at one. . . .

St Leger would look on in the months ahead as Imperial policy, under Alfred Milner's prodding, developed on lines diametrically opposed to his own counsels of patience and moderation. But now he was in the thick of a strenuous and rowdy election campaign, addressing several meetings a day, in the docks, at the Salt River railway workshops and in the suburbs.

St Leger stood as an Innes Progressive on an ill-assorted ticket

10. A cartoon in *Cape Punch*, 22 February, 1888, after Frederick York St Leger had won a libel action against an Eastern Province newspaper, the *Kaffrarian Watchman*, which had claimed that the *Cape Times* parliamentary reports were slanted. The *Watchman* referred to the *Cape Times* as 'our bilious contemporary'.

11. Frederick Luke St Leger

Cape Times Library

12. Robert Arthur St Leger

Cape Times Library

13. J. D. Logan

Library of Parliament

14. F. Rutherfoord Harris

From a group photograph in the
Cecil Sibbett Collection

of three which included his friend T. L. Graham and John A. Faure, an out-and-out Rhodes man who enjoyed Rhodes's support. There was also an independent, T. J. O'Reilly, a colourful Cape Town Irishman, who was to be Mayor of Cape Town in 1900–1, and a fifth candidate, M. L. Neethling, official candidate of the Afrikaner Bond. The five were in competition for three seats.

O'Reilly, whom the *Cape Times* described as the 'licensed victuallers' candidate', denied strenuously that his election expenses were being paid by brewers' interests. The temperance vote was a factor in the campaign. St Leger went to the Metropolitan Hall to address a meeting of temperance organizations, which gave him a vote of confidence. St Leger told the temperance workers that he spoke to them as one who had not altogether weaned himself from the apostolic permission to take a little wine for his stomach's sake. But he pledged his full support for Innes's restrictive Liquor Bill.

For the most part, candidates lined up for or against Cecil John Rhodes. Rhodes himself emerged into the open on the eve of polling day to assume the leadership of the Progressives, with the vociferous backing of the stridently imperialist South African League group in the party. Garrett and the *Cape Times* had played a major part in forcing Rhodes into the open as a Progressive. As the *Cape Times* had written in January 1898: 'We hold that Mr Rhodes cannot lurk unsuspected and that he had much better not lurk at all.' James Rose Innes stuck to his belief, which was soon vindicated, that Rhodes's return to Cape politics would fan jingo emotions to fever pitch.

Garrett, however, was determined to get Rhodes back into the fray, arguing that there was no one else who could unite the opposition against the Afrikaner Bond. For Rhodes to emerge as a Progressive would obviously call for a political volte-face. Rhodes would have to disavow his previously held attitudes on tariff issues, having previously advocated protective duties on imported foodstuffs to help the farmers and now having to appeal for electoral support to a mostly urban constituency, heavily burdened by the cost-of-living.

This was a time, as J. H. Hofmeyr caustically expressed it, when the name of Rhodes could not be even mentioned 'without calling forth thunderous applause'. Garrett argued that you could no more ignore Rhodes than you could ignore Table Mountain. It was better that he come into the open as the leader of the Progressives.

In this atmosphere, St Leger's campaign for the election to the Upper House was on a somewhat uneasy footing. His radical views on the total abolition of duties on the necessities of life went much further than Rhodes was prepared to go in modifying the policies advocated in the years of his alliance with the Afrikaner Bond. And the campaign was dominated by jingo enthusiasms.

A report in the *Cape Times* of a meeting in the Claremont Municipal Hall, addressed by T. J. O'Reilly, gives something of the atmosphere of the campaign:

Mr O'Reilly, who was received with cheers mixed with groans, began by saying that he would not allow any larrikins from Claremont to interrupt his meeting (cheers). He had noticed that in a speech by St Leger—(loud and continuous cheering)—at Observatory that gentleman had said that his (Mr O'Reilly's) only plank was Mr Rhodes. Well, he said, it was better to have that plank than none at all. Mr O'Reilly went on to say that Mr St Leger made jokes which only he laughed at himself. (Uproar, during which a gentleman from the audience approached the chairman, with whom he held a conference, and by whom he was eventually waved back to his seat, while the hubbub continued.) . . . He was in favour of the entire abolition of the duties on the necessaries of life, especially wheat, meat and flour. (A voice: What about beer?) . . . He was in favour of an excise on brandy, but he was not in favour of a tax on beer. (A voice: Why?) Why? Because a glass of beer was good for a man, and if the man who asked that question stuck to beer he would be a good deal better man than he was. (Loud laughter). . . . He would not support the Innes Liquor Bill. (Cries of 'Shame'). . . .

The meeting broke up in disorder, with the leading citizens of Claremont adjourning to the Claremont Club, where they passed a belated vote of confidence in the chair. St Leger seems to have cut an unusual figure as a candidate. He declined steadfastly to ask people to vote for him but exhorted them to use their own good judgment. He was not returned. Although polling well, he was defeated by what the *Cape Times* described as 'the exasperating mystery of the cumulative vote'. St Leger himself attributed his defeat to Cecil Rhodes. He wrote to James Rose Innes on 19 March 1898, thanking Innes for a letter of sympathy:

> I have at least the consolation of knowing that I was a true prophet if not an adept at election tactics. . . . As for the result of the election and how it was brought about, I have my theory—'By order of the Czar'.

After his defeat, St Leger was not enthusiastic about accepting nomination to stand again in the elections for the Lower House, the Legislative Assembly, as Rose Innes was pressing him to do. He wrote to Rose Innes on 3 April:

> Some features in this recent business are so painful as to cause a revulsion against any thought of public life; but I would rather not decide finally under the influence of this feeling.

St Leger's letters at this time suggest that he was deeply depressed. Even his political opponents regretted St Leger's defeat. John X. Merriman, speaking at a dinner given in honour of J. H. Hofmeyr on 28 March 1898, said he was sorry St Leger had not been returned. Perhaps the fact that Mr St Leger was not 'sound on the main point' might have had something to do with it. Mr St Leger was no extreme man and was not a man to rush into conflict with the Republics. (*Cape Times*, 29 March 1898.)

St Leger's old throat trouble had now returned At an eve-of-poll election rally on 13 March in the Good Hope Hall, he had not spoken at all, the chairman explaining that owing to the state of his voice he felt unequal to addressing so large an audience.

His disillusion with Rhodes seems to have been pretty well complete. But he did, eventually, agree to accept nomination, supported by the South African Political Association, for the Legislative Assembly elections. Edmund Garrett, in spite of objections from Harris, was also a candidate in this campaign and, while he was away electioneering at Victoria East, St Leger returned for brief spells to the editorial chair of the *Cape Times*. At this time, Rhodes was attacking his former political associates in bitter terms, and he was sharply criticized by the *Cape Times*. G. A. L. Green fancied that this led to 'indirect expostulations' from Rhodes. St Leger thereupon sent a haughty letter to Rhodes in which he said that he owed him nothing at all and told Rhodes that it was he who had changed his opinion about the Afrikaner Bond—not some of the people whom he contemptuously termed mugwumps.

Meanwhile, Rhodes, speaking at Barkly West, was sneering at James Rose Innes—'his idea for me is a hermit's cell somewhere on the Zambesi'—and railing against 'Krugerism' in the course of an election campaign of feverish intensity. Rose Innes noted in later years that he could remember no period in South African history, apart from the war itself, when (English–Afrikaner) racial feeling ran higher than in 1896–9. The Afrikaner Bond was returned to power in the Cape Parliament in these elections with a narrow majority, in spite of an extraordinary outlay in money and energy by Rhodes's Progressives.

St Leger was returned as a member of the Legislative Assembly, topping the poll in the Cape Town seat. He seems to have profited by a surge of electoral affection, as Cape Town had been shocked and surprised by his failure to gain election to the Upper House. But the campaign left him exhausted. His voice was gone and he was in severe pain. He went to England to consult a specialist, who at first diagnosed cancer. But the consensus of medical opinion was against cancer and an operation was postponed.

Earlier in 1898, St Leger had presided at the first meeting of the Board of Directors and the first general meeting of shareholders of the *Cape Times*, which had been converted into a limited liability company with St Leger and Rutherfoord Harris remaining the principal shareholders and some shares going to members of the staff. The first directors were St Leger (Chairman), E. R. Syfret and T. E. (later Sir Thomas) Fuller.

E. R. Syfret, then a 38-year-old accountant, who was to found Syfret's Trust Company in 1919, came on to the Board, it seems, to represent the Rutherfoord Harris financial interest. His financial sagacity and integrity would mean a great deal to the *Cape Times* in the 37 years of his chairmanship of the Board of Directors, which began a few years later. Sir Thomas Fuller, a Cape liberal politician, was an early friend of Cecil John Rhodes and wrote an affectionate and admiring memoir of Rhodes a few years after his death.

Those who attended the first meeting of shareholders were St Leger, Syfret, C. E. Solomon, E. J. Edwards, T. G. Clarke, P. Day, C. R. Goodspeed, C. H. Simpson, W. J. Wheeler and Fred St Leger, Manager. Edwards was Managing Editor of the *Cape Times* and Goodspeed was the Works Manager. The others were all members of the editorial, commercial and works staff of the newspaper.

Back in Cape Town after medical treatment in Britain, St Leger took his seat in the 1899 session of the Cape Parliament. By now, the spectre of war had become menacing indeed. The Rhodes–Kruger duel had given way to the diplomatic battle of wills between Alfred Milner, representing the now strongly assertive Imperial factor, and Paul Kruger, more determined than ever to defend the independence of his country. Moderates such as Innes still clung to the hope that war could be averted. But the atmosphere was charged with foreboding.

St Leger spoke several times during the session but only at the cost of great pain, having difficulty in making himself heard. Eventually, it was only by the generous forbearance of members that he could be heard at all. He gave up further attempts to speak in the House.

By the time the session adjourned in October, the war had begun. Members returned to their constituencies after a final appeal by the Prime Minister of the Cape, W. P. Schreiner, to 'seek peace within our own borders, even if we have not been able to secure it in South Africa'. St Leger, although urged by his family to return for further treatment in Britain, remained in Cape Town.

Just before the outbreak of war, Edmund Garrett's health had also broken down and St Leger had given him leave to recuperate in Europe. He resigned the editorship in January 1900.

The day-to-day running of the *Cape Times* was now in the hands of E. J. Edwards, under the advice of St Leger as Editor-in-Chief. The 1900 session of Parliament found St Leger in his seat, listening day after day to debates in which he could not take part. The obituaries speak of him enduring 'vicious taunts' and attacks on his newspaper—and he could not reply. On one occasion a member, J. C. Molteno, revived the charge about Rhodes's control of the *Cape Times*, and the following exchange is recorded in *Hansard*:

> Mr Molteno said a most deliberate attempt had been made by the Press of the country to work up feeling against the Dutch people. He did not like to refer to the campaign of lies— (loud Opposition cheers)—that had been instituted with the avowed object of urging the Imperial Government to go to war. (Renewed cheers.) The right hon. member for Barkly West (Mr Rhodes) had said that he intended to take constitutional means to effect his purpose, and he had gone about it by means of the Press of South Africa, working in conjunction with the Press purchased in England. A great many men did not know the inner working of the Press but, when they came to inquire, they found the great bulk of English papers in this country were held by the Rhodes-ian group of capitalists, and there they had the reason for the attitude it took up. He declared that the *Cape Argus*, the Johannesburg *Star*, the Bulawayo *Chronicle* and other Rhodes-ian papers and the *African Review* in London were all in the hands of the Rhodes–Eckstein group, and recently the Bloemfontein *Post* had come under the same control. And now he would come to the *Cape Times*, which was supposed to be the most influential paper in South Africa. It had come under the control of the same body of

capitalists and one of its largest shareholders was Dr Rutherfoord Harris, a well-known director of the Chartered Company. . . . Quoting from a pamphlet, of which he did not give the name, but which he described as a record of the association of the Rhodes-ian group with the papers of England and South Africa, he said that a young man who knew nothing whatever about the affairs of South Africa had been brought out by Mr Rhodes to edit the principal paper.

Mr Oats: 'I rise to a point of order. My hon. friend the Member for Cape Town (Mr St Leger), whose voice is gone, asks me to state that as far as the *Cape Times* is concerned the record is absolutely false.' (Ministerial cheers.)

Mr J. C. Molteno: 'Oh, we will take that contradiction for what it is worth.'

Mr J. T. Molteno: 'Hear, hear; hear, hear.'

Mr J. C. Molteno: 'It is a well-known fact that the Rhodes-ian group are largely interested in the *Cape Times*. Whether they have a half share or a three-quarter share, I am not in a position to say, but they are largely interested. . . .'

St Leger was now dying of cancer of the throat. He missed the last few days of the session, paired with an Opposition member, and quietly withdrew from public life. His doctors performed a tracheotomy on 4 October 1900, which brought some relief. There were two further operations, but to no avail. He could no longer speak and he spent many hours listening to sacred and classical music played by his wife, who took turns with the organist of St George's Cathedral, Barrow Dowling, in keeping him company. In the last five months of his life, St Leger was in great pain. In the last years, as South Africa rushed headlong into war, there had also been great anguish of mind.

The jingo hysteria of the post-Raid years had reached fever-pitch as war broke out. A reader of the *Cape Times*, M. S. Maurice, in a tribute published in the newspaper said that it almost seemed as if, with St Leger's death, the light of 'true British instincts' south of the Equator had dimmed:

Our erstwhile sound British atmosphere shadows forth

much that is un-English and quasi-British. Living and moving among us during the last days of his retirement, what a mind-struggle he must have experienced; with what scorn and contempt would he not have repudiated the signs that point to the self-seeking spirit, the narrow-mindedness, the smallness of aspirations, the debasing under-current of intolerance. . . .

St Leger's 85-year-old granddaughter Constance—Sister Mary of the Sacred Heart of Pretoria, a Roman Catholic nun—recalled in 1974 that St Leger did not in any way show that he was in pain. She used to visit him at his home, Clyst Hazel, Newlands, and would find him sitting with great dignity in his chair in the study or drawing-room. He would greet her with a smile and to any question asked would write down the answer on a slate, being unable to talk since his operation.

St Leger died at Clyst Hazel on 28 March 1901, at the age of 68. He was buried on the following day in the Camp Ground cemetery, now the churchyard of St Thomas's Church, Rondebosch. As his granddaughter Constance recalled, Clyst Hazel was overwhelmed by people who came to pay their respects. When the head of the funeral procession reached the chapel in Rondebosch, people were seen still coming out at the gates of his home in Newlands.

The pall-bearers were James Rose Innes (who had become Attorney-General in the Sprigg Cabinet) and T. L. Graham (Colonial Secretary), Sir Thomas Fuller and E. R. Syfret, his fellow directors of the *Cape Times*, Mr J. A. Reid, the firm's attorney, and E. J. Edwards, a colleague of many years' standing.

The great and famous of the Peninsula were present, including Sir Gordon Sprigg, again Prime Minister of the Cape, W. P. Schreiner, members of the Cabinet, the Bench and the leaders of commerce and the professions in the Peninsula. And there was St Leger's old opponent of the 1898 election, T. J. O'Reilly, Mayor of Cape Town.

The Very Reverend C. W. Barnett Clarke, the Dean of Cape Town, officiated, assisted by leading clergy of the diocese.

And a year later a memorial plaque, subscribed by employees of the *Cape Times*, was unveiled in St George's Cathedral.

The independent *Midland News* of Cradock noted St Leger's death in an editorial:

> The late Mr St Leger raised the *Cape Times* to the position of the leading paper in the country and whilst under his personal control that paper was a safe guide to the peaceful development of South Africa. When his health began to fail, he retired from active service on the paper, but still took a keen interest in the affairs of the country. Possessed of a true patriotism, a sound judgement, clear perception of the trend of various forces working in South Africa and a facile pen, he did much to shape its destinies; and our regret is that through failing health the influence of his guiding hand was lost during recent critical years. . . . South Africa has lost one of its truest patriots (29 March 1901).

St Leger's will was filed on 3 April 1901. He directed that his *Cape Times* shares were to be left undisturbed in the lifetime of his wife, thereafter they were to be divided among the St Leger children and their heirs. The St Leger family connection with the newspaper remained strong, although Fred, who was not an outstanding success as Manager, soon relinquished this post.

In terms of an agreement with the company, negotiated by E. R. Syfret in 1907, Fred was given leave of absence for 12 months on full pay, 'the intention being that he should reside in England or elsewhere abroad and devote some of his attention to the inspection of modern machinery and newspaper working'.

Fred St Leger was to take steps immediately to free himself of his private financial liabilities. He was likewise to undertake to withdraw from all connection with horseracing. Fred St Leger remained on the Board of Directors until 1935. The minutes record that from time to time he expressed dissatisfaction with the quality of the newspaper's racing coverage.

R. A. St Leger, who continued to take a close interest in the welfare of the newspaper, was a Director until 1951, when his place was taken by Anthony York St Leger, F. Y. St Leger's youngest son, who died in January 1963, at the age of 89 years.

Frederick York St Leger's death was followed by a rapid

decline in the standing and influence of the *Cape Times*. A few weeks before he died, a new Editor had been appointed to succeed Edmund Garrett. He was J. Saxon Mills, whose term of office was to be brief but inglorious. It was not until the arrival of Maitland Park in 1902 that the *Cape Times* started on the road to recovery.

CHAPTER 8

EDMUND GARRETT

. . . a man with a weak chest and strong convictions . . .
Francis Dormer, Editor of the *Star*, on
Edmund Garrett, 1895

EDMUND GARRETT's editorship of the *Cape Times* spanned the fateful years of 1895–9 and justifies closer examination than has been possible in the account of the final years of St Leger's life. So it is necessary to return to June 1895, when Garrett returned to South Africa with high hopes of rebuilding a career cut short by tuberculosis.

He was also optimistic about the prospects of steady, evolutionary growth towards South African union. But, as he had noted in 1890, 'we must not hurry'. His hopes were to be dashed on both counts. Six months after his return, there was the precipitate folly of the Jameson Raid. And his health would break down again on the eve of the South African War.

Fydell Edmund Garrett was born on 20 July 1865, the son of John Garrett, Rector of Elton, Derbyshire, in the heart of the Peak District. His mother died of consumption when Garrett was seven. His father, who died seven years later, appears to have been broken in spirit by the death of his wife.

Garrett's cousin Agnes assumed charge of the young family— Garrett was the third child of his father's second marriage—and it was to her and another cousin, Millicent Garrett Fawcett, that Edmund Garrett owed his education at Rossall, aided by a scholarship, and at Trinity College, Cambridge.

Dame Millicent Garrett Fawcett, a leader in the women's suffrage cause, had a considerable influence on the young Garrett. He himself became an advocate of the women's movement and many years later helped to sponsor a Bill in the Cape Parliament to protect young women from exploitation.

In the October term of 1884 Garrett went up to Cambridge. He was to graduate in 1887 with a third class in classics. But he

61

shone in debate at the Cambridge Union, becoming President of the Union in 1887. His brother-in-law, J. H. Badley, recalled Garrett at Cambridge as 'a light, supple figure in the crowded debating hall, with boyish face and wealth of light hair, tossed back as he developed his argument, now sweeping his hearers along with an outburst of poetic fervour, now delighting even his opponents with flashes of wit'.

He spent much time with his cousins Millicent and Agnes in London. Dame Millicent Garrett Fawcett's biographer recalls that his charm and wit made him welcome everywhere. His cousins thought him rather flighty at college, caring more for outside work and interests than his academic studies. But he took their scoldings meekly and was so lovable and amusing that they could never be angry with him.

Garrett was devoted to his cousins—and to his sisters Amy and Elsie. Amy married J. H. Badley, founder of Bedales School. Elsie, the youngest in the family, was the well-known artist and painter of Cape flora, Mrs E. Garrett Rice, who settled in Cape Town. A letter written to 'my dear little sister' Elsie, on the birth of a son in 1899, survives in the possession of Garrett's niece, Mrs R. Hawthorne of Camps Bay.

Garrett was a model uncle. His nephews, Jock Badley and Gabriel Rice, used to get long, exuberant letters illustrated with Garrett's own pen-and-ink sketches.

Having left Cambridge with an indifferent degree, Garrett had no great prospects of employment. He went to see W. T. Stead, Editor of the *Pall Mall Gazette* and the founder of a new school of bright, controversial journalism. In 1885 Stead had embarked on a vigorous crusade against vice in a series of articles on the 'Maiden Tribute of Modern Babylon' which had resulted in his imprisonment for three months in Holloway.

Stead's campaign against the use of young girls in prostitution helped to achieve a tightening-up of Britain's criminal law. And it attracted the interest and support of the chivalrous young Garrett. Stead was also to become a confidant and supporter of Cecil Rhodes and an executor in his will—until his name was struck out by Rhodes when Stead became a crusading pro-Boer.

The 22-year-old Garrett bearded Stead in his editorial den and asked him for a job. Stead received him kindly but was unforthcoming, so Garrett settled down comfortably in an armchair and drew him into general conversation. He left the office without any promise of a job. 'I saw he didn't think much of me', said Garrett afterwards. 'Why should he? A pasty-faced undergraduate who thought he wrote verses!'

Garrett went away and immediately wrote out a transcript of the interview from memory, illustrated with a pen-and-ink sketch of Stead, as he had found him, with his feet on the mantelpiece. This he posted to Stead and within a few days received a commission to do a descriptive article.

Stead's campaign against vice was now a thing of the past. But Garrett had made an attempt of his own 'to rescue a poor girl', as his biographer puts it: 'From such adventures our Galahad emerged scatheless, but perhaps—as others have done in like case—somewhat disillusioned. It was easy to fight against open foes, but difficult to bear up when those who were to be rescued faltered in the struggle, or even turned upon the rescuer.'

In late 1889 Garrett collapsed with the first bout of the consumption which would sap his vitality, on and off, for the rest of his life. It was at this point that Stead sent him on the journey to South Africa which would restore him to health, for a time at least, and would also make his name as a journalist.

In 1892, his health broke down again. This time he sought recovery in Egypt, unsuccessfully, but his travels again produced a series of articles in the *Pall Mall Gazette*. He met Alfred Milner, who had abandoned journalism for government service and was Under-Secretary of Finance with Lord Cromer in Egypt. There began a friendship which would grow into close collaboration some years later in Cape Town. Garrett was now too ill to return to daily journalism and spent some time in a sanatorium at Nordrach in the Black Forest. where an open-air cure for tuberculosis was in vogue.

Meanwhile, there had been a change of proprietors at the *Pall Mall Gazette* and E. T. Cook, who had succeeded Stead as Editor when the latter left to found the *Review of Reviews*, now resigned with most of his staff. Cook took Garrett with him, as Assistant Editor, to establish the *Westminster Gazette*, which was to be a liberal newspaper, sponsored by Sir George Newnes. But, on account of his health, Garrett's place soon had to be filled by Alfred Spender, who later became a distinguished editor himself.

In April 1895, Garrett received St Leger's cable offering him the editorship of the *Cape Times*. Terms of agreement were signed and a few weeks later Garrett sailed for the Cape. At the age of 30, he now had the chance of his life.

Garrett's first concern was to make good the damage to the newspaper's independent standing that had been caused by the suggestion that he was 'Rhodes's nominee' and that the newspaper had become a tool of Rhodes's interests. He decided to take the bull by the horns in a signed editorial, asserting his independence in rather grandiloquent terms. The leader caused a sensation in Cape Town but was not wholly successful, giving the impression that a bumptious young upstart had succeeded the revered St Leger.

It is a great trust which Mr St Leger has confided to me. I am touched and humbled by it. Coming from the grand English school of open speech, it is strange to me that the giving of independent support to a public man or cause should entail on a journalist the indignity of having to explain that he is not in that man's pocket. I do so because I will not in silence let the fountain of the influence of a great newspaper be puddled at the source.

On the day this appeared—25 June 1895—Garrett was lunching in a club in Cape Town with J. W. Sauer when John X. Merriman stalked into the dining-room, hands in pockets in characteristic fashion. He took a chair opposite Sauer and said at once: 'Who is the young jackanapes who is going to tell us what to do in South Africa?'

'Let me introduce you to the young jackanapes,' said Sauer.

Merriman and Garrett bowed frigidly to each other. Merriman developed a strong dislike for Garrett, as his published letters show.

It took Garrett considerable time and effort to neutralize the harm done by the Rutherfoord Harris connection with the *Cape Times*, as the issue was revived, understandably enough, in the wake of the Jameson Raid.

Inside the office, he had many obstacles to overcome. The staff, like Merriman, were wary of this brash young newcomer whose approach was so different from the impersonal, detached journalism of the newspaper's founder. Fred St Leger, Manager of the paper, was initially deeply suspicious of Garrett but eventually succumbed to his charm and candour.

By July 1896, Garrett was able to report, in a letter to his cousin Agnes in London, that the *Cape Times* had survived the loss of St Leger and the tarnishing of its reputation by the 'conspiratorial fame of Harris'. J. B. Robinson's *South African Telegraph* was 'working his connection with us for all it is worth. But nobody cares because they see I never turn a hair for Harris. . . . We have also survived the millionaire attempt to "smash the *Cape Times*" and are now, instead of dividing the circulation, 33 per cent better than a year ago, both on daily and weekly. . . . We have put on more circulation than the whole circulation of the *South African Telegraph*, at present stationary at 3,300.'

At a dinner which he gave to the editorial staff, attended by St Leger, Garrett thanked the founder for his loyal backing, 'never interfering when I knew he must have huge disquiet about methods, substitution of the bludgeon for the rapier and new for old in every way'. Garrett also thanked the staff for their support.

> I tried to show them, too, how much the tradition of the old man's 20 years of work meant for us, and how it often restrained me, and how there was a deep continuity from his work to my work, in spite of superficial differences.

Garrett was most gratified when the usually uncommunicative St Leger stood up to say a few words himself and congratulated the new Editor on steering the *Cape Times* through the most difficult period in its history.

If he had won the confidence of the staff and of his readers and reinforced himself in St Leger's good opinion, Garrett had still to counter Rutherfoord Harris's persistent, behind-the-scenes efforts to influence the newspaper's editorial policy. As noted, it is probable that the Harris investment in the newspaper was on Rhodes's behalf. The memoir of Sir Thomas Fuller, himself a member of the first Board of Directors of the *Cape Times*, certainly suggests that Rhodes had a substantial share in the paper and this could only have been through Harris's interest.

Fuller tells of meeting Garrett one morning at breakfast at Groote Schuur. Rhodes was in a rather overbearing temper and angry at an article of Garrett's which had appeared the day before. Rhodes said he had a right to look for fair play from a paper 'in which he took so large an interest'.

> Garrett rose from his seat and, looking straight at Mr Rhodes, replied: 'I think it is good for you, Mr Rhodes, that your paper has an Editor who does not care a damn if he pleases you or displeases you.' There was perfect and painful silence for a minute. Then Mr Rhodes said quietly: 'Yes, it is best so and I'm sorry if I seemed to question it. I have never inspired an article in your paper or requested that a given "line" be taken. But you might at least be careful about the facts.'

Garrett's letters to Agnes in London tell of stormy exchanges between Rhodes and himself, with Rhodes, at one point, complaining that the Editor of the *Cape Times* was the 'only man who held him at arm's length'. As he wrote to Agnes in June 1897, Garrett was grateful for the instinct that had saved him—'luckily'—from accepting any money favours or 'any too familiar relations with either R [Rhodes] or the others', all through the Raid crisis and the aftermath, even before he had realized all the undercurrents.

There were frequent disagreements with Rhodes. In August 1898 we find Garrett telling Agnes of his latest session with the great man at Groote Schuur which ended in an animated exchange in Rhodes's bedroom where he had insisted on going for privacy from the others. But this was one discussion which ended in agreement and Rhodes declaring: 'You see, our minds are

15. Edmund Garrett

Frontispiece in *Edmund Garrett: A memoir* by E. T. Cook

TO THE MEMORY OF
FYDELL·EDMUND·GARRETT
MEMBER FOR VICTORIA EAST
IN THE HOUSE OF ASSEMBLY
OF CAPE COLONY 1897-1900
EDITOR OF THE CAPE TIMES
1895-1899
"Where'er I fall-like yonder ripped
Old elm-there lay me-so but one
Small brass hang where the solemn crypt
Gives respite from the Capetown sun.
Hard by the hurrying street, alive
With strength & youth, 'tis all I claim,
That where the heart is there survive
The dust & shadow of a name."
HE LOOKED FORWARD
& MADE SOME BEGINNINGS
Born 1865 Died 1907

16. The memorial to Edmund Garrett in St George's Cathedral, Cape Town, which was designed by Garrett's friend Herbert Baker and his partner F. E. Masey, with lettering by Eric Gill. The monument was erected with funds subscribed by Garrett's friends. The verse and epitaph were written by Garrett himself.

travelling to the same point . . . so it must be right!'

As Garrett commented to Agnes: 'May this happy unanimity last a few weeks to the benefit of South Africa and the promotion of my peace of mind. . . .'

Garrett, from close at hand, had a clear sight of flaws in Rhodes's make-up. As he wrote to Stead late in 1899, it was hard to associate Rhodes with an atmosphere of moral grandeur.

We see him too close, like the valet. He is always surrounded by contemptibles, and they pander; and he insists on taking all men on their lower side. It often revolts me, and when it does his word is always 'unctuous rectitude'. . . .

The previous year (January 1898) he had written to Stead:

We are staking a good bit on Rhodes's cardiac valves. . . . I am far more afraid (in your ear), and so is Milner, of a sort of Kaiser-like *manie des grandeurs* . . . the sort of thing the Greeks said preceded and brought Nemesis, which grows on him—and *may* impair his judgement as it did in 1895–6. Poor old C.J.R.! A big man, among some terribly small ones, and with a petty side, like Napoleon—like *all* big men, apparently.

And yet, in his final study of 'The Character of Cecil Rhodes' (*The Contemporary Review*, June 1902) Garrett was in no doubt that Rhodes was a great man—'who would have been a greater man if he had only expected, and so encouraged, ordinary people to be motivated by ideals more nearly on a level with his own'.

Garrett's independent support was of considerable service to Rhodes, although his candid criticism was not always appreciated. Gordon le Seuer, one of the young secretaries at Groote Schuur, tells of his amusement at the look of dismay on Rhodes's face in the mornings as he scanned a leader in the *Cape Times*.

Garrett treated Rhodes with light-hearted aloofness which Rhodes, unused to such treatment, is said to have rather enjoyed. But Rhodes became increasingly intolerant of opposition of any sort and his rows with Garrett became legendary. Garrett would speak laughingly of his 'education of Mr Rhodes', but Sir Lewis Michell, who was in a position to know, believed that he probably over-estimated his influence on him.

In later years, Garrett's own answer to repeated charges that the Press had been 'bought by Rhodes was to argue that the newspapers were in the hands of their readers.

The Press of South Africa being a thing of the towns and therefore English, did not need to be 'bought' to take the English side in the great duel. If bought, it was bought by the public, which was more Rhodes-ian than Rhodes . . . (*The Contemporary Review*, June 1902).

This was certainly true of the post-Raid period when readers resented even moderate criticism in the *Cape Times* of Jameson's filibustering invasion of the Transvaal. The *South African Telegraph*, taking an uncompromising anti-Rhodes line, lost so much readership that it went out of business.

Garrett's biographer tells the story, on the authority of a *Cape Times* colleague, of 'a certain gentleman who shall be nameless' who called at the Editor's office and took strong exception to a leading article which was to appear in the next day's newspaper. The visitor—obviously Rutherfoord Harris—ordered Garrett to cancel the article and write another according to his own views.

Garrett's anger was blazing. His visitor hesitated a moment as he gazed at the thin, wasted frame; then he went, never to enter the *Cape Times* office again in any capacity.

Garrett's relations with Harris were uniformly disagreeable. And, for the first year or so, there was also Fred St Leger to trouble the young Editor's composure. Garrett accounted it a great victory when he was able to tell Agnes, on 4 August 1897, that he had at last secured himself in the support and affection of the Manager. Fred St Leger had confided in him that 'he believed his father thought he had played him false about Harris's part in the paper'.

St Leger junior, Garrett told Agnes, now agreed 'that in the proposed turning of the *Cape Times* into a limited liability company we must be careful to keep the control in his father's hands, not to let it slide into Harris's through share jugglery'.

Once the company flotation had gone through satisfactorily, wrote Garrett, he would feel that he had 'really won this long struggle, avoided all the pitfalls and come out right at the end, by not giving myself quite away at any point to any of 'em'. He would still have cards to play 'even in the case of the Old Man going out or dying, which I sincerely hope there is no prospect of'. But the 'Old Man' remained his strong suit.

F. Y. St Leger, as we have seen, took particular steps to keep control in his hands when the *Cape Times* became a limited company. His attitude to Garrett, in spite of some uneasy patches, remained everything the Editor could have hoped for. Garrett took pains to make St Leger feel that the *Cape Times*, in spite of modernization and a new approach, was carrying on the founder's independent line.

From the start, Garrett's vigorous conduct of the *Cape Times* had kept J. B. Robinson's *South African Telegraph* at bay with a strong emphasis on news-gathering and, by the standards of those days, bright presentation of news. The newspaper leapt ahead as readers came to appreciate the new Editor's sparkle and flair and his vigorous espousal of public-spirited causes. He involved the *Cape Times* in every controversy of the day. He was insistent on the need for better education for all races, as a corollary of the Cape's non-racial franchise—'to abandon the poor black and brown children to the discipline of the streets would be to pull down with one hand while building up with the other'.

He pleaded for the compulsory notifications of diseases. He crusaded against Cape Town's slums and advocated better working conditions for shop assistants. He argued for the development and extension of art galleries and museums.

Noting the absence of interest in the municipal elections, he wrote a series of articles on the theme that 'Cape Town is worth serving'. He organized a *Cape Times* labour bureau, distributing on incoming ships application forms for newcomers to complete. He helped to advocate the scheme for rebuilding St George's Cathedral, writing on 10 November 1898:

Our surroundings are eloquent of commercial activity, of

industrial progress, of the push-along, keep-moving spirit proper to the age. What we want is more that is beautiful to the eye; more that suggests repose of mind; more that lifts up the spirit from the depressing influences of the struggle for existence—a *sursum corda* in stone. . . .

Garrett was also a pioneer advocate of the preservation of the old buildings of Cape Town and of the promotion of interest in Cape Dutch architecture. In 1898 he brought out a Christmas number on the old Cape houses with the assistance of Mrs A. F. Trotter, whose sketches were later incorporated in the book *Old Cape Colony; a Chronicle of Her Men and Her Houses from 1652 to 1806.*

In his preface to the Christmas number, which described 80 Cape homesteads and their founders and builders, Garrett declared that the Cape was one of the few regions in South Africa where man had done much to complement nature.

Time and the carelessness and penuriousness of modern occupants are playing havoc with these relics. The fire insurance companies are waging pitiless war on the thatch, whose rich soft brown is being replaced on all sides by corrugated iron. At least, while the charm is yet with us, it may do some good to put it upon record; it may even help a little to retard the process of its vanishing.

And in a *Cape Times* leader (25 November 1898) the preservation of Cape Dutch architecture was strongly advocated. In common appreciation of the Colony's own distinctive cultural heritage, English and Dutch could find a meeting ground of sentiment. Garrett also campaigned for the preservation of open spaces. An editorial, 'The Lungs of Cape Town' (17 December 1895), was prompted by a decision by the Bishop of Cape Town to close the grounds of Bishopscourt to the holiday public.

Opportunities of this kind are sadly dwindling for the poorer folk among us. . . . On every side, shades of the prison house begin to close around the humbler truants of Cape Town. . . . Mr Rhodes, who once seemed to threaten them worst, is their great stand-by. He has become a great public institution for securing one side of the mountain to the people's enjoyment, with the additional advantage that the cost of appropriation does not come on the rates. The Town Council may or may not have Mr Rhodes's liberal temper, but it has not his liberal purse. Yet something it might do in response to Mr Bryce's appeal, made in our columns the other day, that Cape Town should not be allowed to become wholly dispossessed of the mountain slopes on the Cape Town side. A jealous eye should be kept on these future lungs of an expanding city. Land that the Municipality already holds there should not be offered for private ownership, and should as far as possible be planted. . . . Our Dutch forebears planted oaks that we might sit under them. Shall we not do the same for those who come after us?

In the larger arena of South African affairs, events had been moving swiftly. A few weeks after becoming Editor of the *Cape Times*, Edmund Garrett had travelled to Pretoria for his second interview with Paul Kruger. In the five years since the first interview, there had been a rush of English settlers into the Transvaal, gold production had forged ahead and railway extensions had provided the communications network for closer South African union.

Natal had been given responsible government, the Orange Free State was prospering and contented. British Bechuanaland had been taken over by the Cape Government. Rhodes's Chartered Company was negotiating for the transfer of the rest of Bechuanaland—the Protectorate—and had already fought the Matabele War and established effective occupation farther north. Suzerainty over Swaziland had been given to the Transvaal, but the land between Swaziland and the sea had been annexed by the British Crown. The conditions might have seemed propitious for steady growth towards union. But this would have been a superficial impression.

In October 1894 there had been a stormy meeting in Pretoria between Paul Kruger and Cecil Rhodes. James Rose Innes believed that it was this meeting that prompted Rhodes to change direction, exchanging the constitutionalism of the statesman for the conspiratorial lawlessness of the revolutionary. Rhodes sought to conciliate Kruger and secure his co-operation. He failed. The interview ended on an unhappy note, with the two men 'shaking their fists at each other'.

Garrett's interview with Kruger attracted considerable interest when published in the *Cape Times* on 22 July 1895 (Appendix 2). It concluded:

Do not suppose that the strenuous old man is done with. In a sense, age is strength to him; I felt a touch of pathos, an impulse of hero worship myself; how much more must his own burghers. If there are two men who know what they want and hold it by the teeth of fate, he is one of the two. . . .

The other, of course, was Cecil John Rhodes, whose Jameson conspiracy was already taking shape. He had already secured the appointment of a High Commissioner, Sir Hercules Robinson, who 'was unlikely to give trouble', as Rose Innes puts it. As 1895 drew to a close there was a sharp increase in tension on the Rand and a general expectation that a revolt of Uitlanders was imminent. In the *Cape Times*, Garrett was now writing about Paul Kruger as 'The Sick Man of South Africa'.

On 26 December Paul Kruger was asked about the rumours of trouble on the Rand. If you want to kill a tortoise, he said, 'you must wait until it puts its head out'.

Rhodes's plot had called for an uprising on the Rand, followed by Dr Jameson riding in at the head of a force of about 500 men, with the High Commissioner then going to the Rand to 'restore order'. The object was to bring down the Kruger regime, removing the last obstacle to South African confederation. But the revolt fizzled. Two emissaries from the Rand reformers—Charles Leonard and Frederick Hamilton—rushed to Cape Town and convinced Rhodes at the last minute to postpone the whole operation. Rhodes agreed and sent off messages to Jameson telling him not to move. But Jameson did move and the result was a fiasco. Jameson's force was surrounded by Piet Joubert's men at Doornkop and captured.

The Jameson Raid, said General Smuts in 1932, was *the*

disaster, making racial trust impossible and creating the 'very mentality' for the South African War. Winston Churchill, writing as a young man, saw it as a 'fountain of ill', dealing a grievous wound to the British reputation throughout the world.

President Kruger, in the wake of the Raid, began transforming the Transvaal into the strongest military power in southern Africa. Suspicion of England and of English-speaking South Africans intensified in the Republics and in the Cape Colony. One historian—Dr Jean van der Poel—has argued in her definitive study of the Jameson Raid that it was not so much the Raid itself that had the worst effects as much as the attempt to free the Imperial authorities of all responsibility. If the complicity of the British Colonial Secretary, Chamberlain, had been fully exposed he would have had to resign office and the Conservative Government might have had to go to the country, losing power to the Liberals in 1896 instead of in 1906. South Africa might have been spared the horror of what amounted to a civil war. And instead of a unitary constitution, South Africa might today have had a slowly-matured federal constitution, far better equipped to accommodate the racial and cultural diversity of its peoples.

Edmund Garrett had written in 1890: 'We must not hurry....' Now Rhodes's desperate haste to sweep Kruger out of his way would transform the South African scene and confront the youthful Editor of the *Cape Times* with the greatest crisis of his career.

CHAPTER 9

THE JAMESON RAID

The Dutch always beat us at politics.

Cecil Rhodes to Edmund Garrett, January 1896

ON Monday afternoon, 30 December 1895, James Rose Innes went home by train with W. P. Schreiner, Attorney-General in the Rhodes Cabinet. As they walked from Rondebosch station, Schreiner told Rose Innes that he had received an extraordinary telegram from the magistrate at Mafeking, reporting a rumoured invasion of the Transvaal.

They parted at the Main Road, Schreiner on his way to Groote Schuur where, later that evening, Rhodes would tell him: 'It is all true. Old Jameson has upset my apple-cart. . . .' This was the interview which Schreiner later related to the Cape Select Committee investigating the Raid which would find that the Prime Minister, Cecil Rhodes, as head of the Chartered Company, De Beers and Goldfields, had erected and created the combination which made the Raid possible.

On Monday evening, Edmund Garrett, in his office at the *Cape Times*, had a visit from J. H. Hofmeyr, who came in search of news of the expected rising in the Transvaal. After much coaxing, he drew from Hofmeyr an interview on the Uitlanders' rights, published in the next day's newspaper, in which Hofmeyr confessed he was 'pulled two ways'. The Transvaal still kept his strong sympathies and affection, though he regretted that no statesmanlike compromise had been arrived at. But 'blood is thicker than water', he said. Neither Garrett nor Hofmeyr at this time had any inkling of Jameson's Raid—their thoughts were turned to Johannesburg and the expected rising.

When the news of the Raid was published in the *Cape Times*, Hofmeyr would no longer be 'pulled both ways'. He would send a telegram to Paul Kruger: 'I hope your burghers will acquit themselves like heroes against Jameson's filibusters.'

Hofmeyr was the first of a succession of callers at the *Cape Times* office on that night, including the two Rand emissaries, Leonard and Hamilton, and subsequently the Imperial Secretary, Sir Graham Bower, who came in looking ill with anxiety, with the question: 'Have you any news?'

By now Garrett had heard—from Leonard and Hamilton—that something was afoot. He told Bower, who then authorized him to disclose that the High Commissioner, Sir Hercules Robinson, had repudiated and recalled Jameson—but this was only to be printed if the *Cape Times* received the news of Jameson's dash from other than official sources.

The news eventually reached the *Cape Times* at 4 a.m. in time for Garrett to expand on his leader for that day's *Cape Times*.

At this point, Hamilton returned and went 'quite hysterical' as Garrett told him that Rhodes and the Government would have to repudiate Jameson's blunder—as would the High Commissioner. Garrett sent for a shorthand writer and dictated the rest of his leader in his visitor's presence. . . . 'The first shot fired in the Transvaal must needs make many people round its fringes hard to hold . . . through all such events the High Commissioner's duty is to stand high above the quarrels—even the just quarrels—of the Uitlanders, for it is to him that all South Africa will look to hold the balance even and to mould the united statesmanship of South Africa into the great settlement which must inevitably ensue upon the struggle. . . .'

As Garrett later recalled:

It was hard to see anything clear in the first rush of surprise, but one thing did seem clear to the writer, and he clung to it accordingly. Though heart and soul with the Johannesburg revolution if only the Uitlanders would make it, he could not see that the Imperial Government had the right to interfere and make it for them. The Johannesburg leader left the office unconvinced and fuming. . . .

At the *Cape Times* office this news, that is the Jameson part of it, and the much later discovery of Mr Rhodes's full relation to that part, was as much a surprise that evening as it was to

Ministers and Cape Town generally when it appeared in print next morning (*The Story of an African Crisis*).

It had been a wild and exhausting night. Garrett walked up Roeland Street to the slopes of Table Mountain and watched the sun rising over Cape Town. At 6 a.m. he called on his friend, Dr Jane Waterston, in Plein Street. She was already up and gave him breakfast. After dossing down on Dr Waterston's sofa for a few hours, Garrett got up to find the *Cape Times* going like wildfire.

Excitement was now intense in Cape Town, sustained for several days as news dribbled in by telegraph. All that was known was that Jameson was on the march. On Wednesday, New Year's Day, it became known that there had been some fighting. But the picture remained confused on Thursday and Friday, with wild and mutually contradictory reports in the newspapers. It was not until Saturday morning that the surrender of Jameson and his band could be firmly reported in the *Cape Times*.

St George's Street was filled with milling crowds throughout the week of the crisis, as people waited for the slips that the papers issued as the confused and broken news came in. Leading politicians jostled the man in the street.

On Tuesday morning, 31 December, there was a battle of wills at Government House with J. H. Hofmeyr insisting that the High Commissioner issue a formal proclamation repudiating Jameson in the name of the Queen. Rhodes and his co-conspirator, Rutherfoord Harris, fought unsuccessfully to prevent such a proclamation being issued. Rhodes, it seems, was still hoping that Jameson might get through to Johannesburg.

Rhodes's hopes soared momentarily when Kruger wired to the High Commissioner to accept his offer to come to Pretoria 'to assist to prevent bloodshed'. He deduced from this, wrongly, that Jameson was still on his way and would reach Johannesburg, where the Uitlanders would rise, setting the scene for the High Commissioner to arrive and effect the settlement that Rhodes was counting on.

On New Year's Day, when the situation was still unclear,

Garrett sat down and wrote to Agnes, setting out everything he knew about the crisis and his deductions of what must have happened. Although the outcome of Jameson's dash into the Transvaal was still unknown, Garrett was clear-sighted about the political consequences. As he told Agnes:

Jameson has spoiled all—given it all away—damned Rhodes and himself and the future of South Africa. . . .

Garrett told Agnes about the plans for a Rand rising and the reformers' decision to postpone the day and to tell Rhodes and Jameson that they were 'not yet ready'. Garrett had been put in the picture by Hamilton and Leonard in their visits to the *Cape Times* office on the night the news broke.

But, as Garrett told Agnes, Jameson, the 'ambitious, unscrupulous hothead', had gone in anyway, seeking to force their hand. 'Rhodes on Sunday evening, Christmas week, gets wire calmly apprising [him] that Chartered Company forces have begun war on the Transvaal (for that's what it is) in order not to help, but to *create* a revolution!! Jameson cut wires and by now is either entering Johannesburg or fighting the Boers on the veldt . . . the beginning perhaps of a race war in South Africa, perhaps Europe too, such as none can see end of. Well, it was irrevocable. Cat's out of bag. Rhodes may say and do what he likes, but on Jameson's luck in the next four-and-twenty hours hangs his career, and perhaps his career in this Colony is past hanging already. All his years of work, some of it not *quite* clean, thrown away. . . .'

The news that Jameson had surrendered was conveyed to Rhodes at Government House when this was still unknown in Cape Town. Garrett happened to be at Government House and saw Rhodes coming out.

His face was horribly changed from the exultant man of the night before. He paused to speak, checked himself, jumped into a cart that was waiting to drive him to Rondebosch, then, as he started, turned the same dreadful face over his shoulder and jerked out in the odd falsetto voice he sometimes has: 'Well, there is a little history being made; that is all.'

It was a most mournful, characteristically English attempt to carry off lightly the sudden crushing ruin of a career. . . .

Garrett himself had become involved in the battle over the proclamation, which had been shown to him by Sir Hercules Robinson at Government House. He suggested a small change in the wording. Garrett felt that the proclamation did not draw a clear distinction between repudiation of Jameson's external intervention, on the one hand, and repudiation of the internal battle for the Uitlanders' rights, on the other hand. He argued that the proclamation should not take sides in the internal quarrel. The alteration led to a delay in the issuing of the proclamation which was afterwards the subject of bitter controversy.

And at one point Garrett's zeal for the Uitlanders' cause ran away with his discretion. He sent the following telegram to the Editor of the *Star*, Johannesburg, after hearing of the coming proclamation:

You must expect, and not misunderstand, a proclamation putting Jameson formally in the wrong. Imperial authorities have no other course. Don't let this weaken or divide you. This merely for your information.

Garrett was to be later cross-examined at some length by the Cape Select Committee after the telegram had come to light and was published by the Transvaal Government in a Green Book. He was asked by John X. Merriman and W. P. Schreiner how he felt himself authorized to water down the Governor's proclamation. Garrett denied that this had been his intention. From his discussions with the reformers' emissaries, Charles Leonard and Frederick Hamilton, he was aware that the proclamation would cause intense feeling against the Imperial Government in Johannesburg. It was absolutely his own idea, said Garrett, not hinted to him by anybody at Government House.

He had sent the telegram, 'partly because I hoped that the revolution would come off and partly because I wanted to put the Imperial Government right with the leaders at Johannesburg'.

Throughout the week, Garrett's leaders in the *Cape Times* tried to keep the Raid and the Uitlanders' struggle distinct, condemning the former and sympathizing with the latter. On the first two days of the crisis, the *Cape Times* leaders—'To all Afrikanders' and 'One Man's Madness'—were printed in both English and Dutch and helped to calm the violent emotions of that phrenetic week.

Jameson's action was denounced by the *Cape Times* as a 'colossal blunder' which had checked the rising sympathy with the Uitlanders.

Had the act not been disowned promptly and fully by the Chartered Company and the Imperial Government, the situation in South Africa today would be very serious.... It was a black responsibility which Dr Jameson took when he crossed the border.... They rode lightly in, with a price upon their heads, a mark that every man who lists may shoot at. There is something in the sheer audacity of the thing that disarms. But it will not disarm the Boer commandos. Today, if uninterrupted, Dr Jameson should be effecting a junction with any forces that Johannesburg may push out to meet him; and nobody supposes that the Boers will allow that junction to be made without bloodshed. It is a grisly thought that for that blood Dr Jameson is likely to be hanged like a felon. Never surely was such a gamester's throw, with the peace of half a continent trembling in the balance. All we can do is wait for news and hope for the best, most of us with sympathies painfully divided ... (*Cape Times*, 1 January 1896).

Garrett, as he himself put it, was now 'riding two horses'. And other *Cape Times* leaders that week, written on incomplete information, misread the situation, concluding that matters still hung in the balance:

It was a wild New Year's Day this; Cape Town half pale with suspense, eager knots discussing news in the streets and the noisy mirth of some of our perambulating coloured friends jarring terribly on strained nerves. But we have hopes now of a less dark sequel to it. The Paramount Power has held the scales firmly even (2 January 1896).

On Friday 3 January, the *Cape Times* could get no news through, neither could the *Argus*. Cape Town utterly refused to believe the real news—of Jameson's surrender—which came through to J. B. Robinson's *South African Telegraph* from a Transvaal Government source. Cape Town was now feverishly jingo and resented the censures of the *Cape Times* on Jameson. A *Cape Times* leader declared: 'Save us from the horrors of a race war in South Africa. There is not one of us so light-hearted or so callous-hearted as not to breathe that prayer.'

Finally, on Saturday, when there was no longer any doubt about Jameson's fate, the *Cape Times* railed bitterly against the pusillanimous Uitlanders 'whose representatives invited Dr Jameson in' and urged signatures for a petition to President Kruger to plead that Jameson's life be spared. Part of every copy of the *Cape Times* was made into a petition form and, within a few days, 10 000 signatures came in. The *Cape Times* petition ran through the Colony.

Garrett had been misled by the so-called 'letter of invitation', a sham document given in advance to Jameson by the reform leaders, urging him to come to the aid of the 'unarmed men, women and children of our race', designed to excuse Jameson's behaviour to the Board of the Chartered Company and not intended for publication.

Rhodes, cynically, gave instructions that a copy of the letter be telegraphed to *The Times* in London, which was done, with Rutherfoord Harris changing the date from 20 December to 28 December. In London the letter called forth a surge of sympathy for Jameson, who emerged as a chivalrous hero riding to the rescue. When the facts about the letter came out, Garrett faced the truth with 'characteristic candour', as James Rose Innes put it, confessing that 'of the theory of chivalrous audacity not a rag remains' (*Cape Times*, 4 May 1896).

The Rhodes–Hofmeyr alliance was now shattered beyond repair. Rhodes did not attempt to conceal from Hofmeyr the fact that he knew rather more about the whole business than appeared on the surface. Friends brought Rhodes and Hofmeyr together to try to effect a reconciliation. Hofmeyr must

obviously have expected some indication of regret from Rhodes.
But none was forthcoming. Garrett, who appears to have been
present, noted how Hofmeyr gave vent to his feelings to Rhodes:

> We have often disagreed, you and I, but I would no more
> have thought of distrusting you than a man and his wife
> think of distrusting each other in any joint undertaking. So
> it was until now; and now you have let me go on being
> apparently intimate while you knew that this was preparing,
> and said nothing.

Rhodes was completely unmoved, according to Garrett, and
always spoke later as if, of the two, it was he and not Hofmeyr
who was the aggrieved party. Rhodes had exposed Hofmeyr to
ridicule among Afrikaners as a dupe of his conspiratorial schemes,
and he had betrayed a friend. But he was unconcerned. And even
so ardent an admirer as Edmund Garrett was repelled.

Rhodes was uneasy and resentful because Garrett continued to
keep on friendly terms with Hofmeyr in spite of political differences. It so happened that Garrett had been in Hofmeyr's company
several times in the same week and had been observed by one of
Rhodes's 'jackals', as Garrett called the hangers-on who made
themselves useful to Rhodes in politics.

At Groote Schuur a few days later, Rhodes nagged away at
Garrett about his friendship with Hofmeyr, 'the Blind Man'—
which was one of Merriman's tags for 'Onze Jan' Hofmeyr.

> 'It's no good talking! The Blind Man's very clever; he's
> too clever for you! The Dutch always beat us at politics. He'll
> get hold of you.'
> 'Well,' I turned on him, nettled at last, 'at any rate I don't
> ride with the Blind Man to Hout Bay and back every Saturday.'
> Mr Rhodes flushed and took an angry turn along the stoep
> before answering; then he burst out: 'Yes, I did that. And in
> those years—I *took the North*!'
> 'But surely you were personal friends?'
> 'Pooh! He thought I was serving his object; he finds he was
> serving mine.'

When Rhodes died, Garrett recalled an evening at Groote Schuur years before when he had first realized that this was a man under a sentence of death. Groote Schuur was full of guests, but they had all gone off to the theatre. Rhodes, dining alone, hailed Garrett, who had called on some political business, as a castaway hails a sail. Suddenly Rhodes threw out his right arm, pulling up his sleeve and resting his hand, palm upwards, on the table.

'Look there,' he said.

Rhodes's pulse stood out like a knot and Garrett could count the throbs by the eye.

'Look! You never saw a man with a pulse like that. . . .'

I can recall that evening well; the quiet, rather sombre dignity of the teak-wainscotted room, the old tapestry and furniture, the wax candles guttering as the mild evening air drew in through the open door off the slope of Table Mountain . . . and in the zone of light at the head of the table, Rhodes. . . . The leonine head, always looking large even on the large loose-knit body; the light crisp hair, grizzling fast at the temples, tumbled impatiently on end above the wide and massive forehead; the face red, tanned, weather-beaten—an outdoor face, the chin and jaw formidable, except when lit by an attractive, almost boyish smile; the prominent light-grey absent-minded eyes—now gloomily looking down at that outstretched wrist on the table and at that menacing throb of pulse . . . (*The Contemporary Review*, June 1902).

Garrett found Rhodes's brutal and cynical attitude to Hofmeyr and Schreiner repulsive. And he acknowledged that his faults— like the rest of him—were on the grand scale. But Garrett held such faults to be 'intelligible, perhaps, in a character eager, masterful and so possessed by a great purpose as to leave no time to be nice about means or squeamish about individual people's feelings'.

Now, in the immediate aftermath of the Jameson Raid, the *Cape Times* acknowledged in an editorial that Rhodes was 'smashed' in Cape politics.

Cape Town. Feb 22nd 1898.
Tuesday.

Dear Garrett

Come to
dinner I will not
bully but remember
I am your host

V (.) Rhodes

---

17. An invitation to dinner at Groote Schuur—a peacemaking gesture after one of the frequent Rhodes–Garrett rows.

18. Agnes Garrett

Mrs R. Hawthorne

19. Olive Schreiner

South African Library

If this Ministry fails to survive its head, we are willing to see the ship of State steered by any of our political leaders—Mr Hofmeyr, Mr Innes, Mr Merriman—who is trusted as an honourable man. The question is, if Rhodes goes, do his work and his policy go with him? Are all the patient and sometimes the very distasteful labours of reconciliation of these ten years thrown away?

At this point there came the famous Kaiser telegram of congratulation to Paul Kruger which aroused a storm of anger in Britain. In the *Cape Times*, Hofmeyr gave Garrett an interview which repudiated 'Kaiser William's blundering utterances'.

In the Transvaal, President Kruger was playing his cards with finesse—and magnanimity. It took a strong man to resist the clamour for vengeance, but Kruger did so, handing Dr Jameson and his confederates over to the British authorities for trial.

Then there was the trial of the reformers, Colonel Rhodes, Phillips, Hammond, Farrar and their colleagues who had planned the rising. Garrett went to Pretoria to describe the scene. Rose Innes was also present, as a legal observer on behalf of the British Government. The main defendants were Colonel Frank Rhodes, Lionel Phillips, John Hays Hammond and George Farrar. As the trial drew to a close, Innes felt a sense of impending tragedy. A movable dock was brought into the court for the exclusive occupation of the four leaders, which Innes believed could mean only one thing—the death sentence was to be passed. It was. The tension was eased by Garrett's 'well-intentioned but wholly irregular exclamation that it was "only a cruel farce". It was, as Garrett well knew, nothing of the kind.'

The gallows beam from Slagter's Nek had been brought to the Transvaal and among the wilder spirits there was an idea that 1815 should be revenged in 1896. Again Kruger stood firm.

The Executive of the Volksraad met on the following day and commuted the sentence on the leaders to 15 years' imprisonment. The *Cape Times* urged that magnanimity should be carried further. Once again, a petition was drawn up which was presented at public meetings throughout the country, arranged by Rose Innes's South African Political Association.

The plea for amnesty, launched by the *Cape Times*, of the prisoners was adopted at a mass meeting in the Good Hope Hall in Cape Town on 29 May. The Cape and Natal Governments and the Associated Chambers of Commerce joined in making representations. Eventually, on 10 June, a deputation of more than 50 mayors mustered in Pretoria.

On 11 June there came the news that amnesty had been granted. The four leaders were to be released immediately on payment of fines of £25 000 each and the signing of an undertaking by the four that they would not take part in politics in the Transvaal for a period of 15 years. The amnesty movement, taken up throughout South Africa, was one of Garrett's most successful undertakings.

Meanwhile, Cecil Rhodes had gone to London. He wanted to safeguard the British South Africa Company's charter, which was in danger of being revoked as a result of the Company's involvement in the Raid. Rhodes, it seems, was also prodding the Colonial Office and Joseph Chamberlain to intensify the pressure on Kruger to make concessions to the Uitlanders. Chamberlain invited Kruger to come to London for talks and, when these overtures were rejected, war-talk began to appear in sections of the British Press.

In a series of *Cape Times* leaders, Garrett argued that it was the duty of the Cape Government and of the High Commissioner, Sir Hercules Robinson, to pull Mr Chamberlain back from the precipice.

We are afraid Mr Chamberlain's dispatches are beginning to play at ultimatum. Now an ultimatum is a very fine thing, but it is not a thing to play at. . . . If President Kruger himself dreamed of conceding the franchise at this moment on top of the so-called revolution, the burghers would simply depose him. There is much else for Mr Chamberlain to press about; but if he once tries to force the Transvaal Government about internal reforms by the threat of war, about which his advisers speak so glibly, we tell him plainly that he will have to fulfil the threat—which is a wicked folly which we do not contemplate—or else take a humiliating rebuff, which will be less wicked but scarcely less foolish and mischievous (*Cape Times*, 1 April 1896).

Garrett's leaders angered jingo enthusiasts in Cape Town and elsewhere. But they helped to calm the atmosphere. The British High Commissioner in Cape Town, Sir Hercules Robinson, shared Garrett's view and exerted his influence to pull Chamberlain back from the brink.

J. H. Hofmeyr wrote to Garrett to urge that the substance of his leading articles be cabled to London. Garrett made a copy of his letter and placed it on file in the *Cape Times* library:

> 22 Camp Street,
> 1 April 1896
>
> Dear Mr Garrett,
> Allow me to cordially thank you for your 'Word to Mr Chamberlain'. I hope it will be cabled to the British Press as coming from a paper which has hitherto been regarded as Mr Rhodes's most thorough-going supporter in the South African Press and that it may tend to thwart the wicked designs of those agitators who currently do not abhor the prospect of seeing the whole of South Africa steeped in blood.
> Yours very truly,
> J. H. Hofmeyr

But Garrett's leaders infuriated Rutherfoord Harris. He cabled instructions to Garrett which the Editor blithely ignored. On 15 April 1896 Garrett wrote to Agnes:

> I have just routed Dr Harris, between ourselves, in an attempt to stop my recent line of protest against war by impudent threat or order cabled out to me. He has quite knuckled under and my position is all right. Cecil J. is going . . . [crazy?] and leading Joseph C, and the rest, all into a bog along with him. I am going to stop him, I hope. He *was* all right in motives but he doesn't know how to take a beating and start afresh.

In a letter on 27 May 1896, Garrett told Agnes of a conversation with James Rose Innes which had encouraged him greatly. Rose Innes had said: 'the people here undoubtedly take their opinion about Rhodes and all that from you.' Garrett took this as a testimonial of the *Cape Times*'s credibility. In another letter, Garrett wondered if 'CJR thinks me a beast for "giving him away" so much'. But he was confident that the standing of the newspaper was again as high as it had been in St Leger's day.

Garrett had also written to Stead in London, arguing that it would be wrong to force matters to a war on the question of internal reforms in the Transvaal 'to cover up recent events and reverse their victory and our blunder'. Stead had been taking a strong line against the Transvaal. But Garrett successfully persuaded him that Chamberlain's forceful policy was sheer folly and could lead to a war which would 'put the clock back for a century or two'.

Three years later Stead would throw these words back in Garrett's face. By this time Stead had become a crusading 'pro-Boer' while Garrett, falling increasingly under the powerful influence of his friend Alfred Milner, had come round to the view that the policy of conciliation had failed and the time had come for vigorous Imperial intervention.

Garrett's championship of Milner's policy in 1899 was vigorous indeed, so much so that there were some who were inclined to blame him as much as anyone else when war eventually broke out. Among Garrett's bitter critics was General Sir William Butler, commander of the Imperial forces in South Africa, who resigned his post in 1899, declaring that the country needed a rest rather than a surgical operation.

And there was Olive Schreiner, whose letters to her brother W. P. Schreiner in late 1899 were passionate in their denunciation of Garrett, who, she believed, had led Milner to take the wrong path. In 1899, Garrett was in favour of increasing pressure on Kruger, confident that the old President would back down when faced with the prospect of armed intervention by Britain.

It was a tragic miscalculation, in which Garrett seems to have completely discounted his own first-hand knowledge of Kruger. He acknowledged that there was a risk of war but argued, to the last, that he did not want war and that there would be no war. And in late 1899, Olive Schreiner had written to W. P. Schreiner: 'After Rhodes, and in a sense more than Rhodes, I blame Garrett. . . .'

But now, in April 1896, Garrett was urging moderation. And, whatever the indiscretion of his meddling in politics outside the office, his conduct of the newspaper in the Raid crisis enhanced its prestige in Cape Town.

The circulation of the *Cape Times* increased steadily and sub-stantially during his first year of editorship..It had been a strenuous year—with little time for outside interests. There were occasional week-ends by the sea at Muizenberg, where Garrett shared a cottage with his friend Herbert Baker. Dr Jane Waterston con-tinued to watch Garrett's health, managing his diet and urging him to spend as much time at Muizenberg as possible. He joined a riding club of Cape Town journalists known as the 'Suicide Riding Brigade' and spent happy hours on the Cape Flats. On his thirty-first birthday, 20 July 1896, he wrote to his cousin Agnes:

> At this moment I feel less of an invalid than for several years past. . . . Some good work has been done. I have never told you of all the difficulties or early doubts and struggles. The other day old Faure, one of the ministers who was up at Pretoria and came to see me in bed when I was ill there just a year ago, said to some members in the lobby of the House: 'Look at this fellow! I visited him on his sick bed in Pretoria, fading away to slow music and looking like a regular "sent out to die"—and here he is, the most dangerous man in Africa!'

Cecil Rhodes, back from London, now went north—and was soon in the headlines again, making peace at the dramatic *indaba* with the Matabele, who had risen in the wake of the Jameson fiasco.

Garrett had sent Vere Stent as a special correspondent to cover the Matabele rising for the *Cape Times*. Stent was gratified by the appointment, as he felt himself to be the last person who would be chosen to represent a newspaper which gave broad support to Rhodes. Stent was *persona non grata* with the Chartered Company. He had not hesitated to attack the 'hideous cruelty' which had accompanied the conquest of Matabeleland. Garrett sympathized with his outlook although he did not believe that Rhodes was personally responsible for the misdeeds of his swashbuckling troopers. In August, Stent was to give the *Cape Times* one of its greatest 'scoops', riding into the Matopos with Rhodes, Dr Hans Sauer and Colenbrander.

His dispatch to the *Cape Times* painted a graphic picture of the four men, with three revolvers among them, 'completely at the mercy of the Matabele should they have wished to murder us'. The chiefs and *indunas* were camped in the hills about five or six kilometres from Rhodes's camp and had sent messages that they were willing to parley.

Without the slightest hesitation Mr Rhodes decided to go. . . . We were to go unarmed, but each of us, excepting Mr Rhodes, carried a small pocket revolver. . . . Mr Rhodes carried only the traditional switch. . . . He faced the whole ordeal with consistent nerve. . . . Mr Rhodes risked his life for the sake of peace and Rhodesia . . . (24 August 1896).

The incident caught the public imagination in Cape Town and elsewhere. Even so fierce an opponent of Cecil Rhodes as John X. Merriman was moved to write a generous letter to the *Cape Times* (29 August 1896). Merriman praised the 'physical and moral courage' shown by Rhodes in his mission to the Matopos insurgents. It was easy to imagine how hard a task it must have been to treat for peace with armed, unsubdued rebels. In so doing, Rhodes had risen above his own natural feelings and had averted the possibility of a great disaster.

This *indaba* seems to have had considerable impact on public opinion. Rhodes was a popular hero, among one section of the population at least. His return from the north became a triumphal progress, with big crowds greeting him at Port Elizabeth, at Kimberley and in the towns of the Boland. Throughout 1896, Garrett had pegged away at Rhodes in leader after leader, urging him to make a public statement, acknowledging his role in the Raid fiasco, confessing his fault and 'facing the music'. But Rhodes had bitterly resented these promptings and had remained 'mute as the Sphinx'.

Now, at Port Elizabeth, he broke his year-long silence, still making no apologies but scoffing at the 'unctuous rectitude' of his critics. The House of Commons select committee was about to begin its inquiry into the Raid, and Rhodes's only reference to the subject was to say: 'I am told I have promoted great disunion. That may be, for the temporary moment. We will leave the question for the future.' The *Cape Times* concluded that Rhodes still had a hand to play.

Early in 1897 Rhodes sailed to England in the *Dunvegan Castle*. Also aboard were Garrett—and Olive Schreiner. On arrival at the quayside, Garrett was interviewed by a reporter of the London *Daily News*:

> It was a little uncomfortable for me on the ship in one way. Olive Schreiner considers I have woefully misused my opportunities for telling Mr Rhodes what is for the good of his soul which she once invited me to do, journalistically. Mr Rhodes, on his part, classes me in Cape Politics with 'the Innes group' (a great honour but not meant so) and even congratulated me on making common cause with the 'unctuous rectitudes'. You will probably say the *Cape Times* has been his best friend. So it has. But those political people never do appreciate best friends who happen to be also 'candid friends'. . . .
>
> But it is idle to talk about the pro-Rhodes feeling in Cape Town—it is strong to unreason. Temperate criticism like that of the *Cape Times* is resented by a very large section of its readers. They have, as I said, temporarily lost their heads. I bought something in a shop just as I was starting. The young man who served me said: 'Tell them in England that we don't care a pin about the Raid, but we want Rhodes back to stand up to old Kruger. . . .'

What then does it all come to, this new revulsion and upheaval in Cape Colony? It comes to this, that Paul Kruger

has lost his chance and Mr Rhodes has taken it, and whether
we like it or whether we don't, we shall all have to 'swallow
Rhodes' again as the British standard-bearer in South Africa—
Raid and all. . . .

So far as the towns are concerned, they don't care a straw
about the Raid. They don't think about its ethics at all, I am
sorry to say, and very little about its policy. They love Mr
Rhodes for having been ready to make it, had certain conditions called for the making of it. They love him for standing up
to the Government which has always flouted and bullied the
Colony.

The question is, can Rhodes work from the base of this
partly racial sentiment and yet keep enough Dutch on his
side to make his career consistent and his politics practical?
Can he? He himself, as always, is supremely confident. He is an
extraordinary man. Only time will show.

Rhodes was to make his political comeback in the elections of
1898 but his Progressive Party was to be narrowly defeated by
the Afrikaner Bond. And as Alfred Milner stepped on to the
South African stage, Rhodes was more in the background. What
time *did* show was that Rhodes was indeed smashed as a politician
who could appeal to broad South African sentiment.

Now, in early 1897, he was about to appear before the South
Africa Committee. Rhodes was determined to save as much of
his political reputation as he could. By now the focus of attention
was on the possibility that the South Africa Committee might
uncover evidence of Imperial complicity—evidence that Joseph
Chamberlain, 'Pushful Joe', was 'in it up to his neck'. But the
fact that Chamberlain himself was a member of the committee
seemed to suggest this line of investigation would not be pushed
very far—as indeed it turned out.

Through an extraordinary concatenation of events, Garrett
himself had helped to swing the spotlight away from Rhodes in
the direction of Chamberlain, earning the latter's fierce enmity.
Later, when Milner wanted Garrett to replace Sir Graham Bower
as Imperial Secretary at the Cape, Chamberlain said he would not
appoint him at any price.

Stead, in London, had decided to bring out a Christmas edition called *The History of the Mystery*. Stead's objective was to shield Chamberlain. He believed that the so-called 'missing cables', which were thought to demonstrate Imperial complicity, were bound to come out. So Stead decided to reveal the existence of the cables in advance, at the same time putting the best possible face upon Mr Chamberlain's part in the conspiracy.

Stead sent Garrett a full set of advance proofs. The two had been corresponding for some time about the project, as Garrett was bringing out his own Christmas number on the Raid, *The Story of a Crisis*, which attempted to set out a complete history of the fiasco. This was also published in London, on the eve of the opening of the inquiry by the South Africa Committee, in a book, *The Story of an African Crisis*, which remains a basic document for any student of the Raid.

As publication day of Stead's 'History' approached, pressure was brought to bear on him—by Rutherfoord Harris among others—to black out the chapter discussing the 'missing cables'. Stead did so.

Garrett, in ignorance of the latest developments in London, reviewed *The History of the Mystery* in the *Cape Times* of 8 December, working from his advance proofs. He quoted—in full—the very chapter that had been blacked out in London! And, in adding a highly indiscreet introduction to his own book when it was published in London, he told the story of the 'blacking out' expedient and how it had backfired in Cape Town. But he expressed his view that the content of the missing cables 'was not compromising enough to hang a dog'. Garrett concluded:

> South Africa—and later London—was thus apprised that what the whole mystery amounted to was simply that Mr Rhodes, and through him others, had been led to form an exaggerated view of the extent of Mr Chamberlain's cognizance and approval of their plans, owing to the terms in which friends or agents in London reported the tenor of conversations at the Colonial Office, mainly or partly in connection with the negotiations for the transfer of the Protectorate, and of the duty of policing the Protectorate, to the Chartered Company.

I think that will be accepted as a fair summary; a fair prose translation of Mr Stead's ingenious and poetical fantasy about the Cable-serpent, which drags its slow length through the Atlantic ooze, and tempts the denizens of a political Eden by repeating broken whispers and condensed perversions of each other's thoughts. . . .

The chapter published in the *Cape Times*—and blacked out in London—said at one point:

Here . . . is Mr Cecil [Rhodes] at Hopetown meditating day and night on how he is to save British interests and promote the union of South Libya when the inevitable insurrection breaks out. He cannot tell Blastus [Chamberlain] straight out what he is worrying over. All he can do is get a confidential friend of both parties to sound Blastus delicately as to what is in the wind. Blastus on his part speaks not less guardedly and then the result, boiled down to cable code dimensions, may and sometimes does, mislead both parties. The cable in this political drama is responsible for making Mr Cecil believe that Blastus knew what was up, and, privately at least, approved heartily of all that was being done.

In a *Cape Times* editorial on the same day, confidence was expressed that the inquiry would unearth nothing to the discredit of the Imperial authorities. If to politicians and journalists in England, including Mr Stead, Chamberlain was only Joe of Birmingham, in South Africa he represented England. 'And the good faith of England must be above suspicion', the editorial declared.

The South Africa Committee did not insist on the production of the 'missing cables'. In this and other particulars its report was a whitewash job and was condemned as such by almost the entire British Press. Alfred Spender of the *Westminster Gazette* called it a 'hushing-up in public'. In our own time, South African historians, notably Dr Jean van der Poel and Professor J. S. Marais, do not doubt that Chamberlain knew what was afoot and connived at the conspiracy, however much he deplored Jameson's impulsive dash across the border.

Garrett's own view, at the time, expressed in a letter to Agnes, was less categorical:

I don't think Joe was in it as much as some suspect, but anyone can see that he has not been quite frank and that Rhodes had excuse for thinking he was looked to to make a *coup* for England. Rhodes thinks me a big prig. I think them all a set of too-clever-by-half fools.

When the South Africa Committee report was eventually published, the *Cape Times* urged the South African Press to 'join us in making a very strong appeal to Mr Rhodes' to publish the missing cables. The newspaper considered it most unlikely that the cables contained anything very extraordinary at all but argued that their publication would clear the air.

We know well that Mr Rhodes was no party, quite the contrary, to the original attacks on the Colonial Office made by people who thought they were doing service to him, if not to truth. But here we have Mr Rhodes suppressing certain messages, and Mr Hawksley, his solicitor, openly using the messages, or the suppression of them, to feed the suspicions against the Colonial Office. That is an impossible situation. It combines all the possible evils of both suppression and publication. . . .

The fact that they [the missing cables] ever existed is only known through Mr Chamberlain having very properly demanded to know what were the messages which Mr Hawksley had spoken of, in some communication to the Colonial Office, as having led some of his clients in South Africa to conclude that the Colonial Office was cognizant of their plans. In reply to this demand, Mr Hawksley had confidentially supplied Mr Chamberlain with copies. Those copies included messages which have, and a few which have not, appeared as a result of the Committee's various requisitions upon witnesses. These few, therefore, are now recoverable as copies; Mr Chamberlain has thrown the onus on Mr Rhodes by stating that he has no objection to their publication . . . (*Cape Times*, 31 August 1897).

But Rhodes was unmoved by the *Cape Times*'s appeal to burst the 'Cable Bubble' by publishing the messages. They remain unpublished to this day. Dr Van der Poel believes it probable that they no longer exist. It has been suggested that a blackmail threat by the Rhodes group to publish the missing cables and other alleged evidence of Colonial Office complicity had been used to ensure that Chamberlain would not revoke Rhodes's charter to develop the north—and to oblige him to 'whitewash' Rhodes, as he did in an adulatory speech in the Commons debate on the Committee's report.

The *Annual Register*, discussing the Commons debate, included this much-quoted comment:

> It was an open secret that throughout the debate, one member, unconnected with either front bench, sat with the famous telegrams in his pocket, and with them certain correspondence relating thereto, which he had been instructed to read in the event of Mr Rhodes's character being aspersed. . . .

On his return to Cape Town in March 1897, Cecil Rhodes was given a hero's welcome at the docks. He said (*Cape Argus*, 20 March 1897) he was happy that 'whatever blame you may attach to me . . . you are yet glad to see me back again'.

> You recognize the higher motive which I had (cheers) and I still hope that constitutionally we shall arrive at that point which we all desire (loud and prolonged cheering). And what is that point? It is not a question of race; it is this—that we desire equal rights for every white man south of the Zambesi (continued cheering) irrespective of race, and then gradually the union of Africa (renewed cheers).

As the crowds sang 'God save the Queen', Rhodes stepped into his Cape cart and drove home to Rondebosch. It would not be long before the equal rights slogan would be adapted for the sake of the Coloured vote, becoming a clarion call for rights for all *civilized* men as Rhodes made his attempted political comeback in the following year.

Before events had moved so far, W. P. Schreiner would have

broken completely with Rhodes, announcing his decision not to
stand again in Barkly West, telling his constituents of 'the evils
experienced and threatened and flowing from the continued
influence of Mr Rhodes upon the institutions and politics of this
colony'.

Schreiner seems to have kept hoping that Rhodes would cry
'*peccavi*' and make public acknowledgement of his fault. But
much had happened since the historic meeting in the library of
Groote Schuur when Rhodes, 'completely broken down', had
told his friend and colleague: 'It is all true. Old Jameson has upset
my apple-cart. . . .' In his evidence before the South Africa
Committee, Schreiner had spoken of Rhodes in terms of frank
regret: 'You cannot trust a man altogether and be absolutely
mistaken in your trust and remain with regard to the rest of the
world just as full of trust and confidence as ever; and that is what
hundreds of people are feeling in South Africa today; they have
lost their leader. . . .' But Schreiner insisted that Rhodes's aim
had been a high one.

Nevertheless, Rhodes had perverted the Chartered Company,
De Beers and the Goldfields Company in the interests of a
revolutionary conspiracy. He had betrayed friends and colleagues
and the patiently-won trust of the Afrikaner Bond. And still he
remained unrepentant and contumacious. Schreiner's attitude
had hardened and, at last, he had come out in public denunciation
of Rhodes.

In an editorial on 26 July 1897, the *Cape Times* was confident
that Schreiner would not drop out of politics: 'We cannot afford
to lose from the active public life of the Colony an honest
politician and a high-minded, generously-meaning man.'

Schreiner, having repudiated Rhodes, was assured of a safe
seat with the support of the Afrikaner Bond, and would now be
dedicated to driving Rhodes out of public life.

CHAPTER 10

RECESSIONAL

For frantic boast and foolish word—
Thy mercy on Thy People, Lord!

Rudyard Kipling, 1897

ON 22 June 1897, the British Empire celebrated the Diamond Jubilee of Queen Victoria. At the age of 78, the Queen emerged from seclusion to drive in procession from Buckingham Palace to St Paul's Cathedral for a service of thanksgiving. It was a day of splendid pageantry. Alfred Harmsworth's *Daily Mail* put its best descriptive writers to work, and one of them, George Warrington Steevens, watched the procession of Colonial statesmen and Colonial troops, with Lord Roberts on a white horse prancing at the head, outside St Paul's:

In the carriages we saw the square, strong, invincibly sensible faces of the men who are building up great nations, new big Englands, on the other side of the world. Between the carriages rode and tramped the men who guard the building and carry British peace and British law into the wildest places of the earth. Lean, hard-knit Canadians, long-legged, yellow Australians, all in one piece with their horses, giant long-eyed Maoris, sitting loosely and leaning back curiously from the waist; burned South Africans; upstanding Sikhs; tiny, lithe Malays and Dyaks; Chinese with a white basin upside-down on their heads; grinning Hausas, so dead black that they shine silver in the sun—white men, yellow men, brown men, black men, every continent, every colour, every race, every speech— and all in arms for the British Empire and the British Queen. ... And you began to understand, as never before, what the Empire amounts to. Not only that we possess all these remote outlandish places, and can bring men from every end of the earth to join us in honouring our Queen, but also that all these

people are working, not simply under us, but with us. . . .
How small you must feel in face of the stupendous whole. . . .

And the *Daily Mail's* leader writer, in a transport of enthusiasm,
declared: 'How many millions of years has the sun stood in
heaven? But the sun never looked down until yesterday on the
embodiment of so much energy and power.'

If the *Daily Mail*, in its strident way, was reflecting the popular
mood, there were some who sensed that the sun of Empire was
at its zenith, that this was a celebration of a glory that was
already beginning to pass. On 17 July, Rudyard Kipling's
Recessional would be published in *The Times*, sounding a prophetic
note.

The Jameson Raid was certainly, in Churchill's phrase, a
'fountain of ill', and the South African War, beginning in 1899,
would further undermine the exalted idea of Empire which had
seemed so fresh and compelling to G. W. Steevens in June 1897.
The Boer Republics would lose their independence after keeping
the might of Empire at bay for weary months and years of war.
But their struggle would in time deal a death-blow to the era of
aggressive, expansionist Imperialism.

At Cape Town, the jubilee saw the revival of a long-cherished
ambition of the *Cape Times* to promote a Cape contribution to
the Royal Navy. The idea had originated in St Leger's day and
had been assiduously promoted by Edmund Garrett, who saw
co-operation in Imperial defence as the groundwork for Imperial
federation. The annual contribution, as proposed in the Cape
Parliament by James Rose Innes in the 1897 session, was hailed
by the *Cape Times*.

Cecil Rhodes was indifferent to the idea but it gained enthusiastic support from John X. Merriman, who supported the Innes
resolution as expressing a true spirit of nationality and freedom.
It was Merriman at his parliamentary best: 'Our young men see
visions and our old men dream dreams; but they would be vain
visions indeed, and idle dreams, if the protecting might of the
sea power of England were withdrawn.'

W. P. Schreiner spoke in similar strain and the resolution was
carried without a division. The Prime Minister, Sir Gordon

Sprigg, went off to attend the celebrations in London with the resolution in his pocket.

But Sprigg, overcome by the excitement of the occasion, exceeded his brief and told the assembled Colonial premiers that the Cape was to present a first-class battleship to the Imperial Navy! The offer caused remarkable enthusiasm in Britain. The Cape Parliament, in fact, voted an annual sum of £30 000 towards the cost of Imperial naval defence and later increased it to £50 000.

Garrett was delighted with the success of the scheme and the cordial support of Merriman and Schreiner, given in spite of the post-Raid atmosphere of animosity and suspicion. But now Merriman and Schreiner were moving closer towards the Afrikaner Bond, making it difficult for Rose Innes to rally moderate English-speaking opinion, which was to be steadily driven into the arms of Rhodes. Rose Innes vowed he could never again be a 'Rhodes man' and became increasingly impotent.

Garrett was pursuing his campaign to bring Rhodes back into politics and eventually—in March 1898—the *Cape Times* published the extended interview which marked Rhodes's return to Cape politics. (Appendix 3.) This was on the eve of polling in the Legislative Council (Upper House) elections. A few months later there was to be the frenzied and bitterly contested Assembly election which Rhodes's Progressives were to lose to the Afrikaner Bond by a narrow majority.

Garrett, as already mentioned, decided to stand for Parliament himself, combining the task of editing a daily paper with political campaigning and, later, membership of the Cape Parliament. It was a rash decision, for the *Cape Times* and for Garrett himself, and would rapidly reduce him to the condition of a semi-invalid, unfit for journalism or politics. At this time, however, Garrett was 'intoxicated with betterness' and he enjoyed campaigning immensely. At first, his boyish appearance had amused the crowds and there were cries at one meeting of 'Go home to your mother'. But Garrett became a rousing orator, bringing crowds to their feet, as one of his listeners at a Kimberley meeting recalled: 'He made me realize what it meant to be an Englishman.'

20. A Penstone cartoon in the *Cape Times* Weekly Edition, 3 June, 1896. Dr Leyds, State Secretary, was regarded in the Cape as a sinister and malevolent influence in Transvaal politics. But the pleas for clemency for the Rand reformers prevailed and on 12 June the *Cape Times* complimented President Kruger on his 'good sense, his good nature and his statesmanship'.

21. Crowds outside the *Cape Times* building in St George's Street, awaiting news of the South African War.

22. A meeting in Greenmarket Square, Cape Town, on 3 April, 1900, which called for the annexation of the Boer Republics.

In the *Cape Times*, Garrett was giving vigorous backing to Cecil Rhodes. A leading article on 26 October 1898 helps to explain how Rhodes was able to arouse such extraordinary enthusiasm among ordinary people. It gives some insight into Rhodes's continued appeal in spite of the Raid and everything else. Rhodes was speaking at an open-air rally in the Good Hope gardens:

> Last night the great Expansionist spoke to Cape Town about what he calls 'the big ideas' under a roof expansive enough for anything; for he spoke practically under the Southern Cross. . . . Last night's speech was characteristic in many ways . . . in its abrupt little confidences, in its blunt expression of personal antagonisms, in its calculated and uncalculated indiscretions. . . . Mr Rhodes's impatience with political and other scruples, as with things which get in the way of large designs and more distant objects, often finds vent (it did yesterday) in a tone which seems to imply that everything in politics is 'unctuous' which is not baldly cynical. The audiences do not mind this tone in the least, though to many of them it must be quite new, as popular speeches and plays and articles are nearly always based on a wholly different convention. To some of them the Rhodes convention must be distinctly less wholesome than the other—but both, after all, are equally conventional. Even Mr Rhodes, who talks at one moment as if independence and 'rectitude' were the bane of politics, the next moment resents being accused of having no rectitude himself and twits the Bond party with its lack of independence. But if this note jars, it makes up for all when Mr Rhodes gets on to his far-off dreams and ambitions, the real ideals of his own rectitude—unctuous or otherwise—and lifts his hearers up with him into the same vast uplands. . . . He takes the current petty matters in the lobby in Cape politics and throws them all against the background of the expansion of Africa; brings them into relation, in short, with his life's work, and with all that to Cape Town audiences he embodies. That is the best thing to see at these gatherings, the lifting of the young fellows in the audience out of themselves and out of our localisms, and

making them feel that they, too, are part of the great mysterious process that is creating a new world out of the chaos of a continent. . . . There is here something of the light that never was on sea or land, the consecration of the poet's dream. It leavens much cynicism; it gives the clue to what is best in the human mixture labelled Rhodes.

But Rhodes's Progressives lost the election. The result demonstrated just how completely the Raid had polarized political opinion on English–Dutch lines. As the *Cape Times* noted (4 April 1899), politics in the Cape had become race politics. An Afrikaner constituency would return a Bond member, and a British or Uitlander constituency, a Progressive member. Where there were exceptions to this rule, it was due to yet another racial factor—the Coloured vote. Where the race preponderance was clear, contest was idle. 'Both sides will deplore this race division; each will blame the other for it. It will generally be found that a test is applied, and a cry is raised, by the party which stands to gain by it, not the party which stands to lose.'

The editorial noted that the underlying theme of the election had been the conflicting attitudes towards Paul Kruger's Transvaal. The Progressives had stood for 'the Uitlander view, the reform view, the equal rights view, the anti-Kruger view, the pro-Imperial view . . .'. The Transvaal question overshadowed all else and Cape politics would be on English–Dutch lines until it was settled. And it would be settled, if settled at all, with the Afrikaner Bond in power at the Cape.

Now Rhodes would be more and more in the wings and would tell an interviewer: 'I had my try at the Transvaal "question" and made a mess of it. This is Sir Alfred Milner's turn.'

Milner had already stepped forward in March 1898, with his celebrated speech at Graaff-Reinet: 'Loyal! Of course you are loyal! It would be monstrous if you were not. . . .'

In his anomalous double role as Governor of the Cape and, at the same time, Her Majesty's High Commissioner in South Africa, Milner would henceforth strike a forceful interventionist posture, reasserting the right of the Imperial factor to protect the interests of British paramountcy. The Imperial factor was now 'in the saddle', as Garrett put it. He now agreed whole-heartedly with Milner's analysis that conciliation of the Transvaal had failed and that the time had come for increasing Imperial pressure on President Kruger to give the Uitlanders their rights. As Milner and Garrett saw it, the Uitlander franchise was the key to control of the Transvaal, which, it was now clear, would in turn dominate the united South Africa of the future, with its immense mineral wealth and industrial potential.

In the South African League, Garrett became an effective advocate of Milner's views, denouncing the unfairness of the Transvaal's denial of franchise to the English in the Transvaal while the Dutch in Cape Colony, enjoying full freedom and franchise rights as British subjects, were able to control the legislature of the Cape.

Garrett's view of the situation had changed radically since the days of April 1896 when J. H. Hofmeyr had congratulated him on his words of warning to Chamberlain. But Garrett, backing Milner, would argue that the situation had changed. He was distressed that the *Cape Times's* London correspondent, J. W. Robertson Scott, was writing in a consistently anti-Milner strain. He sent him a cable: 'My dear chap, you must approve Milner or. . . .' Robertson Scott, who recalls in his memoir of Garrett that he could not bring himself to become an applauder of Milner, cabled back: 'My dear chap, or. . . .' And he found another London correspondent for Garrett.

Meanwhile, the friendship between Garrett and Milner was growing into close collaboration in politics. Both were then unmarried and totally dedicated to a high-minded vision of Imperial responsibility. The austere, gently-spoken Milner, for all his superb administrative intelligence and extraordinary strength of purpose, was a lonely man with little aptitude for getting across to people in the mass. Garrett's championship of his policy meant a great deal to him, as did Garrett's friendship.

Garrett was now spending long hours trying to persuade James Rose Innes to come out in whole-hearted support of Milner. In time, Rose Innes came to admire and respect Milner, if not always to agree with him. Garrett was most gratified when

Rose Innes remarked after hearing Milner speak at a club dinner: 'That man is true as steel and he has a backbone of steel.'

But Milner's shortcomings as a negotiator are today generally acknowledged. As John Buchan noted in his autobiography, Milner 'was not very good at envisaging a world wholly different from his own, and his world and Kruger's at no point intersected. There was a gnarled magnificence in the old Transvaal President, but he saw only a snuffy, mendacious savage.'

After the publication of Milner's celebrated 'helot' dispatch, declaring the case for Imperial intervention to be 'overwhelming', there were to be murmurs in the British Press. Alfred Spender's *Westminster Gazette* came out in strong protest. Garrett cabled his expostulations and followed with a strong letter: 'You old women of Fleet Street, can't you even take a 1,000-to-1 chance of war? . . .'

The scene was set for the Bloemfontein conference with Milner, who had been hailed at Oxford as the 'finest flower of human culture', facing the old President, who at one point would exclaim, with tears running down his cheeks: 'It is not the franchise. . . . It is our country you want, it is our country you want. . . .'

On the eve of the conference, the *Cape Times* had argued (29 May 1899) that the franchise proposals by the Transvaal should be judged by their effects—whether they would alter the centre of gravity in the government of the Transvaal so as to relieve the British Government of the burden of further intervention. To be of any use at all, the vote must be given to Uitlanders on such conditions that those who really wished to throw in their lot with the Transvaal and become citizens would in fact avail themselves of it.

Writing some years later on the Bloemfontein conference, Garrett said that the two South African ideals had reached deadlock when Milner came on the scene. Any sincere reform must inevitably involve an abdication of Boer government and look like an abdication of the Boer people. This was as clear to Kruger as it was to Milner. Before the negotiations it was arguable whether the Boer might surrender his political monopoly without the war alternative. The negotiations had made it clear that he would surrender it only on that alternative. Milner had foreseen as much as he gazed across the table at the old Boer, Kruger, and the young Jan Smuts.

'He came out and paced alone for some time, grave and very pale. . . . Then he re-entered the conference room, firm and erect. His verdict was formed—"complete failure"—as he telegraphed to a friend—and his diplomatic reputation must just fare as it might' (*The Empire and the Century*, 1902).

Milner returned to Cape Town, where feelings were running high. A deputation was organized by Edmund Garrett which went—100 strong—to see Milner at Government House to express thanks for the 'firm stand made by you on behalf of the Uitlander population of the Transvaal'. As the *Cape Times* reported, 'all that is worthiest and most influential in the Cape Peninsula' was represented in the deputation.

But there was a notable absentee—James Rose Innes, who had told the promoters that demonstrations calculated to excite public feeling would increase the difficulty of a peaceful settlement. Milner then called for Rose Innes and told him that he would have accepted Kruger's proposal if he could have felt satisfied that the President was genuinely willing to grant reasonable relief to the Uitlanders.

Rose Innes came away feeling that Milner did not want war, but would not be deterred from pressing his point by the risk of it. The next day, Rose Innes issued a statement to the *Cape Times* in which he urged people who had influence with President Kruger to bring it to bear to induce him to make reasonable concessions. And those who had no influence could at least refrain from doing anything which would make the position more difficult.

On 26 June 1899, the *Cape Times* declared that the policy of conciliation had been given a fair trial and had failed. The evidence of pacific intentions on the British part had been grievously misconstrued.

But for the rooted illusion that British diplomacy would give way, and procrastinate, and compromise, at the first cold glint along the barrel of the Boer rifle, we should not be so close as we are today to the necessity for a glitter of British bayonets upon the border. 'England's threats', quoth the Rev. Mr Vorster at Burghersdorp, 'are those of a man with an unloaded gun.' That unloaded gun, or the belief in it, is at the bottom of the whole trouble. We have now come to this point, that the gun must be loaded, and the aggressive combination calling itself 'the Afrikaner nation' must be made to believe that it is loaded, even by the discharge of it, if no other way succeeds. The first thing, therefore, whether peace is to be broken or not, and all the more as we hope to keep it and be spared the last extremity, must be to reinforce the South African garrisons at least to some sort of equality with the Republican forces.

In late July, Garrett had a relapse, suffering a haemorrhage which nearly killed him. From the sanatorium in Kimberley, he wrote to Rose Innes, urging him again to throw his considerable weight and influence behind Milner:

> I would do anything to strengthen his hand. He has already changed the face of Africa. How? By not caring a fig what happened to his career. He knows he can only intervene *once*. The side ready to go to all lengths wins; he was ready. Hitherto it has been the Boer, every time. Home folks not ready; but Milner's personality has pulled the bluff through so far and now they can't well get out of troops and all, if necessary; whereupon it won't be necessary. If only they stick to it. I don't want war, though I know you don't believe it. But I want failure still less. I want a mild and modest instalment of our rights in a free South Africa—such as six weeks ago or eight weeks you would have said could not be got *without* fighting. . . .

As late as August 1899, Garrett was still arguing that there would be no war. He told the Reverend D. P. Faure: 'We don't want war; and there shall be no war.' Faure recalled in his memoirs that he got the impression that 'they were playing a game of bluff'. He told Garrett that Paul Kruger did not play such games. But now Garrett was obliged to leave South Africa, returning to the sanatorium in the Black Forest which had previously nursed him back to health.

Garrett's last essay in journalism before he sailed was an article, 'The Inevitable in South Africa', which he sent to the *Contemporary Review*. It had been prompted by the publication of Olive Schreiner's 'An English South African's View of the Situation: Words in Season', which argued that the Boers had demonstrated great statesmanship in trying to avert disaster. The pamphlet had stirred W. T. Stead. As his biographer noted, Stead wrote in the October *Review of Reviews* that these were reflections which bachelor politicians like Milner and Garrett were sometimes in danger of under-estimating. To Stead, Olive Schreiner's plea for patience was full of wisdom.

The Schreiner pamphlet was attacked by Garrett as question-begging rhetoric 'however glowing, however sincere' which supported the 'logic of a schoolgirl with the statistics of a romanticist and wraps them both in the lambent fire of a Hebrew prophetess'.

Olive Schreiner had argued that time was blending English and Dutch South Africans into a mutual people. Time was the great healer of differences—'and love is growing faster than time'. But Garrett was in favour of tightening the pressure. He insisted that British intervention—with a war alternative—was not the 'fault' of Chamberlain, Rhodes, Milner or anyone else.

It was, he argued, the inevitable result of forces which were wider and deeper and more long-lived than any human personality. The geological accident that had placed gold on the Witwatersrand meant inevitably that the new population, drawn by the gold, would in time outnumber the old. It would have been high statesmanship on Kruger's part to fuse the old population with the new while it was still malleable. Lord Milner had declared the case for intervention to be 'overwhelming'—this intervention had already changed the face of the whole problem without a shot being fired. Unless the British people faltered, this intervention would yet make it possible to leave the rest to the operation of natural forces.

Garrett was wrong. By the time these words were published—on 19 October 1899—war had begun.

CHAPTER 11

THE SOUTH AFRICAN WAR

The spectacle of anarchy, ruin and hatred that filled South Africa
at the time of his death offers a tragic warning to the practitioners
of a narrowly material statecraft.

The *Manchester Guardian* on the death of
Cecil Rhodes (27 March 1902)

They wanted to pull over Bennie's face
A handkerchief or scarf or something, like
A sort of hood. But Bennie bravely asked,
In English, too, yes he could speak it well—
Whether they couldn't hang him please without it?

C. Louis Leipoldt, 'Oom Gert Vertel',
translated by C. J. D. Harvey

ON 10 October 1899, the Union-Castle mailship *Norman* docked
in Table Bay and George Warrington Steevens, at 30 a veteran
war correspondent of the London *Daily Mail*, stepped ashore.

Steevens, who had been with Kitchener at Khartoum and had
travelled far chronicling the glory of Empire, walked up Adderley
Street and recorded his first impressions of Cape Town on the
eve of war. He noted the clarity of the air, musing that hitherto
he had been breathing mud and looking out on the world through
fog. This, at last, was air. From out to sea, the white line of houses
nestling at the foot of Table Mountain had been hardly visible.
Now, in Adderley Street, he found broad streets fronted with
new-looking ornate buildings of irregular heights and fronts.
As he told his readers:

Cape Town gives you the idea of being neither very rich
nor very poor, neither over-industrious nor over-lazy, decently
successful, reasonably happy, whole-heartedly easy-going. The
public buildings confirm the idea of a placid half-prosperity.
The place is not a baby, but it has hardly taken the trouble to

grow up. It has a Post Office of truly German stability and magnitude. It has a well-organized railway station, and it has the merit of being in Adderley Street, the main thoroughfare of the city; imagine it even possible to bring Euston into the Strand and you will get an idea of the absence of push and crush in Cape Town.

Over everything brooded peace, except over one flamboyant many-winged building of red brick and white stone with a garden about it, an avenue—a Cape Town avenue, shady trees and cool but not large; attractive and not imposing—at one side of it, with a statute of the Queen before and broad-flagged stairs behind.

This was the Legislative Assembly, where they were wrangling about the commandeering of gold and the sjambokking of Johannesburg refugees. . . .

In the Assembly, if nowhere else, there rumbled the menace of coming war. Outside, the only visible reminder was the presence of the refugees themselves, choking the lodging houses, the hotels and the streets and thronging the counters of the shipping offices six-deep. Streams of men filed down to the docks with bundles on their backs—the miners of the Rand who had been 'turned out of work, packed in cattle trucks and had come down in sun by day and icy wind by night'.

On 12 October at 5 p.m., President Kruger's ultimatum expired and South Africa was at war, with Boer commandos riding into Natal and fanning out to the west and south towards Kimberley and Mafeking. But Britain was hardly prepared. General Sir Redvers Buller's Army Corps had not yet left England.

On 14 October, General Buller sailed for the Cape in the *Dunnottar Castle*. Also on board was Winston Churchill, war correspondent, who feared it would all be over before he got there. By the time Churchill arrived on 30 October, in fact, Kimberley and Mafeking had been surrounded, and British forces had suffered reverses in Natal at Talana and Nicholson's Nek. And the war would drag on for two more years, making nonsense of Alfred Milner's hopes of a quick and decisive campaign.

Churchill went to the Mount Nelson Hotel, which he found 'a most excellent and well-appointed establishment, which may be thoroughly appreciated after a sea voyage'. But he lost no time in getting to the Natal front. Steevens was ahead of him—having already reached Ladysmith, taking the long trip by train through the Karoo to East London and thence to Durban. Churchill, to his annoyance, was too late. By the time he reached Estcourt, the Boer army was between him and Sir George White's headquarters.

Steevens, trapped in the besieged town, was able to give his readers a graphic picture of what it was like—'you squirm between iron fingers. Nothing to do but endure'—before dying of enteric fever and being buried at midnight with Boer searchlights illuminating the way for the funeral party.

General Buller had failed in repeated attempts to dislodge the Boer lines of investment. Winston Churchill himself was to be captured within a few weeks in the armoured train escapade at Chieveley. He would escape from the Boers and become a celebrity of the war, being elected Member of Parliament for Oldham while Boer commandos were still in the field.

In December, there were more British reverses at Magersfontein, Stormsberg and Colenso—mourned as 'Black Week' throughout the Empire. It would not be until the following June that Lord Roberts, the new commander-in-chief, would occupy Pretoria. In October 1900 the South African Republic would be formally annexed and in December Roberts would sail from Cape Town, confident that the war was won.

But Boer guerrillas fought on. The peace would not be signed until May 1902, with the British Army having put 448 000 men into the field. And there would be a frightful death-toll in concentration camps and a bitter legacy left in the wake of Kitchener's drives to 'clear the country' and smash guerrilla resistance.

In the first phase of the war, the ailing St Leger returned at intervals to take command of the *Cape Times*, now without an editor and being run from day to day by an Assistant Editor, E. J. Edwards.

The *Cape Times*, concerned about the plight of the Rand

refugees, returned to its perennial theme of the iniquity of the food duties, urging the suspension of the excise on imported meat to bring down prices. It pressed the authorities to relieve the hardships of the refugees, who were arriving in packed trains six times a day, the lucky ones in passenger compartments, those less fortunate in cattle trucks.

Towards the end of November, the newspaper was pleading for common sense in military censorship, pointing out that news of the capture of the armoured train at Chieveley had been held up for three days. The newspaper argued that the publication in Cape Town of a report of the capture of 60 British soldiers could not have given any conceivable advantage to the Boer forces.

The *Cape Times* recognized an obligation not to publish official secrets nor to disseminate information to the advantage of the enemy. The public did not want to know of anything which was likely to jeopardize any project of the military commanders. But it did expect to learn and to be entitled to know what had actually taken place on the field of battle. Suppression of information, in such circumstances, was 'unwarrantable and un-English'.

Again, in December, the *Cape Times* returned to the subject of the censorship—'the almost intolerable action of the military censorship in withholding war news and in manipulating war news to suit some inconceivably stupid purpose'.

The *Cape Times* had organized a corps of war correspondents, dispatching its Sports Editor, Alf Hellawell, to Mafeking. In Kimberley, there was G. A. L. Green. The newspaper was also able to draw on the work of some of the Fleet Street correspondents now in the field, publishing dispatches from Charles Hands and Julian Ralph, who had followed G. W. Steevens for the London *Daily Mail*.

One special correspondent of the *Cape Times* had ridden through the Boer lines from Ladysmith to Estcourt, taking the chance of being shot at or captured by Boer commandos or pickets to get his dispatch to the newspaper. And Hellawell, at Mafeking, had ridden to Kuruman and back to Mafeking through the Boer lines to get his reports to the paper. His dispatches stopped abruptly early in December; and on 8 December the *Cape Times* reported that he had been captured.

As the tide of war turned against the Republics in 1900, a conciliation movement sprang up, advocating peace on the basis of the restoration of independence to the Republics. The movement did not find favour with the *Cape Times*, which argued that peace must come on the basis of equal rights and opportunities for all civilized men, or else there would be no end to South African unrest.

In March, after much heart-searching, James Rose Innes had broken a long silence to advocate the annexation of the Republics. At a public meeting in Claremont on 30 March, Rose Innes argued that, whatever the causes of the war and whatever the apportionment of blame, there could now be no permanent peace without annexation of the Transvaal and the Free State and a period of direct rule, followed in time by full self-government on the same lines as the Cape.

But the capture of Pretoria and the annexation of the Republics merely marked a change in the character of the war. It now raged on as a guerrilla struggle, with thousands of young Cape colonists joining the Boer commandos. The Schreiner Ministry fell after dissension over the treatment of the Cape rebels and the application of martial law in the Colony. Sir Gordon Sprigg was again Prime Minister, with James Rose Innes taking office as Attorney-General.

By April 1901 almost the whole of the Cape, excluding the sea-port cities, was under martial law, with General Kitchener having almost complete jurisdiction. There was trial by court martial and the death penalty for rebellion. Kitchener's draconian use of these powers brought him into conflict with the Sprigg Ministry and notably with Rose Innes.

Kitchener was insisting on the compulsory presence of fellow townspeople at public hangings of rebels, a practice that was later prohibited on orders from London. In September 1901 Rose Innes was fiercely resisting Kitchener's demands that martial law be extended to Cape Town itself. And he was battling to get some means of restraining the military.

As he wrote and telegraphed to Richard Solomon in Pretoria, there was a 'perfect reign of terror' in force in some districts. Influential men were being arrested wholesale—in districts where no military operations were in force—and were being lodged in jail without trial. Several leading men had been arrested in Paarl and sent to Beaufort West without any explanation to anyone— and without any charge.

A leading Dutch Reformed minister, a doctor and several townsmen of Ceres had been arrested and lodged in jail in Malmesbury, again without any charge or explanation. Rose Innes was now refusing to allow such men to be held in Cape jails and insisting that the military make their own arrangements.

On 9 October, martial law was eventually proclaimed in Cape Town—but in a much modified form, as a result of Rose Innes's representations. The *Cape Times* had opposed the extension of martial law to the city unless 'dire necessity' could be demonstrated. The newspaper now acquiesced, assuring readers that the law-abiding element of the community had nothing to fear.

The reckless use of martial-law powers, however, had already created powerful resentment in the Cape and had, in fact, driven many more quiescent colonists into active rebellion. By now, the concentration-camp scandal was also raging, as the disclosures of Emily Hobhouse of the death-rate of women and children in the camps shook public opinion in Britain.

Kitchener's farm-burning policy, scorching the earth, had been designed to smash Boer morale, depriving guerrilla bands of food, shelter and support from the civilian population. It had also made refugee camps essential. But, if anything, it stiffened the Boer will to resist. By September, the death-rate in the camps was horrifying. An official statement, issued to the British Press in October, said that 2 411 people—mostly women and children— had died in September alone.

From a sanatorium at Nayland, Suffolk, Edmund Garrett wrote to James Rose Innes on 1 November expressing uneasiness about the camps and anger at the activities of the military under martial law. Garrett's cousin, Millicent Garrett Fawcett, had already arrived at the Cape at the head of a commission of Englishwomen

which had been instructed to investigate conditions in the camps
and recommend improvements.

Garrett was confident that the commission would at least
establish the facts. But he was horrified by reports of public
executions carried out under martial law, with the family and
relatives of the condemned being compelled to attend. He wrote:

> 'Those Slachters Nekking personally-attended hangings—
> what insanity! . . I suppose the soldiers think they atone for
> muddling their own business by muddling ours past remedy
> as well. This is over now but not its consequences. And I
> suppose fifty other follies since that we don't hear of over here.
> It is only *this* kind of thing that ever scares me as to the
> future. . . .

Garrett raged on for several pages, urging Rose Innes to convince Milner that there should be a perpetual, working revision
of everything done under martial law. This was the only safeguard. Garrett asked Rose Innes to reply and tell him 'how things
are really going' in the Colony.

Rose Innes replied on 4 December, telling Garrett that the
camps, as events drifted, had become inevitable from the point of
view of military necessity as well as mercy. He acknowledged that
the mortality figures were bad and he welcomed the Women's
Commission. Rose Innes was bitter about the military and said
he never again wanted to go through such a time as he had
experienced in the past few months. He was being called a
'd——d rebel' for 'endeavouring in feeble fashion to secure a few
very elementary civil rights for the civil population from the
wreck caused by the working of the military machine'.

But, Rose Innes noted, things were improving. There was
now a Martial Law Board to review complaints. Its existence
was a 'wholesome reminder' to the military. It was also becoming
clear that opinion in England was against the arbitrary administration of martial law.

Rose Innes himself would soon desert politics for the Bench,
going to the Supreme Court in the Transvaal. He had fought in
vain to prevent martial law being extended to Cape Town and

the other port cities. He had met Kitchener in Johannesburg and found him in an impossible mood—'he did not argue, he tried to bully'—but a second meeting produced the compromise by which the powers of the military were circumscribed at the coast. British subjects arrested by the military were to be tried in the ordinary courts, under the direction of the Attorney-General.

The South African War, with months and years of intense sectional emotion and political conflict at the Cape, saw St Leger's *Cape Times* declining sharply in stature. St Leger himself had died in March 1901.

A new Editor, J. Saxon Mills, arrived from Fleet Street in the same month, recruited from the staff of E. T. Cook's vigorously imperialist *Daily News* at the time when that newspaper changed proprietors and policy, becoming a pro-Boer journal owned by a Quaker syndicate. Saxon Mills, a master of arts of St John's College, Cambridge, had been a barrister of the Inner Temple.

His editorship lasted 15 unhappy months. Saxon Mills found himself in a political situation which became increasingly inflamed as the months wore on. His conduct of the paper did little to improve matters. Cape Town was divided into two bitterly hostile camps, with the one calling for an end to hostilities and the other convening 'vigilance' meetings and demanding even more severe measures to put down rebellion.

Earlier, in May 1900, when the first controversy about martial law was at its height, Alfred Milner—now Lord Milner—had first thought of suspending the Cape constitution and ruling without Parliament. There was not much enthusiasm for this idea in Downing Street, and Milner had shelved it. But it again came to the fore as Rhodes and Milner began to look ahead to the period of settlement after the war.

On the last day of 1901, the *Cape Times* came out with a vigorous editorial against suspending the Cape constitution. Such a course would provide rebellion with a respectable *raison d'être*, it said. Direct rule from Downing Street had long ago been replaced by free institutions in every British colony. Nothing could be gained from such a backward step.

This was advocacy of constitutional freedom in the best

23. The arrival of Lord Kitchener at Cape Town docks. He took over command in South Africa on 29 November, 1900.

Cape Archives

24. A photograph first published in the *Cape Times* on 20 May, 1939. General Louis Botha is seated in the centre. Some members of the group were identified by readers, as follows: Lying in front, on right; Commandant Tobias Smuts, (Ermelo); third from left, Commandant Ben Viljoen; fifth from left, Gert C. Fourie, Middelburg; sixth from left, Commandant Hendrik van Rensburg (Zoutpansberg); sitting, in centre, General Botha; Kneeling, second from extreme right; Field Cornet Coen Brits; behind him, Field Cornet Tom Kelly; Back row; 11th from left, Granville Nicholson; fifteenth from left, thought to be Jan Kemp (Krugersdorp volunteers.) The picture was sent to the *Cape Times* by Dr James F. Creighton of Saskatchewan, Canada.

25. A sketch by the *Cape Times* artist, Graham Winch, from the *Cape Times* Christmas Number, December 1896, which was devoted to a history of the Jameson Raid. Sir Jacobus de Wet, the British Agent in Pretoria, summoned before President Kruger at midnight on 31 December 1895, is questioned about rumours of a Rand march on Pretoria.

traditions of the *Cape Times*, which had done much in its formative years to nourish the frail plant of responsible government at the Cape. St Leger's 'Notes in the House' had helped to build the tradition of the old Cape Parliament as a model representative institution. In the 1880s the newspaper had argued that there could be no moral or political health without constitutional liberty, once the stage of dependency was passed. 'We might as well talk of going back to school as of giving up our political independence' (*Cape Times*, 1 July 1882).

There was astonishment in Cape Town, thus, when a few months later the *Cape Times* completely reversed its views on the suspension issue—and began a vigorous campaign *for* suspension. It was a remarkable departure, flying in the face of values and standards that had been preached in the newspaper for decades. It was all the more astonishing as soon the argument of military necessity could no longer be advanced. The Peace of Vereeniging had been signed on 31 May 1902. But the *Cape Times* was now arguing that a rest from party strife was essential in the interests of racial peace.

In the interim, Milner's resolve had hardened and the dying Cecil Rhodes himself had thrown his weight behind the movement, calling a meeting of Progressive members of Parliament to draft a petition to the British Government.

By now, Milner was in Johannesburg, having assumed office as Her Majesty's High Commissioner in the conquered Republics. Milner gave his public endorsement to the suspension petition. Rhodes, for his part, had urged suspension in one of the last acts of his public life.

Both Rhodes and Milner feared that there was no guarantee of a pro-Imperial majority in the Cape Parliament. They feared there would be no majority for indemnity of acts done under martial law. Milner, in particular, feared that a recalcitrant Cape Colony could wreck his plans for settlement. The Transvaal and the Orange Free State were already under Crown Colony rule, and to Milner's tidy administrative mind a Cape Colony similarly governed was necessary and desirable.

The Progressive Party split on the issue, with Thomas (later

Sir Thomas) Smartt leading a strong breakaway group giving vociferous backing to suspension. The Prime Minister, Sir Gordon Sprigg, and Progressive moderates such as T. L. Graham were equally strongly opposed.

In March, Edmund Garrett had written to Rose Innes from Suffolk, saying that he was being importuned to add his name to the suspension petition, an idea which he greatly disliked. Garrett sought Rose Innes's advice, saying that he distrusted 'these Eastern Province shortcuts to British supremacy'. If half the martial-law follies had occurred which one suspected, political capital would be made in Parliament by 'J. X. [Merriman] and Co.' But then sitting on the safety-valve would be all the more dangerous. 'Nor do I like letting the idiots who are guilty off with a general suppression of their misdeeds. They should be indemnified but exposed', said Garrett. Rose Innes's reply is not on record, but Garrett did, in fact, sign the suspension petition with a number of other Progressive members of the Cape Parliament. The petition was published in the *Cape Times* on 30 May 1902.

On the same day, the *Cape Times* gave it strong support in an editorial. Two months of political turmoil followed in the Cape, with Thomas Smartt whipping up support for suspension at public meetings and Sprigg and Graham campaigning against it. But Rhodes had died in April and with his death the movement had lost its most influential advocate. Much was made by the suspensionists of Rhodes's 'dying wishes'. In editorial after editorial, Saxon Mills hammered away at the suspension theme— with as much vigour as he had previously opposed it.

The newspaper's change of direction did not escape derisive public comment. Arthur Douglas, Commissioner of Works in the Sprigg Cabinet, at an anti-suspension movement in Claremont on 4 July, suggested that the Editor of the *Cape Times* was now writing in favour of suspension 'on order'. Discussing the leader of 31 December, he asked—according to the *Cape Times* report on 5 July:

> Was it not the writing of an honest man who had got orders that with the beginning of the new year he had to write to a

certain order on another policy, and that as an honest man he wrote that article as the year was dying. . . .

As the agitation continued in June and July, political feeling reached boiling-point in the Colony. Saxon Mills himself had been on the platform when Thomas Smartt addressed a wildly enthusiastic Drill Hall meeting, declaring his unwillingness to put out the hand of friendship to rebels who had 'prostituted their rights as British citizens'. People who were prepared to sacrifice their own free institutions and privileges for a short period of time had a right to demand that such privileges should also be taken away from people who used them to further the cause of Britain's enemies. Such people should not be allowed to do further mischief by holding free parliament—while withholding support from the Prime Minister in the measures necessary to uphold British supremacy in South Africa.

On the other side of the White racial divide, feelings already inflamed by the war, the concentration camps and martial-law follies were revived to a new pitch of bitterness by the suspensionist propaganda. But Sir Gordon Sprigg's battle to save the constitution was earning warm admiration among Cape Afrikaners. C. J. Langenhoven wrote to the *Cape Times* on 5 June praising Sir Gordon's courage in the face of jingo hysteria. He urged those who were crying out for suspension to think again:

> After a fight, you don't conciliate your adversary by sitting upon his head, but by shaking hands with him. . . . I may perhaps, without immodesty, lay claim to some knowledge of the character of the Colonial Dutch people, and I predict that if Parliament be called together it will be found that the cry for suspension is idle.

Jingo feelings were now running so high that police were present in force at a Wynberg meeting called by T. L. Graham, who was Acting Prime Minister in Sprigg's absence at the coronation of Edward VII in London. Graham, who was heckled and jeered by sections of the crowd, said it was an act of insanity to imagine that you could allay racial feeling by depriving people of their constitutional rights.

On 5 July, the *Cape Times* published a dispatch from the Colonial Secretary, Mr Joseph Chamberlain, to the Governor of the Cape, declaring that suspension of the constitution was likely to produce discontent and agitation rather than pacify race hatred. From now on, suspension was a lost cause. When Parliament met, John X. Merriman moved a resolution, which was carried without a division, recording solemn protest against the agitation for the suppression of Parliament. His speech was an oratorical *tour de force*, pouring scorn on those who sought to establish British institutions on a firm basis by destroying liberty of speech and the Parliament of the country.

Merriman placed the blame for the agitation on the 'Rhodes-ian group' and drew a parallel between the Jameson Raid and another 'raid upon the liberties of this country' which might yet materialize. There was laughter when he remarked on the 'masterly article denouncing suspension' which had appeared on the last day of 1901, in what was now 'the leading organ of suspension in Cape Town'.

But suspension was indeed dead—and by mid-September Saxon Mills was no longer Editor of the *Cape Times*. He had pursued the suspensionist argument valiantly to the last, persisting even after Chamberlain had turned the petitioners down.

Throughout the controversy, the *Cape Times* Board of Directors was divided into two hostile camps. E. R. Syfret, who had succeeded St Leger in the chair, publicly sided with the suspensionists, and was present on the platform with Saxon Mills at Smartt's Drill Hall meeting. So was Fred St Leger, Manager of the newspaper, always an ardent Rhodes supporter and active in the South African League.

The other two members of the board, J. A. S. Watson and R. A. St Leger, joined leading citizens of Cape Town in a Constitution Defence Committee which had been formed to fight the suspension movement. J. A. S. Watson, at one point chairman of the Cape Town Chamber of Commerce, had also written to the *Cape Times* at an early stage expressing misgivings about suspension. The St Leger family was strongly represented on the Constitution Defence Committee. The youngest son,

Anthony York St Leger, was also a member and so was M. W. Searle, F. Y. St Leger's son-in-law.

When Chamberlain's decision was announced, the Constitution Defence Committee issued a statement urging the suspensionists to cease their agitation and expressing confidence that the summoning of Parliament would not inflame racial feeling. The statement was signed by J. A. S. Watson, R. A. St Leger, A. Y. St Leger, M. W. Searle and other leading citizens.

But as far as Saxon Mills was concerned, the battle was 'only beginning', as the *Cape Times* declared in a leader on 11 July. Mr Chamberlain was not properly informed about affairs at the Cape, the newspaper declared.

A week earlier, the suspension controversy had been discussed at a meeting of the Board of Directors. The minutes record that Mr J. A. S. Watson complained of 'certain references' in a leading article. After discussion the matter was allowed to drop. But the minutes record that Fred St Leger had spoken to the Editor about the matter.

The leading article which Watson complained about was probably the one of 1 July which said the people opposing suspension were the 'pro-Boers, the waverers, the weak-kneed, the perfunctory loyalists . . .'.

Meanwhile, the suspensionists were still active. On 19 July, Thomas Smartt had been the guest of honour at a loyalist banquet in the York Room of the Theatre Royal, with the Mayor, Mr W. Thorne, in the chair and E. R. Syfret and F. L. St Leger among the guests.

Smartt, invoking the dying wish of Cecil Rhodes, urged Sir Gordon Sprigg to 'recognize his mistake' at the eleventh hour and suspend the constitution so that the measures could be passed which were necessary to ensure the supremacy of Great Britain. Rhodes had appealed to him, said Smartt, not to allow his life's work to be undermined by the opposition party in the Colony. On the stoep of his cottage at Muizenberg, said Smartt, Rhodes had implored him to take the step he was now taking, saying that the Opposition (Bond) Party had nearly undermined his 'dream' and would do so in the future if loyalists were not alert. Rhodes had implored him to trust Milner and to assist him to establish British institutions in South Africa on a sound and lasting basis. On 24 July, the *Cape Times* was still advocating suspension as a solution which 'might yet be found to be the wisest and most effectual'. On 5 August, it argued that strong measures against sedition and rebellion were necessary. 'If we cannot get these strong measures we must have suspension. There is no other alternative for the self-respecting and loyal subjects of King and Empire.' As the weeks wore on and suspension became a forlorn hope, Saxon Mills stuck to his guns with single-minded obstinacy.

When Parliament met on 20 August, John X. Merriman announced that the Bond Opposition intended to back the Sprigg Ministry. In the interim, Smartt had taken over the leadership of the Progressive Party from Sir Gordon Sprigg and that party was now in opposition. An Indemnity Bill, validating acts done under martial law, was passed.

The *Cape Times* leaders were now shrill with jingo petulance. But Saxon Mills's days in the editorial chair were already numbered. The Board had begun negotiations with Maitland Park, Editor of the *Allahabad Pioneer*, who had sailed from Calcutta for the Cape on 11 August. On 15 July, the Board was told that Park had accepted the post of Assistant Editor. In the minutes, however, the word 'assistant' was struck out, so it appears that by the time the minutes were confirmed in August Maitland Park had already been appointed Editor of the *Cape Times*.

The minutes of a board meeting on 13 October 1902 record that Park arrived in Cape Town on 10 September and 'took over the duties of the Editor on 12 September'.

> The General Manager [Fred St Leger] reported that he saw Mr Saxon Mills and explained the position to him and gave him the opportunity of resigning. Mr Saxon Mills seemed inclined to agree to this at the interview but later on in the day sent down a letter demanding his cheque, which was given him.

In another hand, four words were added, presumably later: 'His services dispensed with.'

So Mr Saxon Mills was sacked. The stature of the newspaper, which declined as St Leger's influence was withdrawn, reached rock-bottom during his brief editorship, so much so that there was a reluctance in later years to acknowledge that he had actually been Editor of the *Cape Times*.

The St Leger tradition was in eclipse and the prestige of the newspaper was badly undermined. The reversal of policy on the suspension of the constitution had dealt a heavy blow to its credibility.

Saxon Mills, it is plain, was ill-equipped to edit an influential daily newspaper in an unfamiliar country in a state of virtual civil war. He seems to have had little grasp of the nuances and complexities of Cape politics. He had been appointed Editor as St Leger was on his death-bed, and there is no evidence that the founder of the newspaper was consulted.

The public split on the suspension issue among members of the Board of Directors had placed Saxon Mills in a precarious position, and he was not the kind of man to rise above the conflicting pressures.

There was also Alfred Milner, by now the dominant figure in English-speaking South Africa, whose influence was exerted at a crucial stage. A collection of Saxon Mills's letters at Cambridge University library throws some light on the matter. There is little doubt, in fact, that it was Milner's direct intervention which caused the *Cape Times* to change course.

On 9 March 1902, Saxon Mills wrote to his friend Benjamin Kidd, a Victorian sociologist whose ideas he admired. He had gone to Johannesburg to see Milner, and wrote to Kidd in London from the Rand Club, telling him that it seemed that the Cape would have to be ruled from Downing Street for a few years. Free institutions were seen to be unworkable and would be so for some years to come.

There is no evidence that Saxon Mills made much attempt to assert his authority as Editor. His letters to Kidd suggest that he was bewildered and miserable at the Cape from the start. Soon after arriving he had written to Kidd that there was talk of suspending the constitution, which would be regrettable but in certain circumstances inevitable. He missed the advice of his friends, he told Kidd.

Saxon Mills saw his role in Cape Town as simply to promote Imperial interests and, as he told Kidd, he was trying hard to vindicate the Imperial policy. Mills married a young English-woman while at the Cape, and he complained bitterly about the cost-of-living, telling Kidd that he spent far more than he earned.

The unhappy Saxon Mills continued hammering away until September, as we have seen, when he was sacked. Later, in writing the biography of E. T. Cook, Saxon Mills made a passing reference to his own brief editorship of the *Cape Times*, saying that, 'for reasons still dark to me', he had become 'embroiled with my proprietors in that most precarious of all countries, South Africa'.

Saxon Mills never again edited a daily newspaper. He returned to England and wrote books, the most notable being his life of Cook.

As the suspension controversy died, Edmund Garrett resigned as a member of the Cape Parliament, writing a letter of farewell to his Victoria East constituency. Garrett told his constituents that he had hoped to return after six months, either as an editor or as a member, if not as both. But there was now no prospect of a return to active public life—although he still hoped to return to South Africa.

He had given his support to the suspension petition with great reluctance, but noted that the Imperial Government had accepted the anti-suspension view pressed upon them by the Sprigg Ministry. He hoped that the conduct of Parliament would prove the Ministry's view correct. 'Let us give our Dutch friends in Parliament a fair opportunity to prove our fears mistaken and to astonish us by their moderation', wrote Garrett.

Garrett paid tribute to Frederick York St Leger—'my late chief and kind friend':

> This is not the place to dwell on his political teachings—a high-minded Imperialism with a strong vein of Christian Socialism. . . . But of his public work let me say this; not a newspaper writer among us but is the better for it, the better

able to rise above all that is tawdry, or servile or unchivalrous. It means much for the broadening river of South African journalism that it flowed near the source with so pure a stream.

Garrett urged his constituents not to be carried away by talk of 'putting down the Bond once and for all', 'putting down the *taal* and so on'. British supremacy meant not the supremacy of the 'Britisher', but of the British flag, which meant political equality. The Bond should accept the new order and learn from moderates such as W. P. Schreiner to reconcile the nationalism of South Africa with the larger nationalism of the Empire.

If this letter was Edmund Garrett's last will and testament in South African politics, his intense interest in South African affairs never flagged. He continued to correspond with friends in South Africa, exchanging letters with Percy Fitzpatrick, whose *Jock of the Bushveld* he read in manuscript.

In 1903 Garrett had married Ellen Marriage, a fellow patient at Dr Jane Walker's East Anglian sanatorium in Wiston near Colchester. They lived in a Devonshire cottage where he continued to write occasional articles on South African affairs. But he was growing steadily weaker. One article, as he said, threatened to cost him 'an inch of lung'.

On 10 May 1907, Edmund Garrett died at the age of 42, at Wiverton Acre, near Plympton, and was buried in the neighbouring churchyard of Brixton. James Rose Innes said in his autobiography that Garrett's intellect and his indomitable courage, had he lived, would have carried him far in the country to which he had come in search of health and which he had learnt to love.

Garrett's story—a personal tragedy of unfulfilled promise and dashed hopes—is inextricably a part of the greater tragedy of the South African War. His attempt to combine the roles of activist politician and newspaper editor in a time of crisis was foredoomed to failure. The attempt destroyed his health. And it hastened the decline of St Leger's *Cape Times*. He had gone on consciously past danger point, as he wrote to Rose Innes in 1899, 'I shed my blood for my country, but the country will never know how well I meant and all I gave up.'

Edmund Garrett, in the words of his biographer, had looked

wistfully for some small remembrance in Cape Town. He wrote his own epitaph, which is inscribed, as he wished, on a small brass memorial which hangs in St George's Cathedral:

> Hard by the hurrying street alive
> With strength and youth; 'tis all I claim,
> That where the heart is, there survive
> The dust and shadow of a name.

Garrett's farewell letter to the people of Victoria East had been published in the *Cape Times* on 15 September 1902, under the headline: 'A Plea for Moderation.' The newspaper endorsed his remarks in an editorial, quoting with approval his view that suspension was dead and that it was 'idle to go on flogging a dead horse'.

The suspension controversy was past and done with, said the *Cape Times*, urging the country to settle down in earnest to the task of reconstruction and consolidation. There was a measured assurance and incisiveness that had been absent from the leading columns since the death of St Leger. Maitland Park had arrived. He would be Editor of the *Cape Times* for 19 years.

CHAPTER 12

OATMEAL AND COMMON SENSE

We stand for the British connection and for progress in South
Africa.

The *Cape Times*, 1903

Mr J. D. Logan is seldom less impressive than when he poses as
the virtuous legislator, the scourge of political hypocrisy and
the sworn foe of scandals of all kinds and degrees.

The *Cape Times*, 1906

The proceedings of Peninsula municipalities of recent years,
and still more clearly of recent months, have been of a kind to
excite the contempt and disgust of all intelligent and self-
respecting citizens.

The *Cape Times*, 1907

RUDYARD KIPLING, spending a few days at his father's
country house in June 1902, was in an irritable and crusty frame
of mind. He had mislaid his fishing-rods on the way to Wiltshire
and the streams were bank-high and unfishable, anyway. So he
sat down and wrote a letter to his friend Dr Jameson.

Through Kipling's good offices the editorship of the *Cape
Times* had just been offered to an old friend from his days in
India on the *Allahabad Pioneer*, Maitland Park.

After complaining about the weather, the state of the country
and of the Empire, Kipling asked Jameson whether Rutherfoord
Harris was writing to Park, as he wanted to write himself—'an
unofficial letter, the kind that Harris wouldn't write'.

Kipling told Jameson the story of his recruitment of Park for
the *Cape Times* and the dismay this had caused in London among
the proprietors of the *Pioneer*. He told Jameson: 'Of course, you
can never judge a fish by the noise it makes coming out of the
water, but it's good beginnings to get a man who leaves some
kind of a hole behind him.'

Kipling did write to Park. In a letter dated 11 July 1902, which is in the Kipling Collection at the Jagger Library, University of Cape Town, Kipling gave Park an outline of conditions at the Cape and in the *Cape Times* office, and told him that the Editor, Saxon Mills, was 'a good little chap, but with a vehement admiration for officialdom in all shapes'.

It was a lazy life at the Cape, said Kipling, and people were 'given to picnics and junketings on slight provocation'. The clubs were decent; one was 'loyal' and one was 'rebel', or had been before the war. 'There is no hot weather; no one goes to the hills and the people are kind and helpful and hopeful. There were no applicants for the post of Editor because that post is not open to public application, any more than the editorship of the *Pi*[oneer]. The directors said they wanted a man to face a new and strange situation, a strong persevering man who could work and organize and control. I said you were that man.' And Kipling added a postscript: 'Jameson will be out before me. He is the man who asked me to get you. *He* represents Rhodes, and Rhodes was Africa.'

The directors of the *Cape Times*, it seems, accepted Kipling's recommendation without hesitation. The Poet of Empire had been a familiar figure in the *Cape Times* office since Garrett's time in 1898, calling on mail-days to chat to the Editor and staff and read the English newspapers. The Woolsack, a house near Groote Schuur, had been offered to him by Cecil Rhodes for his use on his annual visits to the Cape during the English winter.

Kipling, on his own admission, owed a great deal to Maitland Park, whose merciless sub-editing of his first literary efforts in India had taught him much about the writing of English. Park had gone to Allahabad in 1886 after serving his apprenticeship in journalism on the *Glasgow Herald*. The son of a Presbyterian clergyman, the Reverend Hugh Park, Maitland Hall Park was born at Cumbernauld, Dumbartonshire, Scotland, on 10 October 1862, and grew up, it is said, in an atmosphere of oatmeal and common sense.

He was a shy, contained youth, but unusually bright. From the parish school, Park went to high school in Glasgow and then to Glasgow University, earning distinctions in literature, logic and philosophy. In later years, he was honoured by his Alma Mater, receiving a degree of LL.D. (*honoris causa*), and in 1914 he was knighted for his services in the achievement of South African union.

When he came to Cape Town, Park had already earned his spurs in journalism, helping to make the *Pioneer* the major newspaper on the Indian subcontinent. He was 40 years of age, and an early diffidence of manner had given way to a resolute self-assurance. Coming from a long saturation in the Anglo-Indian atmosphere, it is said, he was not disposed to suffer fools gladly.

In style and temperament, the new Editor of the *Cape Times* bore little resemblance to his predecessors. St Leger, oblique and ironical, had always seemed to pursue an enigmatic inner life of his own. Park was blunt and forthright. And there was nothing of Garrett's romanticism in his make-up. Park's was a rigorously practical and down-to-earth cast of mind. His particular gifts were for analysis and logical exposition. He was an Imperialist, no doubt, yet his Imperialism had little ideological content.

His journalistic style was the man—logical, combative and caustic. There were no frills. He used to complain that there were two minds of his acquaintance which worked too swiftly to be followed—Jameson's and Kipling's. They arrived at their conclusions like women, he said, by intuition. And they were usually miraculously right—except when they went wrong.

His contemporaries say that Maitland Park was intensely resolute, even stubborn, once he had made up his mind. He had great dialectical skill and delighted in controversy with correspondents, penning crisp footnotes to letters to the Editor.

If there was a touch of Anglo-Indian testiness on occasion and a severity of judgement, Park's intellectual honesty and fairness quickly won the respect of influential Cape figures such as John X. Merriman, who in later years would mourn him as a chivalrous opponent and cherished friend.

In his conduct of the *Cape Times*, Maitland Park would return to the St Leger practice of editorial anonymity. He would take no public role in party politics. But he would become a member of the Council of the South African College and play a leading part in the establishment of the University of Cape Town in 1918.

Like St Leger and Garrett, Park enjoyed the club life which flourished in Cape Town at the turn of the century, belonging to the Civil Service and City Clubs. He was a witty after-dinner speaker, notably at Burns' Nicht festivities. He relished the outdoor life and played tennis, bowls and golf when he could find the time. But his great love was sea angling. His favourite fishing-spot was Hermanus where, on one occasion, he caught a record bag of red stumpnose, finishing with two splendid biskop of more than 15 kilograms each. Of his fishing contemporaries, only W. P. Schreiner, a master of the craft, was said to have been more skilful. Park delighted to fish from the most dangerous spots and would shake himself like a St Bernard and roar with laughter after being doused by spray on the rocks.

Park married twice, and it was his second wife, Anna Baillie, who bore him his only son, Maitland Elphinstone Park, a captain in the Black Watch, who won the DSO in the First World War.

In June 1902, when he was first offered the editorship of the *Cape Times*, Maitland Park knew nothing at all about South Africa. His recruitment on the Imperial old boy network and his translation from Allahabad to Cape Town were unremarkable in the atmosphere of the time. But it does seem remarkable, in retrospect, that he should have been so successful, so rapidly, in a totally unfamiliar society.

On the voyage from Calcutta, Park had read everything available about South Africa. On arrival in Cape Town, he is said to have sat down with the files of the *Cape Times* from its inception in 1876 until 1902, reading every single leading article and pronouncing himself in broad agreement with the principles and practice of the newspaper.

In the months ahead, he would constantly draw on precedents from the time of St Leger to bolster his arguments, restoring the newspaper's intellectual consistency and steadily rebuilding its authority and reputation.

Park's first editorial, the opening salvo of many exhilarating dialectical battles with John X. Merriman, was published on

15 September 1902. The *cognoscenti* were waiting for Park to put a foot wrong. But he had done his homework with extraordinary diligence.

There was, in fact, one glaring bloomer in that first editorial. It escaped detection. Park had described J. H. Hofmeyr as the 'late, lamented' leader of 'Afrikanerism'—in the confident belief that 'Onze Jan' was dead. Fortunately, however, the phrase was taken as an ironical reference to Hofmeyr's withdrawal from public life.

Park quickly vindicated Kipling's confidence. He had arrived in a political atmosphere which was raw and bitter in the aftermath of war and, as a newcomer, he had taken a detached view of the situation, seeking to calm and moderate the intense emotions of the time as, a few years later, he would set himself to neutralize the danger of a vengeful jingoism reasserting itself in reaction to the generous terms of the post-war settlement.

The transition took place smoothly and efficiently, although a few months after the new Editor's arrival a typographical error caused him acute embarrassment. The occasion was a reception at Groot Constantia given in honour of the Colonial Secretary, Joseph Chamberlain, who was on his post-war visit to South Africa. A *Cape Times* reporter, in describing the reception, wrote in rather facetious style of the motor cars at the scene. The forerunners of the modern car were still, in 1903, the subject of much derisive comment in the newspapers. But a compositor dropped a few lines of type into the wrong position, with ludicrous results:

> On the stoep of the grand old homestead were assembled all the rank and fashion of the Peninsula. panting painfully with that distressful monotony peculiar to the breed, and emitting a pungent odour, which, on the still atmosphere of a hot summer's day, was more obtrusive than pleasant.

The paragraph went round the world and was immortalized in *Punch*. Park's first reaction was that this was a deliberate plot to make a fool of him. But it was a genuine error and he quickly accepted it as such.

Soon after arriving in Cape Town, Park recruited his nephew,

Ian Duncan Colvin, as Assistant Editor. Colvin, like Park a son
of the manse, had worked with him on the *Pioneer* and was a
remarkably fine journalist, a writer of grace and distinction,
who had been a gold medallist in literature and history at Edinburgh University.

Colvin, reserved and quietly-spoken, was 26 years of age when
he joined Park in Cape Town. He arrived in a blaze of publicity,
his ship, the *Umona*, having been wrecked in the Maldive Islands
on the way from India. Colvin had spent nine days in an open
boat, sailing to Colombo, Ceylon, to seek help for the castaways.

Like Garrett, Colvin was a skilled interviewer and his feature-
writing brightened the columns of the *Cape Times* and did much
to restore the newspaper's reputation for fine English prose. In
April 1904, for example, he interviewed Captain J. C. Voss, who
was sailing round the world in the 10-metre *Tillikum*, com-
missioned by a Canadian newspaper to uphold the honour of the
British Empire in competition with America's Captain Slocum.

> Some may say of Captain Voss that his task is useless, and
> that all his labours lead to nothing. But the Captain may answer
> with philosophy that the labours of the most useful of us lead
> to very little, and, however we spend our time, we come to a
> like end. With all his hardships and all his perils, he is not
> unhappy. He sees life and all the wonders of the world and he
> is so in love with the sea that he cannot settle down upon the
> land.

The Cape Peninsula made an enduring impression on the
sensitive and romantic young Colvin, himself a wanderer like
his hero Captain Voss. As he recalled many years later, he found
something 'magical and poetic in that town under the mountain'
and in South African history a fascination that never lost its hold.
With G. H. Wilson, Ian Colvin explored the South African
Library, discovering old volumes of travel and adventure. He
was befriended by H. C. V. Leibbrandt, the Archivist, who
laboured in the cellars beneath the Houses of Parliament, and
he wrote historical sketches for the Christmas numbers of the
Cape Times, using a pseudonym, 'Rip van Winkle'.

His artistic collaborator was George Smithard, whose water-colours captured superbly the sunlight and colour of the Cape, reproduced by a new three-colour litho printing process which was the first of its kind to be used in South Africa.

Colvin, in a few years, became an expert on the early sources of South African history and, with Leibbrandt, a vigorous defender of Willem Adriaan van der Stel in the controversy that raged among scholars in the columns of the *Cape Times* in late 1909.

The *Cape Times* Christmas number of 1906, now a collectors' item, featured a study by 'Rip van Winkle' of the art of Anton Anreith—'a tardy act of justice to our first Cape artist'.

Old Cape Town is vanishing away. The pleasant stately white-washed houses of which the city used to be composed remain only here and there, forlorn relics of an age long past. They have shrunk timidly from our main streets into our back thoroughfares and stand as it were upon sufferance, like so many white-washed Rip van Winkles in a world that hustles past them without knowledge or regard. And yet who that takes delight in things of beauty can be insensible to their charm? How noble and simple they are amid the multiplicity of florid and pretentious styles of architecture which now surround them. Their generous doorways with their great teak doors, their quaint fan-lights, their many-paned and green-shuttered windows, their stoeps with corner seats of stone, the glimpse of the courtyard behind, brick-paved and cool with its vine or pomegranate tree and fountain. When they stood in stately and uniform rows shaded by their avenues of oaks, with the sea showing at one end of the street and the mountain at the other, how beautiful and dignified they must have appeared. Now and then upon the broad-angled pediments of those that remain may be seen a piece of worn sculpture in plaster-work, their principal ornament. Here a figure of Mercury with bales of merchandise, there an eagle surrounded by implements of war, a cherub or a swan with couchant lions. And I cannot but think that the best of these were executed by the artist, Anton Anreith. . . . Cape Town is not as proud of him as she ought to be. . . .

Colvin lamented the lack of appreciation of Anreith's work and the fact that there was only a sparse printed record of what he had achieved. The article on Anreith, illustrated with Smithard's delicate pen-and-ink sketches of the pediment on the wine cellar at Constantia, and the pulpits in the Lutheran Church and the Groote Kerk, was the first significant study of the artist's work and the fruit of hours of toil in the Cape archives.

In this kind of work for the *Cape Times*, Ian Colvin did much to awaken Cape Town to its cultural heritage and to make known beyond a narrow circle of scholars the riches of the South African Library. And his superbly-written introduction to Sidney Mendelssohn's *South African Bibliography*, published in 1910, approaching the study of Africana as an enthralling adventure, has passed on his enthusiasm to succeeding generations of South African book-lovers.

Colvin's interests were soon reflected in the leading columns of the *Cape Times*, where Edmund Garrett's concern for the preservation of the old Cape was now strongly reasserted. While Maitland Park busied himself with closely-argued, unadorned analysis of municipal and national politics, Colvin ranged further afield, leavening the leading columns with a lightness and grace of touch reminiscent of Garrett.

But Colvin also wrote on political subjects, notably in his leader on Paul Kruger, who had died in Clarens, Switzerland, on 14 July 1904:

> Paul Kruger, whose long life was so full of conflict, has passed quietly away. He was a very old man and he died in exile. He had outlived all his hopes and ambitions. His ideals and preconceptions were shattered before his eyes. Surely, then, we may assume that his enemies have forgiven him, and that those who fought him with their whole heart while he lived will not let their animosities follow him into the eternal sequels of death. . . . But with all his courage and skill, Kruger failed, and failed miserably. To sit indomitably on the safety valve may be the highest kind of bravery, but it is a line of conduct which inevitably leads to disaster. . . . To sum up the character of Kruger in a few broad generalizations is

impossible. Rhodes said of him that he was the Transvaal. He was the sublimation of the essential qualities of the back-country Boer, strong-minded, shrewd, slow of thought, but with a firm grasp of plain truths, and with, even for a Boer, a prodigious quantity of that 'crooked and sinister wisdom', as Bacon has it, which in South Africa is known as slimness, a trait too much despised by the modern Englishman. To these qualities, as well as to his sincere trust in God and his devotion to his country and his people, his power and his influence were due. Some may deny that he was a statesman, but all will admit that he was a warrior and a man.

The *Cape Times* returned to this theme in November 1904, when the *Batavier VI* docked in Table Bay with Kruger's body on board. Adderley Street was thronged with crowds, and all sections of the community paid their last respects as the cortège moved up Adderley Street to the Huguenot Memorial Hall in Queen Victoria Street, where Paul Kruger lay in state before the train journey north to burial in Pretoria.

He was to the Dutch what Rhodes was to the English, not merely a man but the embodiment of a race . . . the feelings of Englishmen should teach them to understand and sympathize with the mourning of their Dutch fellow countrymen now. . . .

As an author, Colvin is remembered particularly for his celebrated *Life of Jameson*. In later years, his work on the *Morning Post*, London, enhanced that newspaper's reputation. But nothing ever gave him as much satisfaction as his Christmas numbers for the *Cape Times*. 'It may have been an illusion; but we felt the creative joy of producing a work of art', he wrote in 1926 in an article marking the 50th anniversary of the *Cape Times*. A later generation has decided that it was no illusion; the Christmas numbers are now valuable items of Africana.

Ian Colvin remained on the *Cape Times* until 1907, when he had a serious nervous breakdown. There was at this time talk of offering him the editorship of the *Transvaal Leader*, a Johannesburg newspaper which had been acquired by the *Cape Times*

Company. Colvin, it seems, wanted a completely free hand in editorial policy and was not satisfied with the terms initially offered him. In any event, he turned down the appointment, giving his health as the reason, and left for England to join the *Morning Post*. Whatever his reasons for refusing the offer, South African journalism and letters lost an outstanding craftsman.

At the Cape, he had also written à volume of satirical poetry on the politicians of the time, *The Parliament of Beasts*, which is today a rare item of Africana. Many years later, a successor on the *Cape Times*, Anthony Delius, would follow Colvin's example with his satire, *The Last Division*, published in 1954.

G. H. Wilson recounts that Colvin's departure from the *Cape Times* was the occasion of a convivial farewell dinner at the City Club, with Dr Jameson in the chair and Rudyard Kipling among the guests. The grand finale was a speech by Dr Jameson proposing a toast. Colvin rose to reply, a shy, boyish figure, overwhelmed by the warmth of the sentiments that had been expressed towards him. He beamed round the whole company: then he slid gracefully under the table. Kipling later told Wilson that it was the most perfect reply he had ever heard made on such an occasion.

Colvin's close companion on the *Cape Times* was the poet John Runcie. Other members of the formidable team that quickly gathered around Maitland Park were Lennox Short, Roderick Jones, later Chief Editor of Reuters, and briefly, G. A. L. Green, originally a *Cape Times* man, who was reluctantly allowed to return to the *Diamond Fields Advertiser*, whose management had complained that they could not do without him.

By mid-1903, Maitland Park had chosen his team and had taken the measure of his task. The writer of a *Cape Times* history in 1926 says his editorship speedily aroused indignation or admiration, according to the reader's point of view. His intense dislike of public sham or political fraud brought him into sharp conflict with many institutions which had enjoyed immunity from criticism and 'were astounded and disgusted to find themselves brought under the lash of a finely critical judgement'.

Park tackled the Cape's penal system with a series of articles written by a prisoner on his experiences awaiting trial in Roeland Street jail. This led to Mr John Garlick asking questions in the House of Assembly and an undertaking by Dr Jameson's recently elected Cape Government to investigate prison conditions.

An indignant leading article in the *Cape Times* (25 April 1904) doubted whether there was any other civilized country in the world where juvenile offenders, first offenders and others awaiting trial, as well as psychiatric cases, were herded together with inveterate criminals of the worst type. It was a 'disgrace to the Colony' that this scandal should have been tolerated for so long. The *Cape Times* urged a proper system of classification of prisoners and separation of the convicted and the unconvicted.

But the perennial theme of the early years of Maitland Park's editorship was municipal reform and the need for proper provision for the city's water needs in years ahead—a battle that was not won until the First World War when the Steenbras reservoir was at last constructed.

The *Cape Times* threw its weight behind a group of civic reformers, the Citizens' Guild, which was led by William Duncan Baxter and other leading Cape Town businessmen. Baxter, with Sir James Rose Innes, had been a founder member of the South African Political Association in 1895 and was one of an influential group of Cape moderates. He was later a distinguished member of the Union Parliament.

Park felt that a new regime was needed at the City Hall— where the municipal administration had now moved from the old Town House. And he set about this objective in aggressive fashion, sparing nobody's feelings in the process.

At this time, municipal government in the Peninsula was still divided among separate municipalities—Green–Sea Point, Woodstock, Mowbray, Rondebosch, Claremont, Wynberg and Muizenberg–Kalk Bay as well as Cape Town itself.

In March 1907 a municipal scandal broke into the open in Cape Town with the publication of the report of a committee of inquiry into the circumstances surrounding the award of a substantial road-making contract, worth £200 000 in those days, to a British firm. This disclosed extraordinary laxity in the tender procedures and suggested gross inefficiency on the part of the City Engineer, Mr J. Cook.

The *Cape Times* was not satisfied with the commission's report and subjected it to searching analysis in a series of angry leaders. The Council was too ready to place the sole blame for maladministration on the shoulders of its officials, the *Cape Times* said. It demanded to know who were the three councillors who, according to the report, had wanted to give the contract to a company that had not yet been formed and whose only capital asset was a box number, PO Box 761, Cape Town!

The newspaper scorned the 'splendid vigilance' of the City Fathers in protecting the ratepayers' interests. Whenever it was in trouble, the Council made a raid on its own staff, just to be on the safe side, whether or not there were any grounds for suspecting inefficiency or corruption on the part of the staff.

The Council meeting at which the report was discussed was conducted on extraordinary lines by today's standards of municipal dignity and decorum. The public gallery was packed and all the corridors leading to the Council Chamber were choked with spectators, supporters of the opposing factions on the Council, who cheered or booed speakers in turn. There were some wild exchanges which continued until after midnight.

On 20 March 1907, the *Cape Times* was severe in its comment on the 'amazing' proceedings at the City Hall. As the result of a procedural ruling, a letter of resignation received from the City Engineer—giving his version of the facts—was not made public. A motion was moved, unsuccessfully, demanding the summary dismissal of Mr Cook. The *Cape Times* said that malice and vindictiveness had outweighed all considerations alike of the public interest and ordinary fairness.

When the debate was resumed a week later, again in the presence of a noisy public gallery, the *Cape Times* pointed out that the Council had adopted a resolution which amounted to an endorsement of the inquiry's conclusions. The Council was in the absurd position of applauding, without the smallest attempt at criticism, a document which was as serious an indictment of itself as of the City Engineer.

By mid-1907, Maitland Park had pushed the circulation of the *Cape Times* to 22 000, double the figure which it had reached under Edmund Garrett in the late 1890s. The *Cape Argus*, at 9 000, was not a strong competitor, and the *South African News*, the morning contemporary, could muster a sale of only 4 000, mostly in Cape Town and suburbs.

Maitland Park's vigorous interest in municipal affairs was certainly a factor in increasing circulation. But his vigour was not appreciated at the City Hall. In March 1907, at the height of the row about the road-making contract, the Council had resolved to switch its advertisement contract from the *Cape Times* to its two competitors, arguing that their advertisement charges were lower. When the matter was debated in Council, councillors indulged in what the *Cape Times* called 'cheap abuse' of the newspaper. Maitland Park was unimpressed. The *Cape Times* noted that no criticism of the Council was tolerated unless it consisted of 'uncritical slobber'.

Eventually, the Baxter group made headway in the municipal elections and Duncan Baxter succeeded Hyman Liberman as Mayor. As Baxter was not then married, Mrs Liberman, as Deputy Mayoress, acted as Mr Baxter's hostess at civic events.

The *Cape Times* welcomed the new regime, whose election had vindicated its rapport with its readers and its powers of advocacy. The newspaper paid tribute to Mr Liberman's ungrudging sacrifice of his time and energies in the interests of the city. As readers were aware, the *Cape Times* had felt it to be its duty to criticize Mr Liberman's chairmanship of the Council and also his direction in policy matters. But Mr Liberman, the *Cape Times* imagined, was of too tough a fibre to complain on that score, and the newspaper associated itself with the good wishes being extended to him on his stepping down from the historic chair of Van Riebeeck.

If it had been a tough battle, it was ending in a spirit of amity between the *Cape Times* and the retiring Mayor.

Maitland Park then turned his attention to the suburban municipalities, pointing out that the Mayor of Mowbray, Mr James Parker, had been publicly accused at a ratepayers' meeting of accepting a bribe—yet he was standing for re-election before the matter could come before the courts and his name be cleared.

The *Cape Times* railed against 'slackness, imbecility and effrontery' in municipal administration. Mowbray did not stand alone, said the newspaper on 20 July 1907. It was understood that an inquiry into the affairs of Kalk Bay revealed an appalling laxity in administration. And it was an open secret that the financial affairs of Woodstock, Claremont and Rondebosch were in a most unsatisfactory state.

The *Cape Times* urged the amalgamation of the Peninsula municipalities into a single body. But the successful working of a municipality depended on the citizens themselves. The people f Cape Town were urged to shake off a besetting apathy, to be vigilant in condemning axe-grinding and log-rolling, and to give steady support to men who put the civic interest clearly and unmistakably before all other interests.

It was not until 1913, however, that the amalgamation of the Peninsula municipalities was finally achieved.

Early in 1904, the Progressive Party had returned to power in the Cape Parliament, with Dr Jameson as Prime Minister and a precarious majority of one in the Legislative Council.

There were some who thought that the choice of Dr Jameson as leader of the Progressives was provocative and unwise, given the unhappy associations which his name conjured up in the minds of a large section of the population. But Jameson seems to have been driven by a compulsion to make some sort of amends for the Raid and by the time of Union, six years later, he had, to some extent, lived down his political past. In this he was given considerable backing by Maitland Park and the *Cape Times*.

The Progressive Party had always been split into a moderate wing of Western Province liberals, originating in Rose Innes's South African Political Association, and the stalwart Imperialists of the South African League, which body was strongest in the Eastern Cape. The split had been very much in evidence in the suspension fiasco. Dr Jameson now sought to weld the party into a disciplined unit, and the *Cape Times* threw its full weight behind his efforts.

In the 1904 elections R. A. 'Bob' St Leger, who was one of those who believed that Jameson should be disqualified from political office, decided to stand as an independent in King William's Town, posing a serious threat to the unity of the Progressives. Dr St Leger was still smarting over the role played by the jingo stalwarts in the suspension controversy and was anxious to bring W. P. Schreiner back into political office, believing that his wisdom and moderation were what the country needed in the aftermath of war.

But his programme was in all respects the same as the official Progressive programme. And Dr St Leger, a director of the *Cape Times*, found his own newspaper strongly attacking his candidature! Maitland Park believed that Jameson was the only Cape politician then capable of leading a Progressive Party which had some semblance of unity and he came out emphatically against Dr St Leger's decision to stand as an independent.

Park believed, as did F. Y. St Leger, that independents, apart from the occasional really outstanding figure, were doomed to impotence and futility in a party system. He argued that it was no use having political ideals without recognizing the need for some means of putting them into practice. And the *Cape Times* argued the case on precedents set by its founder and first editor, F. Y. St Leger himself, 'than whom nobody took a steadier or saner view of the political situation in Cape Colony'.

As always, it was Maitland Park's practice, whenever important points of principle arose, to base the *Cape Times's* arguments on the precedents set by its founder. This appeal to the authority of a revered father whose ideals he was determined to uphold was too much for Bob St Leger. He announced his retirement from the contest.

Maitland Park's support of Jameson's Progressive Party remained fiercely independent. In the leading columns of the *Cape Times*, he restated St Leger's dictum that the *Cape Times* was not a party paper. In fact it was not long before the newspaper was in direct conflict with the Progressives on major points of policy as Jameson, following the Rhodes tactic, sought to gain country support at the expense of the cities, cutting across the *Cape Times's* declared views on the iniquity of duties on foodstuffs. These were depression years at the Cape and the city dwellers were again battling to make ends meet. Ian Colvin, in his biography of Jameson, notes that Park nevertheless remained Jameson's staunch friend. And he sympathized profoundly with Jameson's political predicament, dependent as he was on a majority of one in the Legislative Council.

It is at this point that J. D. Logan, of Logan contract fame, re-enters the story. The Laird of Matjiesfontein, as he was now known, was a Progressive member of the Legislative Council. Logan, a young Scots seaman, had been wrecked at Simonstown at the age of 26 and had come ashore, working as a railway porter and later at the Salt River railway workshops. He was an industrious young man and rose to become stationmaster at Cape Town and, catching the eye of Cecil Rhodes, had come into politics in the Worcester constituency. He had also gone into the liquor business, with his headquarters at Matjiesfontein, and he had prospered exceedingly. Although Logan had lost the railway catering contract in the Sivewright scandal in 1893, he had managed to get it back in the following year. And his quick and discerning eye for an opportunity was legendary, in both business and politics.

In spite of his narrow majority, Jameson was determined to get an Additional Representation Bill through Parliament, which would reduce to some extent the imbalance between town and country and give the Progressives a better electoral chance. In the nature of things, it was a strongly contested measure, giving rise to violent debate in both Houses.

In the midst of it all, Logan suddenly announced his intention to go abroad. There was consternation in the Progressive camp. A deputation of no fewer than 250 Progressives waited upon Mr Logan, reminding him that his absence would inevitably mean the defeat of the Additional Representation Bill, which he had pledged himself to support. It seems, from the available evidence, that Logan had put a price on his vote—the renewal of his railway refreshment contract. And he was playing cat and mouse with Jameson. But Jameson refused to play.

Colvin recounts that Jameson was sitting at the bridge-table at Groote Schuur when the Progressive agent Owen Lewis came and told him of Logan's demand. 'Tell Logan to go to hell—no trumps,' said Jameson. Logan could not then afford to vote against the Government and had cast his vote for the Additional Representation Bill. But soon afterwards he fulfilled his threat.

'Notes in the House' recorded on 18 May 1903 that the most interesting incident of the day had nothing whatever to do with the affairs of the Assembly. Mr Logan entered the House and took his seat in the space reserved for members of the Legislative Council. A signal brought Dr Jameson to the seat beside him, and the two remained in earnest conversation for a quarter of an hour. Both seemed to be in high spirits and Mr Burton, Mr Cillie and others in the Opposition benches, who appeared to be taking a keen interest in the meeting, could not have gathered much as to the import of what was passing. At twenty minutes to four, Mr Logan pulled out his watch, called out 'Good-bye' and sped out of the House—down to the Docks.

Colvin says that this incident served to explain what Dr Jameson meant when he wrote to his brother:

> By sitting mum and being polite to swine, I am getting on fairly well in this beastly House. . . .

The session ended on 28 May but Logan remained troublesome for the rest of the life of Dr Jameson's Government, adopting an increasingly independent line and coming out strongly in favour of a tax on the diamond industry! (Jameson, of course, was a director of De Beers.) In 1907, when Logan was standing for re-election—now as an independent—Colonel C. P. Crewe, a member of Jameson's Cabinet, declared that if Logan had still held the refreshment contract there would never have been a word from him about taxing diamonds.

Logan was now asserting that he had seen through the party system and would never be a party man again. He would put the interests of the electors above the interests of De Beers; as long as he had breath in his body he would fight for a 15 per cent tax on diamonds, he said at a meeting at Simonstown in December 1907.

At question time, Logan was asked to comment on Crewe's statement about his loss of the refreshment contract, and the following exchange was recorded in the *Cape Times*:

> The Chairman: 'I think that is a very unfair question to ask the candidate. I don't think—'
> Mr Logan: 'Oh, no. I will answer it. It is absolutely untrue and I defy anyone, Colonel Crewe or any member of the Government, to say so. I never asked the Government for a favour in my life.' (Cheers.)

By 1907, the connection between Logan's political views and his business interests seems to have been obvious to everyone. But in 1904, during the battle for the Additional Representation Bill, what was going on behind the scenes was not public knowledge.

The *Cape Times*, in a number of caustic leaders, had gone as far as it could to explain what was afoot without falling foul of the law of libel. On 18 May 1904, the newspaper suggested that Mr Logan's political views probably had very little to do with his extraordinary behaviour. It was not so much that his convictions had been outraged as that his vanity and self-interest had been wounded. It needed little skill in reading between the lines to detect so much, the newspaper said.

On 20 May 1904, the *Cape Times* noted that Logan had for once kept his word and had sailed in the *Norman* for Britain. The newspaper scorned Logan's professions of concern for the ordinary man and his opposition to Jameson's income-tax proposals. Logan had declared: 'Why should people be allowed to live in luxury in Europe out of the proceeds of De Beers, while the poor people are being taxed?'

The *Cape Times*, in its turn, asked why Mr Logan 'should be allowed to spend in luxurious living on a Scottish estate what he gained in large measure from Government railway refreshment contracts, for which the taxpayer was charged?' But it was superfluous to criticize the views which Mr Logan put forward to explain his defection, when it was abundantly clear that conviction on questions of principle could have little to do with the matter.

Logan had not exhausted his capacity for vengeance. His last act was to thwart Dr Jameson's financial proposals in the Upper House and finally bring down the Government. Dr Jameson announced his resignation on 17 September 1907, and the general election followed which returned John X. Merriman as Prime Minister of a South African Party Government of the Cape.

On 19 September, Rudyard Kipling wrote to Jameson: 'I saw in the papers that the licensed vitteler had done you in the eye at last. There is a great deal of crapulous cock-eyed perseverance about a man who has been thoroughly pickled in whisky for a quarter of a century. . . .'

Logan continued to prosper. He lived near Matjiesfontein at his farm Tweedside, where he died on 30 July 1920. The obituary, published on 31 July, was quite friendly in tone, considering the *Cape Times's* view of Logan's approach to politics and business. Apart from his political career, the obituary spoke of Logan's plans to 'make the desert bloom' at Matjiesfontein and his services to cricket in the Western Province Cricket Association. His death would be keenly felt by the whole of the sporting community.

But Logan had been anathema to the *Cape Times* in his lifetime. And under Park's editorship 'Sivewrightism' was flayed in leading articles as synonymous with questionable standards in the conduct of public business.

Now, in 1908, Maitland Park was being called, in awe or, sometimes, in derision, the 'strong man of St George's Street'. His upright, athletic figure was seen each morning striding down Government Avenue from his home in Oranjezicht to the *Cape Times's* offices.

As always, however, there were politicians who asserted that his newspaper was a tool of De Beers or of mining magnates. In 1903 a member of the British House of Commons, A. B. Markham, had alleged that the political views of the *Cape Times* were subordinate to De Beers and their Rhodesian associates. Whereupon Maitland Park offered to donate £5 000 to the hospitals of South Africa if it could be shown that De Beers held a controlling interest or in fact influenced the policy of the paper.

At this time, in fact, the St Leger estate and the St Leger family probably held the largest single block of shares. The Rutherfoord Harris interest had been steadily reduced and the shares were becoming widely held in small parcels among leaders in the Cape business community and among employees of the newspaper. With the purchase by the *Cape Times* of the *Transvaal Leader* in 1902, however, Messrs Eckstein and Co., forerunners of the Corner House group of gold-mining companies, became major shareholders in the *Cape Times*.

In August 1916, J. H. H. de Waal, member of Parliament and later Speaker of the Assembly, declared in a speech at Swellendam that the *Cape Times* was 'controlled by mining magnates, some of whom were resident in England'.

In a leader a few days later, Maitland Park invited De Waal to repeat his statement, spelling out directly what he appeared to be insinuating—that the editorial opinions of the newspaper were influenced by the said mining magnates. If he did so, the *Cape Times* guaranteed that he would be given an opportunity of substantiating his assertions in a court of law. Meanwhile, the Editor of the *Cape Times* was prepared to hand over £500 to any deserving charity—'under which term is not included *De Burger*'—if Advocate De Waal or anyone else could demonstrate that the Editor of the *Cape Times* had 'on any single occasion been influenced in the remotest degree in the views expressed in the leading columns' by any mining magnate whether resident in England or South Africa.

Mr De Waal, a practised controversialist, declined to accept the challenge. He countered with a letter to the Editor in which he declared that Park pretended to be very indignant. But would the Editor deny that the paper was controlled by mining magnates? And would he deny that the policy of a newspaper was controlled by its owners? In asserting this, Mr De Waal said he did not for a moment desire to impugn the journalistic integrity of the Editor of the *Cape Times*:

I believe the chief editor of our Cape 'Thunderer' to be as honourable a scribe as any member of his honourable profession. This does not, however, remove the fact that an editor is the servant of those he serves, as it is not likely that he would have been selected as their mouthpiece if he were not in entire sympathy with their views. Nor is it likely that they would continue his services longer than the term he has been engaged for, should he displease them.

Park's reply was characteristically forthright. Naturally, the owners of the *Cape Times* would get rid of their Editor if they were dissatisfied with his direction. But it was an essential to the satisfaction of the owners that the Editor adhere to the newspaper's traditions—which Park then set out in a series of quotations from the leading columns of the previous 30 years.

As St Leger had said, the *Cape Times* was 'not the journal of any particular party but of colonists as a whole' (22 October 1880).

CHAPTER 13

UNION OF SOUTH AFRICA

The Cape Colonist is somewhat unduly distrustful of his own ideals in assuming that the men who may stand up for just treatment to the native and coloured races in the Union Parliament will be rapidly suppressed. On the other hand, if there is no union, the chances are that the exclusive sentiment in the other states will grow stronger and stronger as the years go by.

The *Cape Times*, 12 February 1909

THE Union of South Africa was born on 31 May 1910, eight years to the day after the Peace of Vereeniging. The *Cape Times* published a special commemorative supplement, with messages from South African leaders. John X. Merriman's was perhaps the most realistic. It was a great experiment, he said, but those foolish folk who expected the millennium would encounter many obstacles and many disappointments.

Merriman, as one of the principal architects, was more acutely aware than most that the compromise of Union had postponed rather than tackled the fundamental dilemma. But Merriman, with the *Cape Times*, held that these problems would become more tractable in a unified South Africa. Merriman, with Schreiner, Sauer, Hofmeyr and other upholders of the Cape liberal tradition of parliamentary government, would have liked to see the Cape's qualified non-racial franchise extended to the northern provinces. If they had insisted, there would have been no Union.

It was W. P. Schreiner who fought hardest and longest. At an early stage, Merriman, corresponding with Smuts, realized that the best that could be achieved without wrecking Union was for the Cape to retain its own franchise, strongly entrenched against retrogressive amendment. Hofmeyr had wanted an even stronger safeguard than the two-thirds majority provision. And Sauer, at the national convention, was still urging the extension of the non-racial franchise to the north. Schreiner, accompanied by

26. Impressions of Maitland Park by D. C. Boonzaaier.

KIND CARICATURES.

MAITLAND PARK, M.A., Editor of the "Cape Times."

A master I of classic lore,
  I jib at each new-fangled plot;
I'm autocratic more and more,
  Despite depression's murky blot :

A pilot of the ship of State,
  Aye ready ! at the party's call,
I lengthily and idly prate,
  Not thinking for myself at all.

27. Maitland Park, caricatured by 'Chris' in the 'Owl' (6 January, 1905) in the early years of his editorship of the *Cape Times*.

Dr A. Abdurahman, leader of the African People's Organization, had finally carried the fight to Westminster, where he was coldly received, and the South Africa Act received the Royal assent in September 1909.

The constitution of Union, it is plain, was a compromise. But those who had misgivings, like the *Cape Times*, were for the most part confident that the Cape tradition, the oldest South African parliamentary tradition. would steadily infuse its spirit into the whole.

Much had happened since the Peace of Vereeniging. Within a few years of laying down their arms, the conquered Republics had been granted responsible government by Sir Henry Campbell-Bannerman's Liberal Party government in Britain. In 1901, Campbell-Bannerman's denunciation in opposition of 'methods of barbarism' in the South African War had struck a responsive chord.

Men such as Smuts and Botha were reminded of older and sounder British values, a social tradition which would outlive the Imperialistic hubris of the late nineteenth century. And they had responded with extraordinary generosity of spirit. Eight years after Campbell-Bannerman's 1901 speech, Louis Botha would dine with Alfred Spender in London and would tell him as they parted, says Spender's biographer: 'Three words made peace and union in South Africa—methods of barbarism.'

In his first speech as Prime Minister of the Transvaal, Louis Botha was to declare that the British people, in granting a free constitution, had trusted the Transvaal in a manner unequalled in history. Was it ever possible for the Boers to forget such generosity?

The *Cape Times* had been unhappy about the terms of the new constitution, however, noting the provision for manhood suffrage rather than a qualified franchise. The Peace of Vereeniging had left the question of franchise rights for Blacks to be decided after the granting of self-government. This would be up to the Transvaal to decide for itself, and it was hardly realistic to expect that the established aversion to political rights for Blacks would be rapidly reversed.

But the *Cape Times* was concerned about the future, noting that the problem of Black political rights was being made even more formidable by the Transvaal's commitment to an unqualified franchise for Whites. In January 1907, Dr Abdurahman, addressing a congress of the African People's Organization at Oudtshoorn, had condemned the Imperial Government for declining to touch the question of a Coloured franchise in the new constitutions for the Free State and the Transvaal.

The *Cape Times*, commenting on 8 January 1907, said the exclusion of qualified Coloured men and Africans from any share of government in the new colonies was neither a final nor a satisfactory solution. But the remedy should be left to the growth of a greater sense of confidence among both the White races.

The *Cape Times* noted that Dr Abdurahman accepted assurances that no movement towards Union would be allowed to prejudice the privileges which the Coloured people already enjoyed in the Cape. Dr Abdurahman was urged to carry this confidence further and throw his whole weight on the side of Union.

A unified or a federated South African parliament is far more likely to deal with the native or coloured problem on broad and liberal lines than the parliaments of some of the separate states: for a Union parliament will find out sooner than any other that it is only on these lines that such questions can be effectively treated.

This would be Maitland Park's consistent theme in the next few years, demonstrating great confidence in the virility of the Cape tradition and the capacity of free, representative institutions, given time, to get to grips with intractable problems.

Park's attitude to Botha and Smuts, which had been wary and suspicious in the years immediately after the war and at times downright hostile, changed radically in mid-1907 after Botha had committed himself to fostering a 'general South African spirit' on the path to Union. In May, Botha had attended the Imperial Conference in London and had established an excellent rapport, remarkably enough, with the Prime Minister of the Cape, Dr

Jameson. He had been accorded an overwhelming reception by the British public as the hero of the hour, so much so that some of his followers in the Transvaal were becoming restive.

When Botha returned from London, passing through Cape Town, the *Cape Times* noted that the city had seen with pride and satisfaction the dignity and address with which the Transvaal Prime Minister had borne himself at the Imperial Conference. Botha had responded generously to a generous reception, declaring that all had turned their backs on an unfortunate past.

In November 1907 the *Cape Times* said of General Smuts that he was likely to become 'one of South Africa's foremost statesmen' if the future bore out the promise of the present. 'Meanwhile, he is unquestionably one of our supplest and most adroit politicians.' Cape Town's mood, as reflected in the *Cape Times*, had undergone a remarkable transformation since 1899–1902.

By 1908, with Smuts and Botha's Het Volk in power in a self-governing Transvaal, President Steyn's Oranje Unie in the saddle in the Orange Free State and John X. Merriman's South African Party ruling the Cape, the reversal was complete. The way was clear for unification.

Maitland Park now brought the weight of the *Cape Times* to bear to promote conciliation and South African union. And he tried to create a climate which would favour a non-party administration as the first government of the Union, believing that Jameson and Botha should form a best-man Cabinet—or else the *Boer–Brit* battle would be perpetuated in a party alignment on the existing group lines.

In February 1909 the newspaper published the full text of the draft constitution as approved by the national convention, whose sittings had finally ended a few days before. There had been misgivings. But the compromise on the franchise was now felt by the *Cape Times* to be moderate and reasonable. The provision which restricted membership of the South African Parliament to Whites was still regretted as a 'rock of offence' which should have been omitted.

Nevertheless, the rights of Coloured and African voters in the Cape had been entrenched behind a 'double barricade', and the

Cape Times was confident that the constitution would ensure a
united South Africa on broad and liberal lines. A few days later,
on 12 February, the *Cape Times* published a telegraphed statement from W. P. Schreiner in Natal expressing his deep disquiet
about the franchise compromise.

The views of Mr Schreiner, said the *Cape Times*, deserved the
most careful and respectful consideration—as a South African
patriot with whom politics were as much a matter of conscience
as the Ten Commandments. It was most regrettable that
Schreiner's undertaking to appear as defence counsel in the trial
of Dinizulu in Natal should have led him to resign his seat on the
convention before it had begun its work. He had been prevented
by this conflict of obligations from arguing his points at a time
when his unsurpassed advocacy would have been most effective.

The *Cape Times* agreed with Schreiner that the provision for
Whites only as members of Parliament was a mistake for which
there was no justification. And there was much to be said for
Mr Schreiner's assertion that the convention's conception of what
constituted 'the people of South Africa' was 'narrow and illiberal'.
It was one thing to erect franchise barriers against 'such an influx
of the semi-civilized into the legislative assemblies of the land
as might swamp the civilized; but it is quite another thing to draw
a definite colour line which bars colour from all participation in
the councils of the country, merely because it is colour'.

Schreiner had argued that the rights and future of the great
majority of South Africans (those who were not White) were
neither adequately provided for nor safeguarded in the constitution. But the *Cape Times* felt that the safeguard for the Cape
franchise was 'a pretty strong barricade to our way of thinking'.
Unless a considerable majority of Cape representatives themselves voted against their own system, its security was 'certain'.
There was no reason why the Cape Parliament should not argue
for a further strengthening of the safeguard.

But Mr Schreiner and those who felt like him had lost sight
of an important perspective.

In a free assembly it seems to us fair and reasonable to hope
and presume that a liberal policy will make headway the more

frequently it is argued; so that the Cape Colonist is somewhat unduly distrustful of his own ideals in assuming that the men who may stand up for just treatment to the native and coloured races in the Union Parliament will be rapidly suppressed. On the other hand, if there is no union, the chances are that the exclusive sentiment in the other states will grow stronger and stronger as the years go by.

The *Cape Times* proceeded to campaign vigorously for acceptance of the constitution in spite of its shortcomings. The draft was yet to be ratified by the Cape, Transvaal and Free State Parliaments and by a referendum in Natal.

In the early part of 1909 the correspondence columns of the *Cape Times* were filled with letters on the franchise controversy, and the newspaper returned to the subject in its leading columns on 22 February, dealing with arguments advanced by Theo Schreiner, brother of Olive and W. P., among others.

Surely a consideration of the practicable is an indispensable element of true statesmanship, and Mr [Theo] Schreiner must know there is no more chance of persuading the Orange Colony and the Transvaal to enter a union which distinctly provided for a coloured and native franchise within their borders than there is of a successful aeroplane passage to the moon.

Did Mr Schreiner believe that the Cape should rather have stood aside from Union entirely? Blacks outside the Cape Colony were not likely to obtain political rights more rapidly if they were left entirely to the tender mercies of governments which at present believed they ought to have no rights at all.

In April 1909 the draft constitution came before the Cape House of Assembly for ratification and W. P. Schreiner, in a memorable speech, denounced the franchise proposals as a 'blot' on the constitution.

The last ten years have taught me a lesson I never understood before. We should have been spared the war if Pretoria had not refused the Uitlanders human rights. By accepting the doctrine of the non-recognition of human rights, we shall be led into great danger. . . .

Schreiner had spoken of the franchise proposals as treacherous and dishonourable. But the *Cape Times* felt there was no justification for such language. If there was, 'we should advise every honest citizen in Parliament and out of it to fight against Union to the last ditch'. As the *Cape Times* had repeatedly argued, the disqualification of any but Whites as members of Parliament was indeed a blot on the constitution—in the sense that it was unwise and impolitic. But it was one thing to adopt this attitude and it was another thing to stigmatize the arrangement proposed in the draft act of Union as either treacherous or dishonourable.

Since the time when representative institutions had been established in the Cape, the general policy of the Government had been to maintain political equality irrespective of the colour of the citizen's skin. This had proved to be a wise, prudent and successful policy; and it had the sanction of half a century's experience. But Mr Schreiner was reckless to speak as if grave impolicy was the same thing as treachery or dishonour.

The *Cape Times* was still campaigning for a best-man Cabinet in the first Union Parliament and as late as January 1910 was still maintaining that this was in the realm of practical politics. W. P. Schreiner was now arguing on similar lines, declaring that the national convention had demonstrated that co-operation between the leaders of the existing political parties was not only possible but also desirable for the achievement of great national ends.

On 17 January 1910, the *Cape Times* said that the party cleavage on English–Dutch lines should no longer be regarded as fundamental. Botha and Jameson were both reasonable men and, if both were convinced of the need for co-operation, neither was likely to impose impossible conditions upon the other.

It was a forlorn hope. Such an arrangement would have been political suicide for Botha. The convention 'spirit' had certainly been remarkable, in the light of all that had passed. But the tension and mistrust of previous decades, and the tragedy of the South African War, could hardly have been so rapidly transcended. As

Professor Leonard Thompson has noted in his monumental study, *The Unification of South Africa*, there were not in fact many men like Botha, Smuts and Merriman to whom the ideal of an Anglo-Boer fusion was a reality. Milnerist aspirations were still alive and a man like Percy Fitzpatrick, great South African that he was, nevertheless still thought in terms of a South Africanism 'essentially British in culture and feeling'.

The Republican yearning had not died out in Afrikaner hearts. In the wake of the war, there was to be a flowering of Afrikaans poetry with Leipoldt, Totius and Jan Celliers giving expression to Afrikanerdom's traumatic experience of suffering. The cultural revival and its significance escaped many contemporary observers. But even before Union, 'Hertzogism' had become a bogy among English-speaking South Africans, with General J. B. M. Hertzog's insistence on compulsory bilingualism in education in the Free State being seen as a departure from the spirit of the language clauses agreed at the convention.

On 23 May 1910, a week before Union Day, the *Cape Times* noted that General Botha had been called upon to form a Cabinet. While the Cape would regret that the choice had not fallen on Merriman, neither the propriety nor the wisdom of Lord Gladstone's choice of Botha could fairly be called in question.

The *Cape Times*, however, was still unhappy about the prospect of a perpetuation of the lines of *Boer–Brit* cleavage in the Union's first administration:

> If it is irrational . . . it is also dangerous, because an adminis-tration on a strictly party basis will be tempted to appeal, directly or indirectly, to racial prejudice as the readiest material for party cement.

On 26 May it was accepted that General Botha was now at the head of what would certainly be a strictly party administra-tion and that the only course for Dr Jameson's Progressives, now called Unionists, was to return to Parliament as many representa-tives as their numbers warranted. Such a course could do no possible harm to General Botha's administration. The newspaper drew attention to the 'narrow and shortsighted, though no doubt perfectly honest' educational ideals advanced by General Hertzog for the Orange Free State. The only path of security for the Unionists would be to return an opposition which would strengthen General Botha's hands if any attempt was made to assist General Hertzog in his avowed aim of extending Free State educational principles to the whole of South Africa.

This, in fact, was to be the pattern of South African politics in the first years of Union, as General Hertzog broke away from the South African Party, convinced that the cultural identity of his people was endangered in the hands of Botha and Smuts.

In the general election of September 1910, 'Hertzogism' was the dominant issue. General Hertzog's fiery speeches at Smithfield and elsewhere dismayed General Botha and evoked a frenzied response in kind from Unionist extremists. At Smithfield, Hertzog had recalled the Jameson Raid and Jameson's support of the suspension movement, and declared that Jameson's espousal of conciliation was not genuine. The *Cape Times* lashed out at the Smithfield speech as an exercise in 'vulgar and insolent abuse'.

As the campaign proceeded, each side protested its own innocence and blamed the other for stirring up 'racialism', repeating the pattern of the 1898–9 Cape elections and generating an electoral dynamic that has still not exhausted itself in South African politics.

The optimism of those who urged a 'best-man' Government to launch the Union of South Africa had been understandable in the convention atmosphere. But such hopes had been unrealistic. A polarization of voting on group lines had taken place in the Cape in the wake of the Jameson Raid, and the *Cape Times* had noted in April 1899 that it was clear that henceforth 'an Afrikander constituency will return a Bond member and a British or Uitlander constituency vice-versa'.

The South African War had intervened, intensifying the sectional emotions let loose by the Raid. In the 1910 elections this pattern was perpetuated. An overwhelming majority of the English-speaking electorate voted for Dr Jameson's Unionists, for the Labour Party or for independents, while almost all Afrikaners voted for the candidates supporting the Botha Government.

It would be another ten years before the Unionist Party would dissolve itself, urging its supporters to throw in their lot with the Botha–Smuts South African Party. In the interim, there would be the crisis of the First World War and the rebellion, giving tremendous impetus to General Hertzog's Nationalists.

In all this, Maitland Park and the *Cape Times* would play a considerable role, moderating the sectionalist enthusiasms of Unionist extremists and urging acceptance of the good faith of Botha and Smuts. Maitland Park had seen the unwisdom and futility of an appeal to sectionalist sentiment.

Before being obliged by illness to withdraw from the editorial chair in 1921, Maitland Park would have the satisfaction of seeing the Unionists merged with the South African Party. This was a development that General Smuts himself, now Prime Minister after the death of Botha, saw as a historic step forward. As Smuts expressed it in a letter to the young J. H. Hofmeyr on 5 November 1920: 'The dissolution of the party of Rhodes and Jameson is one of the greatest victories yet achieved on the road of South Africanism. . . .'

The story of Maitland Park's editorship from the time of Union until 1921 is beyond the scope of this memoir. But there is no doubt that his achievement was considerable, as newspaper and other tributes noted at the time.

The *Natal Mercury* said that Park had lived just long enough to see the fruition of his hopes and the justification of his policy in the 'creation under General Smuts of a great party, neither predominantly Dutch nor predominantly British, but essentially South African'.

The *Friend*, Bloemfontein, said that Sir Maitland Park had not been a journalist of the '*mbongo*' type, the pawn of a political party.

He was the first of those editors who, despite party ties, saw the greatness and goodness of General Botha and his policy . . . who appealed to his own countrymen to drop the racial blinkers that obscured their full vision. . . . He was at first misunderstood by his own people but the result has justified his independence of thought and proved his wisdom and insight. . . .

If he lived to see the birth of a greater South African Party 'neither predominantly Dutch nor predominantly British', Maitland Park did not foresee the erosion and eventually the destruction of the Cape non-racial franchise. The confident expectation of the *Cape Times* that the attitudes of the old Cape would gain ground in a united South Africa was not justified by events. But it would not be until the 1950s that the Coloured people of the Cape would finally lose their parliamentary franchise rights on the common roll as, a few years later, the remnant of the Black parliamentary franchise would also be abolished by the Nationalist Government of Dr H. F. Verwoerd. And the British connection, staunchly upheld by Sir Maitland Park, would be severed in 1961 with the advent of the Republic of South Africa.

With the advantage of hindsight, it is now easier to understand why the optimism of the convention time was so grievously misplaced. For one thing, there had been a major failure of insight on the part of English-speaking South Africa—a failure to understand the shattering psychological impact of the Jameson Raid. It was the Jameson Raid, more than anything else, which destroyed the basis of trust between Afrikaner and Englishman, in the Cape particularly. The *Cape Times*, in common with most of the rest of English-speaking South Africa, failed to grasp this.

When, eventually, the party of Jameson and Rhodes disappeared into the South African Party, this source of mistrust did not disappear with it but was inherited by the party of Smuts and Botha, to the enduring disadvantage of that party. Even the experience of fusion, with Hertzog and Smuts together in the United South African Party, could not exorcize the spectre and Dr D. F. Malan led his followers into the wilderness.

The evil effects have been legion, notably in the question of Black political rights. Hence the destruction of the Cape non-racial parliamentary franchise—which Nationalist Afrikanerdom feared as a political mechanism for a ganging-up of the English section and the Blacks in alliance against them.

One South African who did understand this was the brilliant young J. H. Hofmeyr, who, as the biographer of his uncle 'Onze Jan', had a better grasp of the politics of 1877–1910 than most of his contemporaries.

In October 1938 J. H. Hofmeyr wrote a thoughtful article in the journal *Forum*, urging English-speaking South Africans to make an effort of sympathetic insight in understanding South African history. He noted the roots of the Afrikaans cultural movement in the South African War, pointing out that its leaders had been children at the time of the war and had grown up amid its sufferings. They had turned instinctively to the protection of their distinctive culture and traditions, resisting Milnerization. But had not an even balance been struck by the magnanimity of the Campbell-Bannerman administration? Yes, it had, said Hofmeyr. But analysis had to go deeper than this— and examine the mentality already in existence on the eve of the war as a result of the Jameson Raid.

The chief significance of the Raid was not that it had been an unprovoked attack on a friendly community. It lay in the fact that the Raid had been 'nothing less than an act of treachery on the part of the outstanding English-speaking South Africans of the time'. The first great experiment in national unity had begun when Rhodes and 'Onze Jan' joined forces in the old Cape Colony. 'Onze Jan' had given Rhodes his unreserved friendship. The Afrikaner Bond had given Rhodes its unqualified support. It had made him Prime Minister and loyally assisted him in his schemes in the Cape Colony and in his North.

In this atmosphere of trust and co-operation, Rhodes had committed an act of treachery, and in large measure the act was condoned and white-washed in England and by English-speaking South Africans. Rhodes's act had the deepest psychological consequences. Not even the statesmanship of Campbell-Bannerman could efface those effects. . . .'

It might seem remarkable that J. H. Hofmeyr should have felt it necessary to make these points so vehemently as late as 1938, nearly 50 years after the Jameson Raid. But the files of the *Cape Times* down the years betray little evidence that it shared

Hofmeyr's insight. The Jameson Raid was put aside as an episode best forgotten. And the evidence confirms that the English-speaking intelligentsia, until comparatively recently, did not fully grasp the enduring effects of the Raid on the South African psyche.

As late as 1932, Sarah Gertrude Millin could write of the Jameson Raid in such a way as to provoke this comment from General Smuts, to whom she had shown the manuscript of her book on Rhodes: 'You are surely wrong in thinking the Jameson Raid not very significant in its consequences. It was *the* disaster. It inflamed the national psychology of the Boers, made racial trust impossible, and created the very mentality for the Boer War.'

Edmund Garrett, in the midst of the Raid crisis, had sought to neutralize its traumatic effect on Rhodes's Afrikaner supporters in the Afrikaner Bond. He had urged Rhodes, unsuccessfully, to acknowledge his fault and make amends. Yet his faith in Rhodes had remained unquenchable. And Maitland Park, in his support for Dr Jameson, had disagreed with those, like R. A. St Leger, who believed that Jameson should abandon politics.

Hindsight suggests that a sharp disavowal of the Rhodes–Jameson motif might have done much to restore the fabric of English–Afrikaner trust. Yet Maitland Park's achievement remains notable and it can be argued that his choice of a gradualist rather than a radical change of political direction towards the South African Party was the only practical course, given the sectionalist emotions of the time.

Park's most enduring achievement was the restoration of St Leger's *Cape Times* as an authoritative, independent organ of English South African opinion. His successors inherited a soundly re-established tradition, owing allegiance to the public interest rather than special interest groups. In the news and correspondence columns, the rule was *audi alteram partem*, however forceful the argument in the leading columns.

Sir Maitland Park died at the age of 59 in Cape Town on 15 March 1921, after a long and painful illness. The Prime Minister, General Smuts, was a pallbearer at his funeral.

Five years later, General Smuts would send a special message to the *Cape Times* on the occasion of its fiftieth anniversary. The *Cape Times*, he said, had enjoyed the priceless advantage of a succession of great editors—St Leger, Garrett and Maitland Park—who had infused a fine spirit into the newspaper and 'established a tradition and set a standard which had meant much in the building of the young South African nation'.

POSTSCRIPT

The policy of this paper is not a shirking one; if it were, this would be a party paper—which it is not—and not a record of public opinion, which it is.

The Cape Times, *16 April 1879*

If the government is inclined to accept our representations of what is passing in the public mind as being more accurate and trustworthy than those of some other journals, we shall in a degree be compensated for our exertions to make this not the journal of any particular party, but of colonists as a whole.

The Cape Times, *22 October 1880*

ON 29 December 1929, General Smuts was on board the Berengaria, on his way to the United States after completing a strenuous programme in Britain and delivering the Rhodes Lectures at Oxford.

On board ship, Smuts wrote a letter to his wife Isie. Smuts had been hurt by criticism of his lectures in the Cape Times and told Mrs Smuts that he could not understand why the Cape Times was attacking him in his absence. The newspaper, though strongly supporting Smuts's South African Party, had been scathing about his final Rhodes Lecture.

The ordinary Englishman, reading the lecture, said the Cape Times, might conclude that territorial segregation was an accomplished fact in South Africa, that adequate African reserves had already been established and that all the large towns already had ample locations, harbouring contented self-governing African populations. The segregation plan had broken down time and again, the newspaper said. On 25 November 1929, the Cape Times spoke of the Smuts lectures in England as 'intensely disillusioning in South Africa'. The picture of the 'native question' outlined by Smuts 'seemed to South Africans to have almost scandalously little resemblance to local realities'.

In November, General Smuts had received the honorary degree of Doctor of Common Law of Oxford University, where he had been lionized by undergraduates and acclaimed by the public orator as a 'pillar of Empire'.

But at home he was being criticized by the Cape Times. Smuts told Isie that he thought Dr C. Louis Leipoldt might be responsible for the critical articles. 'I know he writes for the Cape Times.' The author of 'Oom Gert Vertel' was, in fact, a regular contributor to the newspaper but he wrote mostly on cultural or medical topics. Smuts's guess was probably off the mark. The author was more likely to have been the Editor himself, Basil Kellett Long, who had succeeded Sir Maitland Park in 1921 and was carrying on the practice of outspoken editorial comment.

160

B. K. Long earned first-class honours in the School of Modern History at Oxford, migrated to the Cape from England in 1905, practised at the Cape Bar and entered the Cape Parliament in 1908. He served as a law adviser at the national convention and from 1913 to 1921 was the Dominions Editor of The Times, *London. It was B. K. Long who wrote the notorious leader 'Nil Nisi Malum' (7 November 1929) commenting on the terms of Sir J. B. Robinson's will, which contained no public bequests, in language of extraordinary violence and intemperance which is still quoted today.*

But 'Nil Nisi Malum' was merely an incident in B. K. Long's 14-year editorship of the Cape Times, *the story of which must be left to a later chronicler of the newspaper, as must the subsequent editorships. He gave Smuts powerful backing in opposition and, after Fusion, backed the United Party of Hertzog and Smuts. After relinquishing the editorship in 1935, he became a member of Parliament and delivered an outstanding speech in the war debate in 1939 which, some say, helped to sway a majority in the House against neutrality and gave Smuts the 13-vote majority which took South Africa into the Second World War. He sat as a United Party member in the House of Assembly until 1943.*

In 1936, the Cape Times *celebrated its sixtieth anniversary with G. H. Wilson, appropriately, in the editorial chair. Wilson, who joined as a young reporter from England in January 1896, had written 'Notes in the House' for three decades, starting in the old Cape Assembly and carrying on in the Union Parliament until Victor Norton moved into the Press Gallery in his place in 1935.*

George Wilson served the Cape Times *for five decades, linking the foundation years of St Leger and Garrett with the editorship of Victor Norton, who succeeded him in 1944. Wilson, kindly, gentle-natured and discreet, was a confidant of Generals Smuts and Hertzog. After 1944 he remained Consulting Editor of the* Cape Times, *completing 50 years of unbroken service in December 1945, having done much to maintain the newspaper's continuity of outlook and attitude.*

Victor Norton's editorship spanned the years of the National Party victory at the polls in 1948, the constitutional crisis over the scrapping of the Coloured franchise in the 1950s, the Sharpeville and Langa state of emergency, the Republican referendum and South Africa's departure from the British Commonwealth of nations. In the constitutional crisis, the Cape Times *repeatedly recalled the solemn undertakings of the national convention in 1910. If the battle to save the Coloured common-roll franchise was ultimately lost, it was fought in the leading columns of the* Cape Times *with an eloquence and brilliance of advocacy that had seldom been equalled in the newspaper's long history.*

The theme throughout Norton's editorship was the defence of civil liberties. Although there was legislation on the Statute Book which limited the newspapers' right to publish in certain areas—the Defence Act and the Prisons

Act, for example—the South African Press remained, basically, free and Norton did much in his 27 years of editorship to strengthen public awareness of the value of a free Press, particularly in a situation where large sections of the population were without parliamentary representation. In April 1973, in retirement, Norton was honoured by Rhodes University, receiving the degree of Doctor of Literature (honoris causa). With Victor Norton, throughout his editorship, were Dudley D'Ewes, Assistant Editor, and George Aschman, Managing Editor, comprising a triumvirate which steered the Cape Times through the post-war years, more than doubling the circulation, which had been static in the thirties at around 25 000.

These were also the years of the Press Commission and sharp attacks on the English-language newspapers, which had to exert themselves to maintain public confidence as the old taunts of dictation of editorial policy by 'mining magnates' were renewed and intensified. The control of the Cape Times was subjected to searching investigation by the Commission, a body which laboured for 13 years before producing a 20-volume report.

The commission found that the largest single block of shareholders were the employees themselves, who held shares in terms of an endowment trust set up in 1914. The rest of the shares were distributed among 55 shareholders with between 1 000 and 5 000 shares each and 597 shareholders, each holding fewer than 1 000 shares.

There had been a time when the Corner House—the Central Mining and Investment Company—had been a substantial shareholder and had nominated directors to the board of the newspaper, bringing men like Max Honnet, Sir Evelyn Wallers, Sir Drummond Chaplin and Sir Alfred Hennessy on to the Board at different times to represent their interest. The Corner House continued to play a role in the affairs of the Cape Times until 1927, when its shareholding was sold, becoming widely dispersed in small parcels of shares. John Martin, Chairman of the Argus Company, had at this time also become the head of Corner House, which might well have been the reason for the Corner House decision to withdraw from the Cape Times.

In the 1950s, at the time of the Press Commission investigation, the shares were still widely distributed, as we have noted. After an exhaustive study, the Press Commission concluded that Syfret's Trust 'from the nature of its business and its past relationship with the Cape Times, could possibly, if it wished, control the Cape Times Ltd'. This was a fair conclusion, by all accounts. The relationship between the Cape Times and Syfrets had been close and enduring, with E. R. Syfret's long chairmanship of both companies setting a pattern that would be followed by Gerald Orpen and by Clive Corder, who were both in the chair of both companies. Although Syfrets itself held only 8 588 shares in the Cape Times in 1955, the Press Commission pointed out that it could, if so directed, exercise proxies on behalf of its many clients who themselves held shares in the newspaper.

28. Rudyard Kipling

29. Maitland Park

Private

P.S. Jameson will be
not before me. He is the get you.
man who asked me to get Rhodes
He represents Rhodes and S. africa.

THE ELMS,
ROTTINGDEAN,
SUSSEX.

July. 11. 1902.

Dear Park

During business by cut in these
circumstances has its drawbacks but
your affairs are sorted out at last.
Newspaper offices are alike the world over.

I understand that you sail on Aug. 11th
Good luck be with you Sir, all being well,
its a big career that you have entered upon
and you should go far.
There were no applicants for the post of editor,
because that post is not open to public application
any time than the editorship of the Ti: the direction said
that they wanted a man to face a new &
strange situation — a strong persevering man who
could work and organize & control. I said you
were that man.
Ever yours
Rudyard Kipling.

30. Sections of the first and last pages of Rudyard Kipling's letter to
Maitland Park on 11 July, 1902, telling Park that he was to be
appointed Editor of the *Cape Times*. The directors, said Kipling,
wanted a 'strong persevering man who could work and organize
and control. I said you were that man.'

31. Frederick York St Leger, founder and first Editor of the *Cape Times*. Chairman of the Board of Directors from 1898.
Cape Times Library

32. Edmund Garrett, Editor 1895–9.

33. Sir Maitland Park, Editor 1902–21.

34. B. K. Long, Editor 1921–35.

35. G. H. Wilson, Editor 1935–44.

36. Victor Norton, Editor 1944–71.

37. A. H. Heard, Editor 1971–

Chairmen and Editors of the *Cape Times* from 1876 to 1975. No picture could be traced of J. Saxon Mills, Editor 1901–2.

38. E. R. Syfret, Chairman 1902–37.

39. Gerald Orpen, Chairman 1937–56.

40. Sir Alfred Hennessy, Chairman 1957–58.

41. Clive Corder, Chairman 1958–

And the Press Commission noted that the trustees of the Cape Times Employment Endowment Trust normally gave the Chairman of the Cape Times Ltd a proxy for the shares they held. For most of the time, excepting the brief chairmanship of Sir Alfred Hennessy in 1957–8, the Chairman of the Cape Times and of Syfrets were one and the same man. The association between Syfrets and the Cape Times had never been a secret. So the Press Commission's conclusion was hardly a bombshell.

The Press Commission's findings were quickly overtaken by events. In July 1963 South African Associated Newspapers (SAAN), publishers of the Rand Daily Mail, the Sunday Times and other newspapers, acquired a 20 per cent holding in the Cape Times Ltd. There had been a long association between the Cape Times and the Rand Daily Mail. In 1915 the Cape Times Company had sold the Transvaal Leader, which it had owned since 1902, to the Rand Daily Mail and became a shareholder in the Rand Daily Mail. A close association had been maintained down the years with the Cape Times and the Rand Daily Mail sharing services with other morning newspapers.

In 1973, South African Associated Newspapers acquired the remaining 80 per cent of the shares in the Cape Times Ltd, and the newspaper thus became an integral part of the company with which it had long been associated.

There were regrets at the Cape Times office, obviously, but incorporation in a large newspaper group would probably have become inevitable in time and, in the circumstances, the acquisition of the Cape Times by SAAN was seen as a happy and fortunate outcome. The Cape Times noted in an editorial on 16 March 1973 that the newspaper had been paying its way, as always, and was economically buoyant; but it would become increasingly difficult for unattached newspapers like the Cape Times to remain strong and independent in the television era. The Cape Times noted that the Managing Director of SAAN, Mr Leycester Walton, had unhesitatingly pledged editorial independence to the Cape Times as a member of the SAAN group. The newspaper believed its sturdy traditions of editorial independence would continue to flourish under the SAAN group.

In early 1975 the major interest in SAAN (36,56 per cent) was held by the estate of the late Sir Abe Bailey, the Rand mining magnate, the Abe Bailey Trust and allied interests. The Argus Company was also a substantial minority shareholder, with 31,25 per cent. The administrators of the Bailey estate were Mr G. K. Lindsay (Chairman); Mr H. W. Middelmann; Mr R. G. Welsh; Mr D. A. St C. Hennessy; and Mr J. R. A. Bailey. The Chairman of the Abe Bailey Trust was Mr Clive Corder and the members were Dr J. P. Duminy, Sir Derrick Louis Bailey, Mr D. A. St C. Hennessy and Dr Anton Rupert. Mr E. V. E. Howes and the Reverend W. A. Landman were alternates.

The members of the Abe Bailey Trust are nominated by the Rhodes Trust, on the advice of Syfrets, who are agents of the Rhodes Trust and act as secretaries to the Bailey interests. There has been a close association down the years between Syfrets and the Bailey interests. And so the Cape Times, *in spite of its purchase by SAAN, retains something of its traditional link with Syfrets Trust, which was founded in 1919 by St Leger's successor as Chairman of the* Cape Times, *E. R. Syfret.*

As the Cape Times *neared its centenary, the Press in South Africa was again under severe strain. There were intensified pressures on the political front, from politicians on both the Government and Opposition benches. And there were also economic problems, as newsprint prices soared, forcing newspapers to go up in price and hence lose circulation. The economic pressures were also threatening to undermine standards, with fierce competition for circulation and survival in the TV era.*

In nearly a century of publication, there had been ups and downs. But the Cape Times, *for most of its existence, had been spared the debilitating battles between editors and proprietors that have sapped the vitality of many journals. At the beginning, the editor and the proprietor had been the same man, F. Y. St Leger. And in the seven decades since the death of St Leger there had been only four chairmen of the Board (E. R. Syfret, Gerald Orpen, Sir Alfred Hennessy and Clive Corder) and six editors. Such a record had been possible only in an atmosphere of mutual confidence between the editor and his employers, the members of the Board of Directors.*

The ideal basis for relations between editor and proprietor will always be a common commitment to uphold the tradition of the newspaper. An editor is never more than the temporary custodian of his newspaper's tradition, as Garrett had argued in 1896, in his declaration that the Cape Times *was a 'weapon for good' which had been shaped by others and put in his hands for the time being.*

As Maitland Park wrote in 1914, the proprietors would indeed get rid of the editor if they no longer approved of his direction. But, said Maitland Park, it was an essential to the satisfaction of the proprietors of the Cape Times *that the editor should adhere to the traditions of the newspaper.*

This provision, in fact, is still written into the contract which the Editor of the Cape Times *is given by his employers. He is required to carry out any instructions from time to time given by the Chairman of the Board of Directors 'provided that they do not involve any departure from the established and recognized policy and practice of the* Cape Times'. *The tradition of the newspaper establishes very clearly and forcibly that the expression of opinion and the direction of the editorial activities of the newspaper are the function of the Editor.*

When he retired in August 1971, Victor Norton said at a lunch given in his honour by the Board of Directors that the Editor of the Cape Times, *and the Editor only, was responsible for maintaining the traditions and practices of the newspaper—'and the Editor is the man who decides what are these traditions and practices. This is not only the theory which is written into the constitution of our newspaper but also very much the practice down all the years I have been in office', he said.*

Dr Norton spoke before the Cape Times *became a wholly-owned subsidiary of South African Associated Newspapers in 1973. But the change in ownership brought with it no change in what Dr Norton has called the 'constitution' of the newspaper. And so the new custodian of the tradition is Dr Norton's successor, Anthony Heard, who is likewise required by his contract to uphold the established traditions of the newspaper.*

Frederick York St Leger had sought to make his newspaper a record of public opinion, 'not the journal of any particular party, but the colonists as a whole'. He was insistent that his newspaper should remain independent of political parties and special interest groups while upholding ideals of constitutional liberty. St Leger knew that the public trust in the Cape Times, *which had grown up slowly over decades, was the newspaper's greatest strength and its most enduring asset. His newspaper's chances of surviving another 100 years would rest, in large measure, on the ability of his successors to keep the confidence and trust of the readers of the* Cape Times.

APPENDIX 1

Directors of the Cape Times Limited, 1975

C. S. Corder (Chairman); W. Judge (Managing); G. M. C. Cronwright; D. A. St C. Hennessy; I. G. MacPherson; H. C. Payne; L. H. Walton. Alternates: C. R. Judd; F. R. Meredith.

Directors of S.A. Associated Newspapers Limited, 1975

I. G. MacPherson (Chairman); L. H. Walton (Managing); J. R. A. Bailey; Dr F. J. C. Cronje; G. M. C. Cronwright; D. A. St C. Hennessy; H. C. Payne; J. D. Robinson. Alternates: W. A. Rowley, K. W. Stuart.

A PLAIN TALK WITH OOM PAUL

This is the text of an interview between Edmund Garrett and
Paul Kruger at Pretoria which was published in the *Cape Times*
on 22 July 1895, a few weeks after Garrett had become Editor of
the *Cape Times*. It was Garrett's second interview with Kruger.

IT is six years, roughly, since I last picked my way across the streets
of Pretoria—six o'clock of a sultry January morning it was, I remember—for the honour of a chat with President Kruger. In these six
years much has happened in the President's republic; more in some
ways if less in others than sanguine folk expected.

Materially, things have come true which I was able then, on due
inquiry from those who knew, to promulgate as bold forecasts. The
railways have come in with a rush, and the gold output gone up with
steady strides. Long before the baptism of fireworks of the Delagoa
Bay line, which the President then swore must come first, the Cape
trunk line, let in by famine and tumult, has enabled the then bankrupt
Rand to pay its way and that of the Republic; to rebuild Pretoria,
and to change the lodgings of Oom Paul's Executive from Van
Erkom's tobacco store to the great Raadzaal, which now dominates
Church Square. And that extraordinary mortgage on the future
known as "Deep Levels"—the boring, at colossal cost, of a second set
of holes beside the first along the miles of the great *banket* reef—this
is one of many new signs that all this material development has come
to stay, that the industrial *Uitlander*, outnumbering the pastoral Boer,
is a feature of the situation absolutely permanent.

Yet politically it is "as you were." The Johannesburger is only a
politician in lean times; and these are fat ones. The mob, despite two
or three moments of crisis when a random shot would have fired
South Africa, is still practically voiceless; the handful still rules; the
impossible quietly continues; the Boer, rifle and *biltong* at saddle-bow,
is still the man who counts across the Vaal. And Stephanus Johannes
Paulus Kruger is still President, President for the third time; though
there was talk of gerrymandering at the last election, and though some
of Piet Joubert's men are said to have taken an oath, Boer-like, that
they would not wash till they had shot Paul—and, as some say, kept it.

So at three o'clock of a crisp July afternoon, I once more sought the
low-pitched bungalow-looking house opposite the little Dopper
Church, for a talk with Paul Kruger. With me was the same interpreter as before, my good friend Johann Rissik. The six years have
made him State Surveyor-General, and a rich man to boot, they tell

me; but they have not touched Mr. Rissik's simple readiness to take trouble for other people, nor his transparent straightforwardness, nor the President's complete trust of him, even as interpreter for a *courantschryver.*

A little more grizzled, a little more bent is Paul Kruger at seventy than he was at sixty-five; but he is still Paul Kruger, every inch of him.

In the stiff though homely parlour—just such a parlour as one knows in certain old countrified places in England, with just such rugs, just such antimacassars—the old man motioned us to a pair of chairs, and pulling up an armchair point-blank to them, sat down himself and faced us with the characteristic Boer air of masked vigilance. As he did so, he lit the inevitable long pipe and began puffing at it.

How stolid he looks! How ox-eyed! (And the comparison Homer meant as a compliment to a goddess may be permitted for the President of a pastoral Republic.) How mildly ruminative! But give him one little opening for the point he wants to make, and down he comes upon you, in under your guard, flashing and relentless as a rapier. "Great men," said Mr. Chamberlain of another grand old man, "are like great mountains": if so, the Paulberg is certainly a sleeping volcano.

"The next talk we have" (I had to open somehow) "I hope, President, to be able to speak to you in the *taal.* Hitherto, I have had no opportunity to learn it."

"Humph!"

A guttural and phlegmatic response showed me that my good intentions towards the cherished *patois* were discounted.

I reverted to our last meeting, and hastened to drag in the blessed word Swaziland—once a sure conventional "open sesame." "I told you then, President, that you would get Swaziland as soon as people at home understood what you would do in return. Well, you have got it."

The President fixed deep-set eyes on the interpreter while the words were translated; then suddenly, and with characteristic vehemence, he brought up that official phrase about Swaziland not being "actually incorporated in the Republic." Heaven knows what the phrase means.

"But, President, you know that is purely a question of words— diplomatic language meant to hoodwink a few people who want to be hoodwinked. You must understand that with our party-government a thing of this kind, that is in the teeth of certain prejudices, has to be done gingerly. There is a section of people in England—very good people—who become quite unreasonable on the least pretext where natives are concerned; a Government has to think of them."

"But *I* have also my difficult people to think of. I have done my part, all the same; only the British Government have not done theirs.

I risked my position here—yes, I risked it—carrying out what I promised, because I had promised."...

" 'Damping the trek,' you mean?"

"Yes; it was a risk for me, but I did it; and then the British Government have got out of their promise."

"But surely you have, or are on the point of having, everything that is of any use to you in Swaziland?"

"Swaziland? Swaziland is nothing . . . Swaziland is nothing at all . . . There is a little gold, perhaps; that is nothing to me; and some grazing; but Swaziland in itself is nothing at all!"

The sentences were given out with immense force and *intention*, the pipe being clutched in the right hand and withdrawn only momentarily for each sentence from the teeth, which closed upon each statement like a guillotine, then sent after it a great jet of smoke.

"But, sir, you did not say Swaziland was exactly *nothing* . . . six years ago. . . ." I ventured.

"I always said it was nothing save as a way to the sea. I said that all along, and it was well understood. And now they no sooner give it to me than they take away altogether the only thing that made it worth having—the way to the sea."

I knew of course that we must come to the Zambaan and Umbegiza business soon; but I could not have the Swaziland cession whistled down the wind so coolly; so I interjected the excellent Boer formula for all doubtful cases—*Wacht en beitje!*

"Wait a moment, President, I beg you. You used a phrase to me six years ago: 'Each hand must wash the other.' You could not expect to get everything for nothing. Swaziland, as I understood it, was for 'damping the trek'; expansion eastward for giving up claims to expand northward. The way to the sea surely was to be for a further *quid pro quo*: to wit, for joining the Customs Union."

"See, it was like this!" the old man burst in so soon as he had grasped my statement of the case. "There is the *trek* and there is the *haven*"—he actually laid down his pipe for a moment, and putting up two fingers of his right hand, no dapper one, ticked them off with the left.

"No! no!" I interjected, determined not to be mistaken, and copying his pantomime: "here is the *trek*, and here is Swaziland only; then *here* (a third finger) is your haven against (fourth finger) our Customs Union."

The President gave up the hand and fell back on still quainter symbols. Turning to the table, he seized a great leather tobacco-case which lay there close to the enormous family bible, and catching up in the other hand a matchbox, he set them up against each other like a man bartering.

"This" (the tobacco-pouch) "is the way to the sea, including Swaziland (he hurried on), which is only useful as *part* of the way to the sea. *This* (the matchbox) is the piece of coast with means to make a port—*that* certainly is something more than the way to the sea. For *that* (match-box again) *vryhandel*: (free trade, meaning customs union); but for *this* (tobacco-pouch) I have already given what I promised, and you have not yet given it me (brusquely withdrawing it, and throwing it on the table), you have made it now quite impossible."

He recovered the pouch, refilled his pipe which had gone out, and puffed forth volumes of smoke, while his meaning was being made clear to me.

"This is to me quite a new conception of the case, President," I rejoined. "Granted, the way to the sea was always part of the bargain; but it was a distinct part, and belonged to the coast side, not the Swaziland side of the business."

"I assure you it was as I say; it was clearly understood so in conversation after conversation with British statesmen."

"But President"—a bright idea coming to my rescue—"we gave you a chance of your way to the sea as well in the 1890 Convention; and your Raad rejected it. Then in the new Convention the chance was not repeated. But you had it, and lost it. How was that?"

The shot told. What the President would have liked to say was perhaps something about his recalcitrant Raad. What he did say was simply that the Raad did not consider the way to the sea which was then proposed acceptable in its method of arrangement. I asked what they really did want, and jumping up with the alacrity of excitement, the old man fetched from the next room a large school-map on a roller. We went to the table, where he spread it out, and talked rapidly over it, laying his hand now over Swaziland, now over the coast, now over that fateful little strip between the two which the recent annexation has turned into a "No Road" notice-board. He depreciated the road to Kosi Bay proposed in the abortive Convention; it ran over ground not feasible: he depreciated Kosi Bay itself, talking of its shallowness and sandiness till I asked myself, "Has the old man really grasped the utter futility of the dream of Kosi Harbour!" He wandered down the coast to Sordwana Bay, which is just opposite the point where the Republic most projects towards the coast, south of Swaziland and much more coastward—only forty miles off, in fact: but that bay surely is part of Zululand and a clear reversion of Natal's; Natal would always see to it that there should be an Imperial non-possumus there. He traced with one broad finger the northward course of the Pongo River, which connects this same south-east corner of the Republic, through the Tonga lowlands, with a southern coign of Delagoa Bay—as if it would really profit him to have a second string, besides the semi-Portuguese railway, to the wholly Portuguese port. But finally he made it clear that what he really yearns for is free leave to drive a wedge of Republican territory through the new annexation and the Tonga protectorate to anywhere that suits best on the coast between the Portuguese frontier and Zululand.

"But what is the use of talking—after this annexation?" He always came back to his point. "They practically say to me, 'You are shut in—shut into a *kraal* for ever!'"

He put his two hands together to make the kraal, just as he had done six years ago over the same expression. And as then, so now again, voice and gesture had a certain pathos, the note of an old man against Fate; and I noticed once more the sad gap on the rough left hand where the thumb should be—and recalled, with teeth on edge, the story of how the boy Paul amputated it himself long ago with his pocket-knife out on the lonely veldt. Truly that boy was father of this hard old man before me, who never forgets, never relents, always suspects.

"For ever is a long time, President. What if the British Government has only made its title clear to this strip of country so as to be able to bargain better—to have no questions next time which side the asset really belongs to?"

"I have been played with so often," was the gloomy reply. "Great Britain holds a thing out, and says: 'We will consider the Republic's rights favourably, only you must just do something more'; then again it says: '*Now* you positively get it, only first there is one small thing we must have from you'; and so it goes on. . . ."

What could I answer? The very expressions almost that I have written over and over again these dilatory years past. The President's sarcastic sketch of our diplomacy on the Swaziland question was an uncomfortably speaking likeness.

I turned the tobacco-pouch over in my hand rather stupidly, remembering in a vague way that the French *blague* means at once "tobacco-pouch" and "humbug." To be sure, the dangling as of a bunch of carrots has not been all on one side in Transvaal *pourparlers*.

In my embarrassment I caught up the President's other symbol again, the match-box, and copying his own dumbshow of bartering the one against the other, I said:

"I think, President, you and we have been like two savages exchanging treasurers. Neither hand liked to give credit; neither would be the first to let go its prize before closing on the return value."

The President was rolling up the map. We went back to our chairs, I assuring him earnestly that there was no real hostility to his sea ambitions in England, and quite a cordial feeling growing up in these latter days towards himself.

"You should visit England again, President, if you like being banqueted——"

"I have always found, when people banquet me, they want something out of me," quoth the unmitigable old cynic without the ghost of a smile. And, after a smoky pause, he burst out again at the annexation grievance: "It was the way it was done. I was never told—never consulted—never warned even."

It must out. It was a thing I had come to say—the unpalatable truth that the oft-threatened annexation fell when it did fall simply as a sharp *riposte* to the German intriguing of Mr. Kruger and his late inspirers.

"It was, after all, President, a kind of rude tit for tat."

"Tit for tat! What had I done? What had I done, or failed to do, since the Swaziland Convention which this simply makes nothing of?"

Of course there was but one possible answer to the challenge. Generalities would not serve here. That *gauche* speech of the President's at the *Kaiser-Kommers* playing off Germany against England was the easiest thing to name. I promptly named it.

Then did President Paul Kruger wax very wroth. He began with a volley against newspaper reports. Newspapers had to make something startling for their readers. He was utterly misrepresented. If I had been there I should have seen at once that his meaning was a perfectly harmless one.

Might I ask what it really was?

The explanation was tortuous. To my dull apprehension, it amounted to saying—well, pretty much what the papers always said he said. That did not surprise me. But the gloss was to the effect that, whatever he *said*, the President meant only a little joke, and his little joke was as much at the expense of Germany *versus* England as of England *versus* Germany. He would expect either to prevent his head being punched (were such a design conceivable) by the other. There was no mischievous bringing in of Germany—not more than of England. In fact (the President rounded off with this suggestion) the whole thing was after dinner.

"But on your own showing, President, I must join issue with your view of the German position here. We cannot allow that Germany has any right to be brought in here on a footing equal with England. What has Germany to do in this *galère* with any footing at all?"

"Do you deny my right to look to other Powers for moral support?"

"Certainly; it is treason to South African unity! . . ."

"Suppose England wanted to cut my throat! I do not for a moment say she ever would, but supposing! Should I not then have a right to moral support from Germany?"

"Giving you your independence does not look like cutting your throat; and as for moral support, what moral support got you that independence? Not German; not European at all; but just the moral support of your kinsmen, my friends down there in Cape Colony. You looked to them then, and surely it is them you should look to now, if support you want: not to France or Germany or *any* Power outside South Africa, President!"

"I know what they did! I do not forget their support! I do not wish to bring in European powers unnecessarily," insisted the President with rising disquiet; and feeling I had the advantage of him, this time I pressed him for a pronouncement.

"Will you not say frankly, President, that you adopt the South African standpoint—the only one I hear taken in the Free State as well as the Colony: that every other European Power, beyond the maritime power of England which keeps the coasts, is an exotic, an intruder in the South African States and colonies. You are angry with England just now over this annexation; but you know that country is not lost to South Africa, as Madagascar is lost when France steps in, as Damara is lost when Germany steps in; it is only kept warm some day to be handed over as British Bechuanaland is being handed to Cape Colony, as Zululand will be handed to Natal——"

"It does not help me to have country taken from me and handed to Natal," said the President hotly. . . .

"And as Swaziland has been to the Republic," I closed up my argument; "as this very strip may yet be, for value received."

"Swaziland was by right ours already! They were all ours! Natal itself was ours! It is like stealing my watch"—he pulled out a great clock, disengaging the chain and seals with trembling fingers, and thrust it into my embarrassed hands: "You take my watch, then you say, 'Look! we give you this. Here is a nice present for you; be grateful'! I will not say anything unfriendly to Germany!" Then, as if he had committed himself too far, he went on pettishly: "I do not wish this conversation printed. It must not be published. I inform you that I was only giving you a friendly chat. . . ."

Here was a pretty kettle of fish! It is ill to argue with the master of interviews, as of legions. I had won the argument, so I fondly told myself, and lost my paper the interview. I had angered Oom Paul; he knew his German speech was a blunder, and he was determined to punish me. Was he inexorable? Not at all, when the moment's testiness had been got over. There were explanations and apologies; the temperature resumed the normal; fairness and good temper reasserted themselves; the embargo on publication was removed; and my interview was saved by the skin of its teeth.

The old man, remembering his Boer hospitality, went out to order coffee, and on his return hastened to leave the dangerous topic for more attractive ground.

"President, will you bargain with me a moment for your seaport, as you did six years ago for Swaziland? I want another outspoken message to the English people. Imagine me plenipotentiary for them— all we journalists are that in a sense. . . ."

"Well?"

"First, there is the railway question. . . ."

The President frowned slightly.

"The Cape asks for too much. We cannot agree for so much. We have not yet a basis of agreement."

"Granted. But after we have had all the lines working together, with no cutting down prices, so as to see where the trade will naturally run—say eighteen months or two years hence: suppose it were possible for a committee of railway experts to apportion the profits on the ascertained facts: would you consider the idea of a general pooling of the railway systems and of the customs at the same time—for customs are an asset in a railway fight, and *vice versa*—if the same conference which achieved this gave you out of hand and at once your port, your access, everything you want to get to the sea? No promises, mind; no more nonsense about 'good will' on either side; but cash down— harbour for rail-and-customs union?"

Needless to say it took the President some time and a great deal of tobacco smoke to digest this portentous offer, which has all the sweeping largeness of the irresponsible diplomat.

"I cannot well say yes or no without knowing more of the Railway and Customs Union. All would depend on the terms," he answered at last. "Hitherto in all the unions proposed, this Republic has had all to give and nothing to gain."

"But if it had the sea to gain, and union were the only condition? Put yourself for a moment in *Oma's* place," I pleaded (*Oma*, Grand- mother, is colloquial Boer for Her Britannic Majesty's Government). "*Oma* has to think of her children. Natal and the Cape may say, 'Why give the Transvaal a port which might be used to cut us out? The Transvaal is rich; we are poor; but we have our ports.' "

"But I don't want a port to cut them out. I only want it to prevent them from joining together to bleed me."

"Then surely you can have no objection to getting your port on terms which simply lay that down. Once come with a Customs and Railway Union, and any hostile action between the various ports is impossible. Surely you don't ask us for a port, and in the same breath refuse guarantees that the giver of the port shall not suffer by it?"

"I will give any guarantee of equal treatment at the port that England demands," exclaimed the President. "I will promise that it shall never be less favourably open to English or English Colonial trade than to any other in the world."

"Not even by the expedient of differential railway rates?"

"No; that is also a point which can be settled beforehand, when we come to discuss the harbour."

"Then, in effect, you are not opposed in principle to such a simultaneous settlement of all these open questions as I suggest?"

"I am in favour of a settlement. I have always been in favour of a settlement, so it be only fair and reasonable; then it is for the benefit of the republics as well as the colonies; it will help us all together."

With this very proper sentiment the President evidently meant the interview to close. It had indeed lasted well over an hour, and I felt I must not abuse the old gentleman's courtesy longer. Yet there was one question yet in the bottom of the wallet that must out. I could not go away without a word about the franchise and the *Uitlander*. We had settled up South Africa; but the internal affairs of the Transvaal we had been ignoring.

"One thing more I must ask, President—and understand, please, that I speak now not in an English character. England claims no voice in your private affairs on the Rand or elsewhere."

The President nodded slowly, and resigned himself to the unwelcome line of country.

"No doubt, you have there among the rest some of the scum of the earth," I pursued, anxious to get out at once all my credentials of moderation. "But you have also——"

Tramp, tramp, tramp! At this point in came half a dozen members of the Volksraad, evidently keeping an appointment with the President. They drowned my sentence unfinished. He rose to welcome them, and Mr. Rissik to go. I surveyed the situation, and with a bold stroke brought the intruders into the conversation.

"Let us ask these gentlemen," said I, turning to a bearded farmer in broadcloth: "I appeal to your own burghers, President. Are there not, besides the scum of the earth in Johannesburg, thousands of honest folk who are building houses, and rearing children, and meaning to spend their lives here, and could be safely *inspanned* as citizens?"

The half-dozen must have all this translated, of course. There was handshaking and introductions; the talk became general. Platitudes were poured forth, and the President slyly dropped out of the conversation. At last I carried off Mr. Rissik in triumph, and got back to his Honour.

"There are our own Afrikanders [*sic*] from Cape Colony, too, President. Surely *they* can be trusted with your independence. I know you suspect them as *Engelsche gesind*——"

"I have no hatred of the English," was the wary answer. "See this ring. . . ." And he began working away at a big plain gold ring on his finger, wetting it and trying to push it off. I knew that old ring. It was a gift from an English sympathiser on one of the President's visits to us in the 'seventies or 'eighties. Bother the ring! I mentally ejaculated.

"Surely you could trust the Afrikanders [*sic*] with a vote," I persisted, escaping from a vicious, if golden, circle.

"They can vote already," said the President, impatiently enough. "After only two years, they can vote for a Landdrost and a Commandant, and the Second Raad, which has to do with many important things, and will have more still given to it. . . ."

"President, if I had cast my lot in with your Republic I should be willing to exchange British citizenship for yours; but I would not be put off with half-citizenship. I should not care a straw, if you will excuse me, about your Landdrost and your Second Raad; I should demand a voice in the real government of the country. As it is, you are less of a Republic here in reality than we in the Cape Colony."

"What!" exclaimed the President; "you can only vote for one Raad in the Colony. . . ."

And he launched into a constitutional disquisition from which it appeared that he imagined that at the Cape the Assembly co-opts the Council.

I assured him the Council was elected by the very same voters as the popular chamber; whereon he fell back on comparing himself, directly elected by the people, with the Governor and the Prime Minister whom the Colony does not elect directly. I rejoined that we could at any rate make our Prime Minister responsible for his mistakes and turn him out. And so on and so forth. It was characteristic of much that, when at a loss for any other argument of Transvaal constitutional superiority, the President fell back on colour. "You in the colony," said he, "are governed by black men. You let black men vote!"

At last we escaped from the constitution and returned to the point.

I asked him plainly what he would do if the Orange Free State proposed an assimilation of the oligarchical Transvaal franchise to their own liberal one as a condition precedent of the much-talked-of inter-Republican federation? He at once and firmly declined to discuss the question.

There was a pause; then Oom Paul said gravely, "See, I will tell you what is the truth about this *stemregt*. I know neither English nor Dutch, Afrikander nor *Uitlander*; I only know good people and bad people. You yourself say, some of these people in the towns are the scum of the earth. Very well. We cannot let people in without proving them. We let them in once before the war, and therefore the war came; for it was people let in on this easy plan who misled the English Government into coming in and annexing us. Therefore we must first *prove* this population—we must *prove* them to see if they are good people or bad people. Then . . . we shall see."

A most characteristic pronouncement! Derive from it, O reader, what sap thou may'st. Around, the faithful burghers sat drinking it in with heavy concentration; puffs of smoke were the commas, and the full-stops—well, you know how a Boer puts in the stops in a conversation . . . till you scarcely know where to tuck your feet.

We rose to go.

And so, with thanks on my side and mutual expressions of good will, ended my latest—not, I hope, my last—plain talk with the "grand old man" of the Transvaal.

"Oom Paul is a bad enemy, as we have learned to our cost. He has proved to us of late that he can also be a leal friend. Slowly but surely, I believe, my countrymen are coming to realise that his friendship is worth having." So I wrote six years ago, after a talk at Pretoria. My countrymen so far agreed with me that they gave Oom Paul Swaziland. If they now grumble that they have seen little friendship since, I answer that they got what they were promised, and that they dangled the gift too long for any further graciousness to cling to it. Do not suppose that now the strenuous old man is done with. In a sense, age is strength to him: I felt a touch of pathos, an impulse of hero-worship myself; how much more must his own burghers.

If there are two just men in South Africa who know what they want and hold by it in the teeth of fate, he is one of the two. For the *Uitlander* in the Transvaal, Oom Paul will do just so much as he is forced to, when he is forced: no sooner and no more. As well talk to the Paarl rock! But for a frank and bold policy of South African amity outside, may not the one strong man be as good to bargain with as ever the *Uitlander* in his thousands is likely to prove, when the *Uitlander* has come by his own? Be that as it may, I have the honour to offer President Kruger's words, through the *Cape Times*, to the consideration of England and South Africa.

CECIL RHODES

This *Cape Times* interview with Cecil Rhodes in March 1898 embodied the substance of several conversations with Edmund Garrett at Groote Schuur and marked Rhodes's return to Cape politics on the eve of the 1898 elections.

"SPEAK? Of course I'm willing to speak if I'm wanted. I don't like speaking, as you know. I don't speak by choice. But if there's a definite purpose, if it's going to help in the election, and I'm asked to speak—why, what do you suppose I am waiting about here for? I am waiting over the election simply on the chance that one's influence may be of use to help the Progressive party. If I followed my own wishes, do you think I should be messing about down here?"

That set my eyes travelling from the broad white-pillared stoep of Groote Schuur away up past the trim Dutch garden, past the faint blue hydrangeas in the spinney, past the oaks and the pines, up the hill to the steep purple bluffs of the mountain, with the old Blockhouse at its edge—Mr. Rhodes has just had a tree felled to open his view to the Blockhouse. I suggested that Groote Schuur grounds, even when shared with all Cape Town, as Mr. Rhodes shares them, were not such a very bad place to be "messing about" in.

"Yes, yes—it's a picture here, a picture one never tires of; but life isn't all looking at pictures, and I want to get back to my North, you see. They want one there, everything is moving; I ought not really to have left. Here one sits talking and talking and seeing people. Here it's all talking—in the North it's *doing*. Away on the veld I am always happy. Can't you see that if it was not for a purpose I should have been back there weeks ago?"

He threw himself on to one of the big sofas in the stoep with a bang.

"But, Mr. Rhodes, you can hardly grudge, if you are going to take a leading place again in Cape politics——"

He bounced up again from the sofa even more impatiently than he had bounced into it.

"Don't talk as if it was *I* who want your Cape politics. You want *me*. You can't do without me. You discuss 'Ought Rhodes to do this?' and 'Will Rhodes keep in the background?' and so on—*I* am quite willing to keep out, but you have to take the feeling of the people, and the feeling of the people—you may think it egoism, but there are the facts—is that somebody is wanted to fight a certain thing for them, and there is nobody else able and willing to fight it. You say, 'Oh, but that's your ambition; you want to get back into power——' "

"I never said——"

"Well, somebody else says it then. I reply, quite fairly, No humanly speaking, *qua* ambition at the Cape, one has had everything. There is no more to offer, only work and worry. *Qua* the North——"

He paused. This somewhat elliptical use of "qua" is very Rhodes-ian, by the by.

"*Qua* the North—well, there we are really *creating* a country. It's interesting to create, I can tell you; much more interesting than politics. We've had the war and rinderpest and rebellion and drought and so on, and now everything is pushing on; and there's the native question to solve and the new constitution to get under way; and that tariff arrangement I wanted to make—the treaties were in the way, but Laurier has got rid of them; and I have a big irrigation scheme on; and then the development to make way for a population—— You will say, If it comes out all right; but I don't bother about that; I know the country too well, and with Heany crushing twenty penny-weights in May—I can wait. Then the railway and the telegraph—you know that telegraph of mine that the British public wouldn't look at. There is imagination in that. It is really an immense thing, only you people won't see it——"

Here a protest against the "you" as quite incorrect passes unnoticed.

"You won't see it, though it was the dream of the ancients to pierce through this continent; and, if you look you will see Alexander got so far, and Cambyses so far—got to Memphis, didn't he, and then went mad?—and Napoleon so far—there's a tablet his soldiers stuck up at Philae, and we are pushing up from the other end right through. They used to say I was too soon, but the danger now is being too late in connecting, with the French cutting in. Really there are many other things to think of besides Cape Town parish pump."

"Of course (I admitted) Cape Town is parish pump, if you take it as a localism apart from the broader unity; Bulawayo is even more parish pump, and Salisbury parish pump *in excelsis!*"

"Quite true. You have it exactly. Do you know our people up there are no more thinking about uniting than the people here, or at Johannesburg. They're hoeing their own patch for all they're worth; of course they are, and as for unity with the Cape, they look on the Cape as a sort of Bond-ridden place—Bond, varied by unctuous rectitude and all sorts of wobbling; and as to my ideas of working in with the Cape as to railway, and so on, I really believe they say 'Oh, this is Rhodes's amiable lunacy—we must humour him because after all he does work for the country.' You see, it's very amusing. Localism here and in Johannesburg, and in Natal and in Cape Colony; and that's where I think, to be frank, that one *is* perhaps able to be of a certain use, because one has a certain influence with a good many people in all these places, and you know my idea—Colonial Federation. One was trying the general federation before, with the Republics in; only Kruger and Leyds made it impossible, and then in the middle of the mess they had made one made a mistake, on the top, and so the whole plan is altered."

"You say 'made a mistake.' The 'unctuous rectitude' of some of us has consisted in wanting you just to say so much to your former Dutch supporters."

"I said so much at Westminster; but I am not going on saying it, and crawling in the dust to please you or anybody, so I told some Dutch constituents of mine who made advances, after abusing one like a pickpocket at the time. 'Oh,' they said, 'do say you repent! Only *tell* us you repent!' 'That's *my* business,' I answered. I know what my idea was—no race feeling at all—and what my motive was, and it all went wrong, and I and others made mistakes, and that's all about it."

I now pass to Mr. Rhodes's very frank and simple treatment of the supposed difficulty of his position in Cape internal politics.

We took the thorny points first, beginning with the Food Duties; but as about these the conversation took a rather argumentative turn, I prefer not to try to reproduce the *ipsissima verba,* but to leave Mr. Rhodes's exact position to be stated by himself on Saturday. Broadly, however, his position is this. The meat duty he is prepared to abolish, recognising that the duty is at present pinching the families of working men in the towns without being the slightest protection to the farmer, who has no stock left to protect*; that it will take long to re-stock the country; and that a legislator's duty is to deal with the present. On food-stuffs apart from meat he is evidently prepared to make something of a new departure, though not nearly so large a one as his urban admirers would like. He frankly declines to give up his strong feeling that the community at large ought to be ready to sacrifice something to keep white men settled on the land, which he holds can only be secured in Cape Colony by giving *some* special consideration to the products of the soil; but he declares that the form and the amount of such consideration he has always treated purely as a question of degree and of fair adjustment between the claims of the various classes of the population. The times have changed. He once voted for an increase of duties; that is now utterly out of the question. He fully owns that any change in the present state of things must be in the other

* The rinderpest year was '97–8

direction; and I think if the party strongly unites on the 50 per cent. compromise adopted by the League—which itself contains many farmers—Mr. Rhodes will see his way to pledge himself to that extent of reduction. Fortunately, Mr. Rhodes's tendency to consider each local question, not only as between local producers and consumers, but with a view to the broader South African scheme, helps in this case on the right side. In 1895 he distinctly made use of the argument that increased duties would help to keep the Free State in the Customs Union. To-day his federal scheme looks rather towards Natal, and Natal still stands, though not so sharply as formerly, for low duties.

On all the other planks of the Progressive platform, Mr. Rhodes claimed that, so far from having a past to bury, his record includes nearly all the real Progressive measures that have been actually carried in the Colony. The Rhodes Ministry passed the Scab Act, in the teeth of what Sir Gordon Sprigg called "the demons of prejudice and ignorance," to improve the staple product of the colony. It also passed the Glen Grey Act, which took the first great step for the progress of the native in our social and economic scheme, by giving him an individual hold on the land.

"What about the Excise?"

"I voted against the Excise when it was levied in the wrong way, that is with a minimum of revenue and a maximum of irritation to the farmers with their small stills, but I have long had a plan for the Excise to be levied from the canteens and really paid by the consumer."

"What about the Innes Liquor Bill for keeping drink from the aboriginal native?"

"Keeping drink from the native? Why, I might say that that has been my whole life. I have run De Beers on ginger beer. In Rhodesia the Native Liquor Law is the most stringent in South Africa. In the Transkei I found the traffic only checked by a fine, and substituted confiscation because the sellers could afford to pay the fine and go on. If anybody in South Africa has done more than I have to keep drink from the native, I should like to know his name."

"And education?"

"Of course any one can see that education is the key to progress among us. As you know, I wanted to found a real South African University, and put the scheme aside only in deference to the susceptibilities of Stellenbosch, which you may call vested interests."

"But what of the Progressive party's demand for compulsory education in centres?"

"I have a scheme for what I would call permissive compulsory education. That is to say, compulsory for the individual when adopted by the district and assisted by the consolidated fund on the £ for £ principle. The Colony might be divided into seven districts, of which five would adopt the permissive compulsory right away, and the others would have the strongest inducement to follow suit."

Needless to say, Mr. Rhodes is strong for redistribution. No need to enlarge on that.

"I do not pretend to be a town politician," he says, summing up. "Production interests me. My sympathy with the farmer is natural. Look at my own pursuits and tastes. I can conceive a time when the people in the towns who have stood by me so well in my time of failure, and for whose fair demands I hope to do something now, will say that I am too moderate for them in my politics. I say my Progressive record already is pretty good, considering that I was working with the Bond and for the Northern Extension, and you cannot do everything at once. To-day what is the Bond—I mean the official Bond, the Bond which rejects Dutchmen like Faure and Bellingan because they are not narrow enough? It is not only against progress, it is against equality, against unity, and it is domineered by that continental gang from Pretoria. It is not a case of whether the Bond will forgive me. It is I who will have no compromise with them and their continental gang. You may find Mr. Hofmeyr very moderate and very nice, but I take 'Ons Land,' which represents Mr. Hofmeyr among his own people. Look at the line it takes. They talk of race hatred! Some of my greatest friends are Dutch; and in what I may call my own country, in Rhodesia, the only thing that is said sometimes is that the Dutch get actually favoured more than my own people. But these others with their eternal whine of Afrikanders [sic], Afrikanders, poor oppressed Afrikanders, and their abuse of England and Englishmen, and their support of everything rotten at Pretoria, they are simply spreading hatred as hard as they can spread it. Those are the people we are going to fight. We shall want all our discipline and all our organisation and unity for that fight, But it will all come right later on. I may not live to see it, but you will all be putting up statues to me."

The reader may be surprised, by the by, to find Mr. Rhodes in his casual talk dipping into the remote past; hitching his telegraph wire on to Cambyses; and picturing himself, with Burns' lady,

<blockquote>
Gone, like Alexander,
To spread his conquests further.
</blockquote>

But this is quite characteristic. I remember once his going to Aristotle to explain experiences in the Matopos. At the historic *indaba*, for instance, he was not afraid because he thought he knew it was all right. That was one kind of courage, the courage of superior knowledge, as defined by Aristotle. In actual fighting, on the other hand, the noise of the elephant-rifle bullets fired close by always made him duck his head, and the sight of men hit and bleeding made him feel sick. In short, "I was in a horrible funk. But I stayed at the front because of being far more afraid to be thought afraid"—which, he explained, corresponded to another Aristotelian classification of courage. Is it not a triumph for Oriel, for Oxford, and for Greats that Cambyses and Aristotle should thus mingle with the thread of the musings of a man of action in the whirl of Cape politics or in the wide spaces of life on the veldt? At any rate it is very quaint and interesting.

THANKS AND ACKNOWLEDGEMENTS

A complete list of people who have given unstinting help and encouragement in the writing of this book would occupy several pages. But I should like to acknowledge a special debt of gratitude to Ian Farlam, who awakened my interest in late-Victorian Cape history and provided invaluable assistance over a long period; Frank Bradlow, who drew my attention to the Garrett letters; Edna Bradlow, Arthur Davey and Schalk Pienaar, all of whom read the manuscript and offered criticisms; Mary Nassimbeni who drew my attention to the Saxon Mills letters; Jeremy Lawrence, a descendant of F. Y. St Leger, whose memorandum supplied much of the biographical data; the personnel of the South African Library, the Jagger Library, the Cape Archives, the Cambridge University Library; the Department of Manuscripts, British Library, London; Peggy van Reenen and the staff of the *Cape Times* Library; George Aschman; the *Cape Times* Photographic Department; Mrs R. Hawthorne, niece of Edmund Garrett, and her daughter, Mrs E. G. Bettesworth, who supplied photographs and invaluable assistance; Canon C. T. Wood, archivist of the Church of the Province of South Africa; the Rev. D. G. V. Topping, St Michael's and All Angels Church, Queenstown; the Editor of the *Cape Times*, Anthony Heard; Clive Corder, Chairman of the Board; Walter Judge, Managing Director; Guy Cronwright, Director and former Managing Director, and their colleagues on the Board of the *Cape Times*, without whose enthusiastic help and support this book could not have been written. Particular thanks are due to Roger Mulholland, Night and Production Editor of the *Cape Times*, who sub-edited the manuscript and read the proofs. The responsibility for the final result is mine.

G.S.

The author acknowledges with thanks permission to use copyright material as follows:

Juta and Company Limited for *An Editor Looks Back* by G. A. L. Green and *Turn Back the Pages* by W. Duncan Baxter.

John Murray (Publishers) Limited for *Millicent Garrett Fawcett* by Ray Strachey.

George Allen and Unwin Limited for *Gone Down the Years* by G. H. Wilson.

The estate of Lord Tweedsmuir for *Memory-Hold-the-Door, The autobiography of John Buchan* (Hodder and Stoughton).

W. H. Allen and Co. Ltd for *We and Me* by J. W. Robertson Scott.

The estate of Frederic Whyte for *Life of Stead* by F. Whyte (Jonathan Cape).

Oxford University Press (by permission of the Oxford University Press Oxford) for *W. P. Schreiner, a South African* by E. A. Walker; *The Unification of South Africa* by Leonard Thompson.

Oxford University Press (Southern Africa) for *The Jameson Raid* by Jean van der Poel; *Autobiography of James Rose Innes* ed. B. A. Tindall; *Afrikaans Poems with English Translations* (A. P. Grové and C. J. D. Harvey).

The Cecil Rhodes Trust for *Life of Jameson* by Ian Colvin (Edward Arnold).

Cassell and Company Limited for *Life, Journalism and Politics* by J. A. Spender; *J. A. Spender* by H. Wilson Harris.

Constable and Company Limited for *Cecil Rhodes* by Basil Williams.

Hamlyn Publishing Group for *My Early Life* by Winston S. Churchilll.

Basil Blackwell for *St. Andrew's College, Grahamstown, 1855–1955* by R. F. Currey.

Longmans (SA) Limited for *My Reminiscences* by Victor Sampson.

The Smuts Archive Trust for *Selections from the Smuts Papers* (ed. Jean van der Poel).

The Van Riebeeck Society for *Sir James Rose Innes, Selected Correspondence (1884–1902)* (ed. Harrison M. Wright); *Selections from the Correspondence of John X. Merriman* (four volumes) (ed. Phyllis Lewsen).

Mrs George Bambridge for letter to Maitland Park from Rudyard Kipling (in the Kipling Collection, Jagger Library, University of Cape Town).

Thanks are also expressed to the following for authority to reproduce photographs or extracts from documents in their custody; the South African Library; the Cape Archives; the Diocesan Office, Grahamstown (the diary of Matthew Norton); the Syndics of the University library, Cambridge (the Saxon Mills letters); the Jagger Library, University of Cape Town (the Cecil Sibbett Collection); the Library of Parliament.

NOTE ON SOURCES

The author acknowledges his debt to the standard South African histories and to the work of Professor G. H. Le May, Dr Jean van der Poel, Professor J. S. Marais, Professor Rodney Davenport, Professor Leonard Thompson, Phyllis Lewsen and Dr Harrison M. Wright. Sources are acknowledged in the source list and/or in the text where possible. Any oversights are regretted.

It should be noted that Edmund Garrett's letters to Agnes Garrett are in the Gordon Papers (Bell Collection) in the British Library. Some excerpts have been quoted by Garrett's biographer, E. T. Cook. Garrett's letters to James Rose Innes are in the Rose Innes papers at the South African Library, as are F. Y. St Leger's letters to Rose Innes, Garrett's letters to W. T. Stead have been quoted by Stead's biographer, Frederic Whyte. Rose Innes's letters to Garrett and others are in his published correspondence (Van Riebeeck Society). Garrett's 1890 travel letters on South Africa were published in *In Afrikanderland*. J. Saxon Mills's letters are in the Kidd Collection at Cambridge University. Quotations from the letters of John X. Merriman are from the selection published by the Van Riebeeck Society. Excerpts from the correspondence of General Smuts are from the published *Selections from the Smuts Papers*, edited by Jean van der Poel. Rudyard Kipling's letter to Jameson on the appointment of Maitland Park was quoted by Ian Colvin (junior) in a *Cape Times* article on 27 October 1956.

SOURCE LIST

I. *Literature*

Colvin, I. D.; *Life of Jameson* (London 1922)

Cook, E. T.; *Edmund Garrett, A Memoir* (London 1909)

Currey, R. F.; *St. Andrew's College, Grahamstown, 1855–1955* (Oxford 1955)

Davenport, T. R. H.; *The Afrikaner Bond: The History of a South African Political Party* (Cape Town 1966)

De Kock, W. J. (ed.); *Dictionary of South African Biography* (Vols 1 & 2)

Garrett, F. E. and Edwards, E. J.; *The Story of an African Crisis* (London 1897) (An expanded version, with introduction added, of 'The Story of a Crisis', Christmas number of the *Cape Times*, 1896)

Hobson, J. A.; *The War in South Africa, Its Causes and Effects* (London 1900)

Hofmeyr, J. H. and Reitz, F. W.; *The Life of Jan Hendrik Hofmeyr* (*Onze Jan*) (Cape Town 1913)

Hofmeyr, J. H.; *South Africa* (second edition revised by J. P. Cope) (London 1952)

Lawrence, J.; Unpublished memorandum on the life of F. Y. St Leger
Le May G. H.; *British Supremacy in South Africa, 1899–1907* (Oxford 1965)
Marais, J. S.; *The Fall of Kruger's Republic* (Oxford 1960)
McDonald, J. G.; *Rhodes, A Life* (London 1941)
Michell, O.; *Life of Rhodes* (London 1910)
Nathan, M.; *Paul Kruger, His Life and Times* (Durban 1942)
Strachey, R.; *Millicent Garrett Fawcett* (London 1931)
Thompson, L. H.; *The Unification of South Africa* (Oxford 1959)
Van der Poel, J.; *The Jameson Raid* (Oxford 1951)
Walker, E. A.; *A History of South Africa* (London 1928)
Walker, E. A.; *W. P. Schreiner, A South African* (Cape Town 1937)
Whyte, F.; *The Life of W. T. Stead* (London 1925)
Williams, B.; *Cecil Rhodes* (London 1921)

II. *Contemporary works and memoirs*

Baxter, W. D.; *Turn Back the Pages: Sixty-eight Years at the Cape* (Cape Town 1954)
Buchan, J.; *Memory-Hold-the-Door: The Autobiography of John Buchan* (London 1940)
Churchill, W. S.; *London to Ladysmith via Pretoria* (London 1900)
Idem; *My Early Life* (London 1930)
Dormer, F.; *Vengeance as a Policy in Afrikanderland: A Plea for a New Beginning* (1901)
Faure, D. P.; *My Life and Times* (Cape Town 1907)
Fuller, T. E.; *The Right Honourable Cecil John Rhodes: A Monograph and a Reminiscence* (London 1910)
Garrett, F. E.; 'In Afrikanderland and the Land of Ophir; Notes and Sketches in Political, Social and Financial South Africa', *Pall Mall Gazette 'Extra'* No. 58 (London 1891)
Garrett, F. E. and various authors; *The Empire and the Century* (London 1905)
Green, G. A. L.; *An Editor Looks Back: South African and Other Memories, 1883–1946* (Cape Town 1947)
Lewsen, P. (ed); *Selections From the Correspondence of John X. Merriman, 1870–1924*
Le Seuer, G.; *Cecil Rhodes* (1913)
Noble, J.; *Official Handbook of the Cape and South Africa* (Cape Town 1878)
Robertson Scott, J. W.; *'We' and Me* (London 1956)
Rose Innes, J.; *Autobiography* (Oxford 1949)
Solomon, W. E. G.; *Saul Solomon, The Member for Cape Town* (Oxford 1948)
Sampson, V.; *My Reminiscences* (London 1926)

Spender, J. A.; *Life, Journalism and Politics* (London 1927)

St Leger, A. Y.; Genealogical chart of the family of St Leger (Cape Town 1951)

Steevens, G. W.; *Cape Town to Ladysmith* (London 1901)

Trollope, A; *South Africa* (London 1878) (A reprint of the 1878 edition, with notes and introduction by J. H. Davidson, was published by A. A. Balkema in 1973.)

Van der Poel, J. (ed); *Selections from the Smuts Papers* (Cambridge 1973)

Wilson, G. H.; *Gone Down the Years* (Cape Town 1947)

Wright, H. M. (ed); *Sir James Rose Innes: Selected Correspondence* (1884–1902) (Cape Town 1972)

III. *Newspaper and periodical sources*

The *Cape Times* library; Files of the newspaper since March 1876; Christmas numbers, annuals and supplements. Clippings from various newspapers and periodicals from 1895, including biographic material on C. J. Rhodes, J. H. Hofmeyr, F. E. Garrett and others

Garrett, F. E.; 'Sir Alfred Milner and His Work' (*Contemporary Review*, 22 August 1900)

Garrett, F. E.; 'The Inevitable in South Africa' (*Ibid.*, 18 October 1899)

Garrett, F. E.; 'The Character of Cecil Rhodes' (*Ibid.*, 19 June 1902)

Hattersley, A. F.; 'Byways of South African Journalism in Victorian Times' (*Quart. Bull*, South African Library, December 1956)

Stent, V.; 'The Personology of Cecil Rhodes' (*Cape Times*, 26 March 1927)

Colvin, I. D. (junior); 'How Kipling Chose the *Cape Times* team' (*Ibid.*, 27 October 1956)

IV. *Manuscript sources*

Minutes of meetings of directors and shareholders of the Cape Times Limited 1898–1910

Garrett letters to Agnes Garrett. In the Gordon Papers (Bell Collection) ADD MSS 45929. Department of Manuscripts, British Library, London.

Saxon Mills letters. In the Kidd Collection, Cambridge University Library.

The Rose Innes Papers. South African Library, Cape Town

INDEX

A

Abdurahman, Dr A., leader African People's Organisation, 147, 148
Additional Representation Bill, 140–2
African People's Organisation, 147, 148
Afrikaanse Patriot, 16
Afrikaner Bond, Hofmeyr control, 16; Rhodes seeks support of, 20, 21, 23; *Cape Times* comment on refusal to accept responsibility, 22; Franchise and Ballot Bill, 24; Rhodes supports Sivewright to ensure support of, 36; 49; 50; past alliance with Rhodes, 52; returned to power, 54; 90; support of Schreiner 95; greater power after Raid, 98; English/Afrikaans split in politics, 100; opposition to suspension, 120, 123; 154, 157; Raid effects, 158
Allahabad Pioneer, Maitland Park ed. of, 120, 125–7
Annual Register, comment on 'missing cables', 94
Anton Anreith, article on in *Cape Times*, 131–2
Argus, The supports Sivewright in Logan affair, 37; attack on Innes, Merriman and Sauer, 39; backs Sivewright indispute with *Cape Times*, 41; Dormer and Rhodes dispute over appointment of Garrett as ed., 46–7; (See also *Cape Argus*)
Aschman, George, 162
Atwell, Mayor of Cape Town, 48

B

Badley, Amy, Garrett's sister, 62
Badley, J. H., founder of Bedales School, 62
Bailey, Sir Abe, interest in SAAN, 163 Abe Bailey Trust, 163, 164; members of, 163; administrators of estate, 163
Daker, Herbert, friend of Garrett, 87
Basutoland, xii; Rhodes's interest and troubles in, 19
Basuto War, 19
Baxter, W, D., leader of Citizens'

Guild, 135; mayor, 137
Bechuanaland, denuded of wood by De Beers—*Cape Times* report, 39–40; taken over by Cape Govt., 71; 91; 174
Bender, Rabbi A. P., member of C.T. Irish Association, 7
Bishopscourt, closing of grounds to public, 70
'Black Week', 109
Blewitt, Horatio Dunsterville; St Leger *vs* Rowles, 25–7
Bloemfontein conference, 102
Boeren Beschermings Vereeniging, xii
Botha, Gen. Louis, attitude to Union, 147–9; 'Het Volk', 149; 152; Anglo-Boer fusion, 153; 154, 155, 156
Bower, Sir Graham, Imperial Secretary, 75, 90
British South Africa Co. (alt. Chartered Co.), Charter to develop Rhodesia, 20; influence on politics, 22; *Cape Times* guards independence against, 25; 30, 57; transfer of Bechuanaland, 71; Jameson Raid, 74, 77, 79, 80, 84; Matabele uprising, 88; 91, 95
Buller, Gen. Sir Redvers, 108; failure to dislodge Boer lines, 109
Burg St., extension of *Cape Times* offices, 9, 43
Burger, Die, 144
Butler, Gen. Sir William, 86

C

Cambridge, Corpus Christi College, 1; Trinity College, 61, 62; St. John's College, 121
Campbell-Bannerman, Sir Henry, 147; administration, 157
Cape Argus, ix, xiii; rival of *Cape Times*, 9; Green ed. of, 10; policy of, 12; report of Isandhlwana, 15; interest bought by Rhodes, 17; 26, 40, 46; accused of being Rhodes-ian, 56; Jameson Raid, 80; circulation, 137
Cape Parliament, xii, xiii; press gallery, 10; speech by Rhodes, 19;

Franchise and Ballot Bill, 24; St
Leger seeks election to, 49, 50;
elections, 52–4, 98; Bill to protect
women, 61; contribution to Royal
Navy, 97–8; 108, 115; suspension
of Constitution issue, 116, 118; 120,
122, 130, 135; 1904 Progressive
Party in power, 138; 140, 141, 143,
151, 161, 177
Cape Punch, cartoon of 'Watchman'
case, 27
Cape Select Committee, investigation
of Jameson Raid, 74; 78
Cape Times, foundation of, 6; cost
and sales, 9; offices of, 9, 43, 44;
circulation and growth, 10, 13, 87,
137; St Leger's editorship of, 11;
newspaper policy, 12; 15; Transvaal
War, 16; editorial on Cetewayo,
17, 18; report of Rhodes's speech,
19; comment on Rhodes's appointment as P.M., 21–2; comment on
Strop Bill, 23; comment on Franchise and Ballot Bill, 24; pinnacle
of success, 25; accusation by Watchman, 25–7; editorial and comment
on Logan contract, 35–7; support
of Rhodes's schemes for Northern
expansion, 39; exploitation and
denudation of Bechuanaland, 40;
feud with Sivewright, 39–42;
Rutherfoord Harris given share in,
44; formed into company, 44–5;
Garrett, editor of, 46, 47; Robinson's attempts to buy, 47; reports
on municipal affairs, 48; first meeting of shareholders, 54; attack by
Molteno, 56, 57; St Leger's death,
59; independent line in involvement in public causes, 69, 70;
preservation of old Cape buildings,
70, 71; articles on Kruger, 72, 132,
133, 168–78; Jameson Raid, 74–9,
82–6, 89; report on Matabele
uprising, 88; comment on Schreiner,
95; promotes contribution to Royal
Navy, 97; articles on Rhodes,
98–100; franchise proposals of Transvaal, 102; South African War,
109–12; decline in stature, 114;
Saxon Mills as editor, 114; views
on suspension of Cape Constitution,
115–17; letter from C. J. Langen-

hoven, 117; decline under Saxon
Mills, 121; Maitland Park as editor,
126–9; Colvin's contribution to,
130, 131; farewell to Colvin, 134;
interest in civic reform, 135–9;
articles on Logan, 142, 143; question
of control by De Beers, 143–4;
Union of South Africa, 146, 147;
franchise controversy, 148, 151, 152;
comment on Smuts, 149; Boer–
British cleavage, 153; comment on
Hertzog, 154; Maitland Park's contribution to, 158; attack on Smuts,
160; Press Commission, 162; members of board, 162; association with
Syfrets and Bailey interests, 163–4;
editorial control, 164–5
Cape Times Employment Endowment Trust, 163
Cape Times Board of Directors,
controversy over suspension, 118;
119, 121, 163–4
Cape Town Chamber of Commerce,
118
Cape Town, Town (City) Council,
48; St Leger resigns from, 50; 71;
inefficiency, 135; intolerance of
criticism, 137
Cape Town Irish Association, 7
Carnarvon, Lord, xii; instructions to
annex Transvaal, 14
Cetewayo, 14; Cape Times calls for
release of, 17–18
Chamberlain, Joseph—British Colonial
Secretary, complicity in Jameson
Raid, 73; aftermath of Jameson
Raid; 84, 85; 86, 90; 'missing
cables', 91–4; 101, 105, 119; visit
to South Africa, 169
Chapman, Sir Drummond, 162
Church of the Province of South
Africa, St Leger's views on establish-
ment of, 4
Churchill, Winston, writing of
Jameson Raid, 73; 97; experiences
during South African War, 108, 109
City Club (Cape Town), St Leger
founder member of, 134
Claremont Club, O'Reilly's meeting,
53
Clarke, Very Rev. C. W. Barnett, 58
Clyst Hazel, (Newlands), St Leger's
home, 58

Colenso, Bishop, Colenso controversy, 3, 4, support of Cetewayo, 18

Colvin, Ian Duncan, appointment as assistant ed., 130; interest in Cape history, 130–2; leader on Kruger, 132; 133; departure, 134; comment on Jameson, 140, 141

Constitution Defence Committee, fight against suspension, 118, 119

Corder, Clive, 162, 163, 164

Corner House (Central Mining and Investment Co.), 144, 162

Currey, R. F., historian of St Andrews, 2

D

Daily Dispatch, comment on Cape Times dispute with Sivewright, 42

De Beers, 'Big Hole' discovery, 5; report in Cape Times re Bechuanaland, 40; Jameson Raid, 74; 95, 141, 142; view that Cape Times tool of, 143, 144

De Villiers, Sir J. H. (later Lord), hears case, St Leger v Rowles and Co. 25–7; refers to Harris's role in securing Rhodes's re-election, 44

De Waal, J. H. H. (Advocate), accusation against Cape Times, 144; 145

D'Ewes, Dudley, assistant ed. of Cape Times, 162

Delius, Anthony, 'Notes in the House', 11; 134

Diamond Fields Advertiser, St Leger's election manifesto, 50; 134

Dormer, Francis, purchase of Cape Argus, 17; quarrel with Rhodes over appointment of Garrett as ed. of Cape Argus, 46; 61

Du Toit, S. J., Afrikaanse Patriot, 16

Duke of Edinburgh's Own Volunteer Rifles, 7

F

Fawcett, Millicent Garrett, cousin of Edmund, 61; 62; head of Women's Commission, 112

FitzPatrick, Percy, letters to Garrett, 123; 153

Frere, Sir Bartle, 15

Friend, The (Bloemfontein), on Maitland Park, 155

Fuller, Sir Thomas, director of board of Cape Times, 55; pallbearer for St Leger, 58; 66

G

Garlick, John, 135

Garrett, Agnes, letters from Garrett, 49, 50, 65, 66, 67, 68, 77, 85, 87, 93; Garrett's youth, 61, 62

Garrett, Edmund, editorship of Cape Times, 7, 44, 45, 61; 8; arrival at Cape, 28; travels in South Africa, 29–30; interviews with Kruger, 30–3, 70–1; 34; return to England, 33, 43; subject to pressure by Harris, 45; question of Rhodes's control, 46; introduction to readers, 47, 48; articles on Rhodes, 51, 52, 73, 88; youth and early career, 61–5; relationship with Rhodes, 67, 68; independent line of Cape Times, 69; preservation of buildings, 70–1; Jameson Raid and aftermath, 74–84; championship of Milner, 86; return to England, 89; 90; backing of Rhodes, 97, 98; stands for Parliament, 98; relationship with Milner, 102, 103; ill-health/involvement in pre-war negotiations, 104–6; letter to Innes about concentration camps, 112–13; resignation from Cape Parliament, 122; later years/death, 123–4; 127, 128; 132, 137

Glasgow Herald, 126

Goldfields Co., Rhodes and Jameson Raid, 74; 95

Goodspeed, C. R., 55

Graham, T. L., stood as Progressive, 51; St Leger's funeral, 58; opposed to suspension, 116, 117

Gray, Robert, Bishop of Cape Town, 1

Green, G. A. L., reminiscences of Cape Times, 10; ed. of Cape Argus, 10; description of St Leger, 11; comment on St Leger, 44; 54; reporter during S.A. War, 110; 134

H

Hamilton, Frederick, emissary from Rand reformers during Raid, 72, 75, 76, 78

Hammond, John Hays, 83

Hands, Charles, 110

Hansard, Molteno's accusation of Rhodes's control of *Cape Times*, 56

Harris, Dr Rutherfoord, shares in *Cape Times*, 44, 46, 144; support of Rhodes, 44, 45; 55, 56, 65; efforts to influence editorial policy of *Cape Times*, 66; relationship with Garrett, 68; controversy over Jameson Raid, 76, 80, 85, 91; 125

Heard, Anthony, foreword, x; 165

Hellawell, Alf, sports ed. of *Cape Times*, 110

Hennessy, Sir Alfred, board of *Cape Times*, 162, 163, 164

Hertzog, Gen. J. B. M.; educational policy, 153, 154; 156, 161

Hobhouse, Emily, concentration camp scandal, 112

Hofmeyr, J. H. (Onze Jan), Afrikaner Bond, 16, 20; support of *Cape Times*, 21; Garrett's meetings with, 29, 74, 75, 83; 40, 49; comment on Rhodes, 52; Jameson Raid, 76; break with Rhodes, 80, 81, 82; letter to Garrett, 85; 101; 129; ext. of non-racial franchise, 146; 157

Hofmeyr, J. H., 155; biography of 'Onze Jan', 157; 158

Honnet, 162

House of Commons (British), inquiry into Raid, 89; speech by Chamberlain, 94; 143

I

Innes, James Rose, Cape politician— friend of St Leger, 78; *Cape Times* comment on, 22; Masters' and Servants' Act, 23; Franchise and Ballot Bill, 24; St Leger *v* Rowles case, 25, 26, 35; Logan contract dispute, 36–9, 41; South African Political Ass., 49; relationship with Rhodes, 51, 54, 98; letters to St Leger, 53; St Leger's funeral, 58; conversation with Schreiner, 74; 80, 83, 86, 97; relationship with Milner, 101–2; pre-South African War negotiations, 103–4; 111, 112; exchange of letters with Garrett, 112–13, 116; 123, 135, 138

J

Jameson, Dr, Rhodes's plot, 72; 74; news of Jameson's raid in Cape

Town, 75, 76; surrender 77; controversy over responsibility for Raid, 78, 79, 80; handed over to British by Kruger, 83; 92, 95; recruitment of Maitland Park, 125, 126; 127, 134; investigation of prison conditions, 135; Prime Minister 1904, 138; 139; Additional Representation Bill, 140; 141, 142; resignation from govt., 143; 148, 149, 152; Hertzog's attack on, 154; 155, 156, 158

Jameson Cabinet, 141

Jameson Raid, xii, xiii, 25; break with Innes and Co., 38, 39; 44, 49, 61, 65, 68; description of Raid, 72; results of, 73; chapter on, 74–95; 'missing cables', 91; 97, 99; effect on Cape politics, 100; 118, 138; Hertzog recalls, 154; 157, 158

Johannesburg, 31, 75, 76, 77, 78, 79, 108, 114, 176, 180, 181

Jones, Roderick, employed on *Cape Times*, 134

Joubert, Piet, captured Jameson's force, 72; against Kruger, 168

K

Kaffrarian Watchman, attack on *Cape Times*, 25–7

Kidd, Benjamin, letters from Saxon Mills, 121–2

Kimberley, xi, 19, 20, 29, 39, 44, 88, 98, 104, 108, 110

Kimberley, Lord (Colonial Secretary), Cetewayo's appeal, 17, 18

Kipling, Rudyard, 'Recessional' published, 97; recruitment of Maitland Park as ed., 125–6; 127, 129, 134, 143

Kitchener, Lord, 107, 109, 111, 112, 114

Kruger, President S. J. P., Rhodes's policy towards, 20; interviews with Garrett, 28, 30–3, 71–2, 168–78; 34; railway negotiations, 40; 42; diplomatic battle with Rhodes/Milner, 55; Jameson Raid and aftermath, 73, 74, 76, 80, 83, 84; 86, 89, 100; Uitlander rights, 101; pre-war negotiations with Milner, 102–5; *Cape Times* leader on, 132–3; death, 133

L

Leibbrandt, H. C. V., archivist, 130, 131
Leipoldt, Dr C. Louis, 107, 153, 160
Leonard, Charles, emissary from Rand reformers during Raid, 72; 75, 76, 78
Leyds, Dr, interview with *Cape Times*, 40; 42, 181
Liberman, Hyman, Mayor, 137
Liquor Bill, 51; O'Reilly's attack on, 52; 182
Loch, Sir Henry, 28
Logan, J. D., dispute over railway contract, 35–40; member of Legislative Council, 140; voting on Additional Representation Bill, 140–1; clash between politics and business, 142, 143
Long, Basil Kellet, editor of *Cape Times*, 160; 161

M

McKenzie, Angus, 'Notes in the House', 11
Majuba, battle of, 16; 29, 31, 32
Malan, Dr D. F., 156
Markham, A. B., 143
Marriage, Ellen, married Garrett, 123
Martial Law Board, 113
Martin, John, chairman Argus Co., 162
Mashonaland, 21
Masters' and Servants' Act, 23
Matabele, war, 71; rising, 87; 'Indaba' with Rhodes, 88
Matjiesfontein, 35; 140; 'Tweedside', home of Logan, 143
Maurice, M. S., tribute to St Leger, 57
Mendelssohn, Sidney, 132
Merriman, John X, description of New Rush Camp, 5; on St Leger, 8; member of Rhodes cabinet, 22; 23, 24; Logan contract dispute, 36–8; 39, 41; meeting with Garrett, 64; 65, 78, 80, 83, 88, 97; closer to Afrikaner Bond, 98; 116; moved resolution against suspension, 118, 120, 127; Park's first battle with, 128; Prime Minister, 143; Union of South Africa, 146; 149; Anglo-Boer fusion, 153
Michell, Sir Lewis, 67

Midland News (Cradock), editorial on St Leger's death, 59
Millin, Sarah Gertrude, writing on Jameson Raid, 158
Mills, J. Saxon, editor of *Cape Times*, 60, 114; writing on suspension, 116; 117; support of suspension, 118, 119; end of editorship, 120–1; letters to Kidd, 122; 126
Milner, Alfred, Lord 50, 55, 67; Garrett's support of, 86; 90; Governor of Cape, 100; views on Uitlanders, 101; character and policy of, 102; pre-South African War negotiations with Kruger, 103, 104; 105, 108, 113; martial law, 114; suspension of constitution, 115; 120; influence on *Cape Times*, 121
Molteno, J. C., attack on *Cape Times*, 56, 57
Morning Post (London), Colvin worked for, 133, 134
Mount Nelson Hotel, 7; Churchill a guest at, 109
Murray, R. W. Jnr, xiii; work on *Cape Times*, 10, 13; recruitment of Garrett, 43

N

Natal Mercury, 155
Norton, Canon Matthew, impression of St Leger, 2
Norton, Dr Victor, 'Notes in the House', 11; ed. of *Cape Times*, 161, 162; policy of *Cape Times* under, 164, 165

O

O'Reilly, T. J., stood as independent, 51; report of address in *Cape Times*, 52; St Leger's funeral, 58
Orpen, Gerald, chairman of *Cape Times* and Syfrets, 162, 164
Oundle School, 1
Oxford, xii; 102; Rhodes lecture by Smuts, 160; School of Modern History, 161; Oriel, 184

P

Pall Mall Gazette, Garrett employed by, 28, 63
Park, Maitland, ix; 60; arrival in Cape as ed., 120; 124; recruitment

as ed. by Kipling, 125–7; style and policy as editor, 127–9; 130, 132; critical policy and resulting conflict, 134; municipal reform, 135; increase in circulation of *Cape Times*, 137; backing of Jameson, 138–40; attack on Logan, 143; reply to accusation against *Cape Times*, 144, 145; attitude to Union, 148, 149; tribute to, 155, 156; death, 158; 159, 160, 164

Phillips, Lionel, 83

Powell, Edmund, ed. of *Cape Argus*, 26

Press Commission, 162, 163

Pretoria News, 36

Progressive (later Unionist) Party, 49, 50; Rhodes as leader, 51, 52; elections, 54; defeated by Bond 1898, 90; 98, 100; suspension issue, 115; 120; returned to power 1904, 138; 139, 140, 141, 153, 154, 155, 182, 183

Punch, extract from *Cape Times*, 129

R

Rand Club, 121

Rand Daily Mail, association with *Cape Times*, 163

Review of Reviews, founded by Stead, 63; 105

Rhodes, Cecil J., xii, xiii; 17; first speech in parliament, 19; expansion to north, 20, 39; conflict of interests, 21, 22; policy of, 23, 24; Garrett's meeting with, 29, 30; Logan contract dispute, 36–8; Harris's association with, 44, 45, 46; quarrel between Rhodes and Dormer, 46; 47, 48; protective duties, 49; 50; support of Faure, 51; leadership of Progressives after elections, 51, 52; 1898 elections, 53; 55; Molteno's accusation of Rhodes's control of *Cape Times*, 56, 57; 64; relationship with Garrett, 66, 67, 68; 70; relationship with Kruger, 71, 72; 73; Jameson Raid and aftermath, 74–7, 80–4; 85, 86; responsibility for South African War, 87; Matabele uprising, 88; inquiry into Raid, 89, 90; political comeback, 90, 98; 'missing cables', 91–4; break with

Schreiner and Bond, 95; 97; speech reported in *Cape Times*, 99–100; 105, 114; dying wish urged suspension, 115–16, 118, 119; 133, 139, 140, 155, 156, 157, 158; interview with Garrett, 179–84

Rhodes Cabinet, 22, 23; moderating influence of Innes, Merriman and Sauer, 24; Logan contract results in break up of, 36

Rhodes, Colonel Frank, 83

Rhodes Trust, 163

Rice, Elsie Garrett, 62

Rissik, Johann, interpreter for interviews between Garrett and Kruger, 31, 168, 169, 176

Roberts, Lord, 96; commander-in-chief, South African War, 109

Robinson, Sir Hercules, 16, 34, 72, 75, 76, 78, 84, 85

Robinson, Sir J. B., 47, 65, 69, 80, 161

Runcie, John, employed by *Cape Times*, 134

S

St Andrew's College (Grahamstown), 1; improvements by St Leger, 2

St George's Cathedral, St Leger's attendance at, 5; 57; plaque in memory of St Leger, 58; scheme for rebuilding, 69; memorial to Garrett in, 124

St Leger, Anthony York, recalls father's resignation, 3; director of *Cape Times* until 1963, 59; member of Constitution Defence Committee, 119

St Leger, Christian Emma, married to St Leger, 1; converted to Catholic faith, 5

St Leger, Ellen Mary, 3

St Leger, Emma Jane, 3; marriage to M. W. Searle, 25

St Leger, Frederick Luke, 3, 6; advises father to give share in *Cape Times* to Harris, 44; 45; shareholders' meeting of *Cape Times*, 55; member of *Cape Times* Board until 1935, 59; 65, 68; support of suspension, 118; 119, 120

St Leger, Frederick York, policy in founding *Cape Times*, ix, xiii; family, education and recruitment to mission field, 1; headmaster of St Andrew's, 2; career in church, 2, 3, 4; resignation from priesthood, 4; move to New Rush Camp, 5; foundation of *Cape Times*, 6; description of, 7; friendship with Rose Innes, 8; newspaper policy, 10–12; 15; attitude to Rhodes, 21, 24; Bond, 22; attack by *Watchman*, 25–7; 39; retirement from editorship of *Cape Times*, 43; financial difficulties of *Cape Times*, 44; 45, 47; interest in public affairs, 48, 49, 50; election campaign, 50–5; ill-health, 55, 57; death and tributes to, 58, 59; relationship with Garrett, 64–6, 69; 86, 97, 109, 114, 115, 118; 121; tribute from Garrett to, 122–3; 124, 127, 128, 139; shares of *Cape Times*, 144; 145, 158, 159, 161, 164; policy for *Cape Times*, 165

St Leger, John, son of F. Y. St Leger, 3; 6

St Leger, Dr Robert Arthur (Bob), 3; recalls New Rush Camp, 5, 6; director of *Cape Times* until 1951, 59; 118, 119; stands as independent, 139; 158

St Leger, Stratford Edward, son of F. Y. St Leger, 3

Sauer, J. W., favoured by *Cape Times* as P.M., 21; 22; against Masters' and Servants' Act, 23; Franchise and Ballot Bill, 24; Logan contract dispute, 36–8; attack on by *Argus*, 39; 41, 64; extension of non-racial franchise, 146

Schreiner, Olive, letter to brother, 86; 87, 89; view on pre-S.A. War situation, 105; 151

Schreiner, Theo, letter to *Cape Times* on franchise, 151

Schreiner, W. P., biography, 46; Prime Minister of Cape, 55; 58; rumours of Raid, 74; 78, 82; letter from Olive, 86, 87; break with Rhodes, 94–5; 97, 98, 123, 128; 1904 elections, 139; extension of non-racial franchise, 146, 151–2; views on constitution of Union govt., 150; 152

Schreiner Ministry, dissension over treatment of Cape rebels, 111

Scott, John, 'Notes in the House', 11

Scott, J. W. Robertson, 101

Searle, M. W. (later Sir Malcolm), 25, 119

Sivewright, Sir James, Bond member of Rhodes Cabinet, 22; railway contract scandal, 23; split in cabinet as result of contract, 36–7; feud between *Cape Times* and, 40–2; 140

Slagter's Nek, 83; 113

Smartt, Sir Thomas, split on suspension among Progressives, 115–16; speaking on suspension, 117, 119; leadership of Progressives, 120

Smithard, George, sketches of Cape, 130, 132

Smuts, Gen. J. C., 72; pre-S.A. War negotiations, 103; 146, 147; attitude to Union, 148; *Cape Times* comment on, 149; Anglo-Boer fusion, 153; 154, 155, 156; comment on Jameson Raid, 158; message to *Cape Times* on 59th Anniversary, 159; ref. to *Cape Times* in letter, 160; 161

Solomon, Richard, 112

Solomon, Saul, ix; xii; *Cape Argus*, 9; political duels with *Cape Times*, 12, 15; relinquished control of *Cape Argus*, 17

South African Associated Newspapers (SAAN), acquired shares in *Cape Times*, 163, 164, 165

South Africa Committee, 44; inquiry into Jameson Raid, 90, 91; 'missing cables', 92; report of, 93; Schreiner evidence, 95

South African League, backs Rhodes, 51; 101, 118, 138, 182

South African Library, 130, 132

South African News, 137

South African Party, xii, 154, 155, 156, 158, 160

South African Political Association, 49, 54, 83, 135, 138

South African Telegraph, threat to *Cape Times*, 47; 65, 69; news of Jameson's surrender, 80

South African War, xii, 55, 56, 61, 73, 97, 106, 107, 108–14, 123, 147, 152, 157

Sprigg, Sir G., 39, 58, 97–8, 111, 116, 117, 119, 120, 182

Sprigg Cabinet, 20, 58, 120, 122
Standard and Diggers' News, comments on Sivewright in dispute with *Cape Times*, 42
Star, The takes Sivewright's part in Logan affair, 37; backs Sivewright in dispute with *Cape Times*, 41, 42; 46, 56; telegram from Garrett, 78
Stead, W. T., 28, 62, 63, 67, 86, 90, 91–2, 105
Steenbras Reservoir, 135
Steevens, George Warrington, 96, 97, 107, 109, 110
Stent, Vere, comment on Logan affair, 36; comment on creation of circumstances for Jameson Raid, 38, 39; covers Matabele rising for *Cape Times*, 87, 88
Strop, Bill, 23
Suicide Riding Brigade, Cape Town journalists' club, 87
Sunday Times, 163
Syfret, E. R., director on board of *Cape Times*, 55; 58; *Cape Times* company, 59; sided with suspension, 118; 119; chairman of *Cape Times* and Syfret's Trust, 162, 164
Syfret's Trust Company, 55; Press Commission, 162; association with *Cape Times*, 163; association with Bailey interests, 164

T

The Times, 80, 97, 161
Transvaal Leader, acquired by Cape Times Co., 133; 144, 163
Trotter, Mrs A. F., sketches of Cape houses in *Cape Times*, 70

U

Uitlanders, 72, 74, 75, 76, 78, 79, 80, 84, 100, 101, 102, 103, 151, 168, 176, 177, 178
Union of South Africa, 138; 146–59
Union Parliament (also South African Parliament), 135, 148, 149, 151, 152, 161
United South African Party, 156, 161

V

Verwoerd, Dr H. F., franchise, 156
Victoria, Queen, 18, 76, 96, 108
Volksraad, 83, 171, 176, 177

W

Wallers, Sir Evelyn, board of *Cape Times*, 162
Walton, Leycester, Managing Director SAAN, 163
Waterson, Dr Jane, friend of Garrett, 76, 87
Watson, J. A. S., board of *Cape Times*, 118; Constitution Defence Committee, 119
Western Province Cricket Association, 143
Westminster Gazette, 64, 92, 102
Wilson, G. H., 'Notes in the House', 11; difficulties in reporting a Sivewright speech, 42; 130; Colvin's departure, 134; ed. of *Cape Times*, 161
Women's Commission, 112; to investigate conditions in Boer concentration camps, 113

Z

Zululand, 17, 18, 171, 172, 174
Zulu War, 15, 17